THE BODLEY HEAD

1887–1987

THE
BODLEY HEAD
1887-1987

J. W. LAMBERT
&
MICHAEL RATCLIFFE

THE BODLEY HEAD

LONDON

To

MAX REINHARDT

British Library Cataloguing
in Publication Data
Lambert, J. W.
The Bodley Head, 1887–1987
1. Bodley Head—History
I. Title   II. Ratcliffe, Michael
338.7'610705'09421   z325.B7
ISBN 0-370-30949-9

© The Bodley Head Ltd 1987

Printed in Great Britain for
The Bodley Head Ltd
32 Bedford Square, London WCIB 3EL
by William Clowes Ltd, Beccles
Set in Monotype Ehrhardt (453) by
Gloucester Typesetting Services
First published 1987

CONTENTS

CONTENTS *CONTINUED*

ILLUSTRATIONS

On tinted paper

Plates: following page 280

ILLUSTRATIONS *CONTINUED*

I

JOHN LANE
AND
THE NINETIES

I

Down on the Farm

In the early summer of 1887 John Lane, thirty-three years old, stocky, brisk, dapper and trimly bearded, walked down an unimpressive London street, saw what he wanted, and consciously or not set about changing the face of the London publishing and indeed literary scene.

He had been looking for premises in which to open, or cause to be opened, a bookshop, which might perhaps itself publish a few volumes; and in Vigo Street, he reported, was the very thing. An acquaintance, one Dunthorne, print-seller and art dealer, was vacating his shop—'a shop and w.c. only', but it could be leased from its landlord, the neighbouring Royal Geographical Society, for a mere £80 or, as it turned out, £86 a year. 'The risk is nothing and the position is a fine one.'

Neither statement was strictly true. London was not short of antiquarian booksellers with a finely spun network of contacts. And Vigo Street, though named in 1733 (as Vigo Lane) after a notably profitable naval engagement in the early eighteenth century, has remained undistinguished to this day, a mere street of convenience lying behind and parallel to Piccadilly on the north side. Its only previous claim to attention was a fire which more or less destroyed it in 1761; and perhaps, too, its use, as a gathering-place for the better class of whore—so convenient for clients from, especially, the Albany, which had opened its doors in 1803 as London's first custom-built set of apartments.

The life John Lane embarked upon with cautious confidence in London could hardly have been more different from that of his childhood and early youth—to which, however, he remained devoted throughout his life; as did his young cousin and heir apparent Allen Lane.

John was born, in 1854, of Devonshire yeoman stock, at the unromantically named but more romantically situated West Putford, twelve miles west of Bideford, deep in the hilly, thickly wooded land between Exmoor to the north-east and Dartmoor to the south-west, a richly fertile world. The Lanes, in fact, were scattered all over north Devon and Cornwall, earning a mention in Charles Kingsley's *Westward Ho!* John Lane's branch grew from an estate called Bocombe, which John derived from Beaucombe, 'because it is a most beautiful combe', a handsome house in a handsome estate. His own father was the youngest of the five sons of an earlier John Lane, of Iddlecot, known as Little Egypt, because it was a land of plenty to a population which took its images from the Bible.

Whatever the vagaries of English agriculture during the nineteenth century, John Lane's forebears, on both sides of the family, prospered steadily in their yeoman fashion, neither pigging nor yet aspiring to the gentry. All the same, John's father Lewis cannot have seemed a notable catch for Isabella Mary Jenn. The Jenns, another prosperous yeoman family, were of Flemish Huguenot descent, settled, according to John, 'since Tudor times', when indeed many such escaped to England from Spanish rule and Roman Catholic hostility in the Low Countries; setting up, for example, the weaving community of Flushing in west Cornwall, on the banks of the River Fal. The Jenns, evidently a vigorous stock, spread all over north Devon and Cornwall.

Mary's father was a farmer, miller, corn merchant, sportsman and churchman; her mother, Isabella Mary Hobbs, from a little farther west, near Bude, was, as John himself was to be, an enthusiastic dancer, and also a ready versifier and a locally celebrated gardener. She boasted, and young John enjoyed, a lively collection of brothers. One was a passionate teetotaller—a thankless role at that time and in that family—who was also mechanically and musically minded; he made his own violin, and played in the string band at the local chapel. He also introduced John to the celebrated sporting parson,

(4)

the Reverend Jack Russell, whom the boy heard preach two sermons, 'with the hounds yapping only a few yards away'.

Another from the same side, by no means a teetotaller, impressed the boy by never doing a day's work in his life, and by leaving all his nephews and nieces £50 in his will. Idle he may have been, but Uncle Josiah was reputed to be the best shot in the county, his exploits regularly recorded in north Devon newspapers. He too was a musician, and played the bass violin in West Putford church. This strain in the family was certainly not inherited by John, who made no secret of his dislike of music, though in middle age he married a musician, abandoning their London house during her musical evenings. Another uncle, and yet another John Lane, who succeeded to the family home, appeared to the boy 'a weird-looking person, with long hair and a cast in his eye'. He was also philosophically inclined, and became a Swedenborgian, following the speculations, if not the Revelation, of that remarkably modern eighteenth-century scientist.

More to his taste, perhaps, was the household of another Lane aunt, Mary Ann, who married Richard Walter of Churston Manor, a former seat of the Prideaux family, their arms above the overmantel in a fine hall. Walter, says Lane,

'was a cheery soul and very stout. He had been a great swimmer and a fine shot, but in later years he took to astronomy, obtained a good telescope and erected a shanty, commonly called an Observatory, on high ground not far from the house, an elevation from which he could see both Exmoor and Dartmoor with the naked eye; and here his spy-glass, as he called it, was an endless delight to himself and his friends ... Indeed I have always felt that my almost emotional love of scenery is largely due to the influence of the surroundings of my birthplace.'

And well it might be. But it was enjoyed by John—along with his picturesque relatives—only on his frequent visits, for he was barely three when Lewis Lane removed his family to another farm—though no less romantic surroundings. Forcewell (his spelling) or Forselle lay less than ten miles north-west of Buckland Brewer as a crow might fly; but even today a stranger might find the journey complex, if not speculative, traversing bleak uplands and steep, deeply tangled valleys. The new farm included both, along with a lively stream which tumbled down to the sea by way of Hartland Abbey, a handsome and secluded country house. In this stream the boy John used to tickle trout (perhaps a useful apprenticeship for coaxing authors); but when he tried it again in later years he found that his hand had lost its cunning.

Forcewell farmhouse stood—and still stands, as a guest-house—with the windswept upland a little above it, and the hill running steeply down to the north-east; a quite handsome house built not long before the Lanes went there as tenants of the Hext family. Hardly a mile to the north, the road dipping over another stream, lies Hartland, very little changed in appearance in nearly two hundred years: a trim village, with a tidy little square containing the chapel of ease which the Lanes attended, though John Lane ungenerously called it 'the ugliest building in Devon' and surprisingly seems to have cared not at all for its ancient, and still reliable, clock, bought for 33s. in 1622 to be installed in the tower—a welcome seamark—of the parish church. This lies west of the town, midway between the village and Hartland Quay, a terrifying dent in the jagged cliffs which outface the swell and fury of the Atlantic. The Quay was built early in the first Elizabeth's reign and was still in use for most of the nineteenth century, a busy and notably alcoholic little settlement.

'In this parish,' wrote John Lane in an all too brief fragment, 'I spent my happy, indeed I might say romantic, youth;' and in this parish, after all the hectic London years between, his ashes lie.

When (which was often) Lane later turned to reminiscence, it was not on his publishing triumphs but on his memories of his father's farm at Hartland, that he chiefly loved to dwell.

Perhaps time gave these memories a golden glow, a Pickwickian charm:

(6)

'I have a vivid recollection of an annual feast or revel at my Hartland home, held by us always on Christmas Eve, to which we invited all our workpeople and their wives, in fact everyone who had lent a helping hand in saving the hay and the corn harvest. The policeman, the postman, the town-crier, the rat and molecatchers, all participated, and the Vicar sat on the right of my mother and said Grace. The table was a long one, added to for the occasion.

'"Good stummick to you all," was the universal greeting, and . . . the table groaned under rounds of beef, roast goose (as for that other Christmas bird, the Turkey, that was unknown in N. Devon at that time), boar's head, suckling pig, and junket . . . There was home-brewed ale and home-made cider ad-lib. below the salt; but I have a recollection of grog being served above in old-fashioned rummers. The spirit was usually the far-famed Plymouth Gin. There was also Metheglin mead as a cordial. After the spread, the family and the Vicar retired to the parlour, but the remainder of the company kept up the festivities rather late, almost invariably till the waifs arrived, singing their Christmas carols and such old-world songs as "Uncle Ned" and "Wait for the Wagon".'

Such were the days that an older John Lane recalled as a respite from the alarms and excursions of publishing. He remembered his father, in a hard winter, cutting ivy from the cob walls of a linhay ivy to feed the hungry sheep: 'Goats, of course, are very fond of ivy, but I never succeeded in finding any confirmation of giving it to sheep until I read *The Winter's Tale*, Act 3, Scene 3: ' "They have scared away two of my best sheep, which I fear the wolf will sooner find than the master; if anywhere I have them, 'tis by the sea-side browsing of ivy." '

Few if any London publishers, then or now, would assert so confidently that goats, *of course*, are very fond of ivy.

This was the little world in which the future publisher of *The Yellow Book* was formed. For schooling he went first to a dame school run by the daughter of the village's Independent minister, then to a boys' school in the village started by one Ellacote, who later went off to join his brother-in-law, another Hartland boy, who had become a successful stockbroker in London. After Ellacote came Matthew Webb, from Chagford, a Dartmoor town, 'a bright and dapper little man with a touch of the tar-brush in him'; he took a kindly interest in the boy. Then came his first spell away from home, for he was sent to Chulmleigh Academy; Chulmleigh is to this day another neat hilltop town some thirty tortuous and beautiful miles away; at the Academy, 'most of the sons of the best yeomen of the county and many professional men were educated.' Though no longer a school, it dominates, a tidy sandstone house, the little central square. It was run by John Wallings Brooks, who combined science and the arts in a way many of today's children might envy. Electricity dominated his thinking on one hand, and in the late 1860s his school had what seemed to young Lane 'a fine laboratory'; on the other hand he was a collector of china and furniture, 'so that it was probably through him that I first became interested in and gained some knowledge of these things.'

This is putting it mildly. Had he not become a publisher, he would surely have made a name for himself as an antique dealer; as it was, his interests in this field later cost his publishing business a great deal of money in handsome, valuable, but not evidently saleable books. His qualifications were considerable—a genuine interest, a quick intelligence, and an instinct for upward mobility. Not that this last, when exercised in combination with his abiding love of his Devon roots, always paid off. While still at school in Chulmleigh, he went out on a school walk which took the group past Lord Portsmouth's orchard, heavy with fruit. Three or four boys got into the orchard; suddenly came the sound of horse's hooves. John Lane shinned up a tree, and beneath him rode, all unnoticing, Lord Portsmouth and his son, Lord Lymington.

'Some forty years later, one night at a party at Lord Portsmouth's house in Mansfield Street, I ventured to tell him of the incident, remarking that the first time I saw him, he luckily did not see me. But I regret to say that he never forgave me, though the story has since amused at least three of his sisters, his mother and one of his brothers.'

It had by those scrumping schooldays become clear that whatever else John Lane might turn out to be, he was not cut out for farming. What else? At a General Election in 1868 Sir Stafford Northcote, pillar of the Tories, came to Hartland to speak. John's father was a staunch Tory, his mother a staunch mother. After the meeting, Lewis Lane was persuaded to speak to Sir Stafford on the boy's behalf, with a further kindly intervention by Sir George Stucley. It worked. Before long a letter came from the Secretary of the Railway Clearing House at Euston, nominating the lad to a junior clerkship in the Clearing House, providing he could pass an examination.

'My presence was requested in London two days later. Meanwhile I had gone on a round of visits to my relations. My mother had given me a little Exmoor pony, on which I made my travels to my relations and places of interest like lovely Clovelly and wild Bude and romantic Morwenstow. And it was with some difficulty that I could be traced. When found, I remember, I was in the hall of Churston Manor, the guest of my uncle Richard Walter.'

Driven back to Hartland, three days later he was taken to London by his mother. It was the first time either of them had been so far from home. Travelling on the Bude line to Waterloo, not Paddington, they took a cab to recommended lodgings at Euston; Mrs Lane was so alarmed at the prospect of crossing the Thames that she gave the cabman an extra sixpence to drive slowly over the bridge.

At sixteen, John Lane, the country boy, was ready to take on the Metropolis.

2

Exploring the Ground

To take it on, but not to take it by storm. Nearly twenty years were to pass before he took his first steps into publishing. First came the Clearing House and its little examination. There were two candidates. The other, James Murray, already had a brother working (or at any rate employed—these young clerks spent a good deal of time playing chess) in this forgotten corner of industrial bureaucracy. Both boys passed and were taken on. They soon became friends—though not without difficulty, since Murray was a minister's son from the Hebridean Isle of Lewis: what with his lilt, and Lane's rounded Devonshire, they were hardly able to understand each other. Lane's accent presumably modified itself in due course, since thirty years later Kenneth Grahame was to write, à propos of one of the assorted uproars which accompanied Lane through life:

'You will find it will assist matters immediately if you will re-acquire, and retain, a strong Devonshire accent. The public like anything that smacks of the soil. By the way, that would be a good title for your next young lady's effusion: "Smacks of the Soil".

Difficult to say whether Lane took notice of this ambiguous recommendation, with or without reference to his 'next young lady's effusion', but a year or so after this letter his house journal *The Bodleian* (price one penny) was cheerfully mocking the founder of the firm for pronouncing 'spoon' as 'spune'.

His mother, doubtless fretting a little at the thought of her ewe lamb at large in the ferocious metropolitan jungle, went back to Devon after helping young John to find suitable lodgings. These were in Gower Place, just south of Euston Road. His rooms were previously occupied by the Italian patriot Mazzini, a signed photograph of whom was proudly displayed by his landlady, formerly a cook, widow of a retired soldier who had worked for University College, and was said to have weighed twenty stone. The illegitimate daughter of a clergyman, she attended the Gower Street Chapel of the Particular Baptists, where the sermons habitually moved her to tears over the subsequent Sunday dinner. John Lane several times went with her to these affecting occasions; but neither they nor his later sermon-sampling seem to have done much to strengthen, or perhaps establish, any religious feelings. The Quakers certainly attracted him for a while; in a secular way he was proud of the Huguenot roots of his mother's family, and all his life supported the Huguenot Hospital, dining annually with its Governors at Hackney.

The walk from his lodgings to his place of work was a short one, but even then not quite free of those dangers which a loving mother must have foreseen. One evening in Euston Square he was accosted with the gentle insinuation, 'Won't you come home with me, Johnny darling?' Surprised at hearing his own name, aware that something, somehow, was not quite right, he answered 'I don't know you' and made off.

London was expanding round the boy, and he rapidly expanded with it. West and north lay Regent's Park and its grandiose Nash terraces, east and north the slum-ridden chaos created by the railway age which was employing him. Near him in discreetly shabby Bloomsbury, amid the down-at-heel Georgian squares, small hotels and boarding houses, stood the British Museum, for one of Lane's temperament an Aladdin's cave of curiosities, in which the bright young man soon made friends with the officials. And then, south of Bloomsbury, across Oxford Street, before the area was cleared up with the creation of Kingsway and all that flowed from it, lay a warren of small streets and small shops, of junk-rich antique dealers, antiquarian bookshops and print-sellers (before they migrated to the Charing Cross Road). And west of this network of alleys lay indeed the West End—fine shops, rich equipages, handsome houses, pillar-proud streets. Shaking, whenever possible, the dust of the Euston Road from his feet, young Lane set about familiarising himself, in a state of equal excitement, with backwater and boulevard.

As Lane readily acknowledged, it was the example, as much as the teaching, of his headmaster in the bow-windowed, portly shape of Chulmleigh Academy which gave his life the sense of direction, or rather directions, which in turn sent him out continually in search of furniture, china, glass, eighteenth-century portraits, books and book-plates; of these last he was to be among the first to make a systematic study.

He always felt his lack of formal education above a homely level (though at least that level prepared him better than is aimed at for most children today with the basic equipment of literacy). A quick mind and a natural gregariousness led him quite quickly in the direction of more experienced fellow-collectors and experts in their various fields. Adaptability was, at least in his early days, his outstanding characteristic. His country ways and dress were soon modified; there emerged a dapper, sandy-bearded young man who passed easily—or at any rate passed—into a wide range of social circles, from the bohemian to the elegant: never perhaps committing himself to any one of them.

By the time he was twenty he had penetrated at any rate some of Bohemia's creeks. He was to be found, for instance, in the rooms of one H. J. de Burgh and his flat-mate Lestocq, a fellow-drudger in the Railway Clearing House who later went into the theatre. This pair, on the outer fringe of Bloomsbury, were hospitable, perhaps to a fault. Another actor, W. S. Penley, led the company in a chorus from Gilbert and Sullivan's *Trial by Jury* to such effect that the tenant on the floor below dashed out on to the landing screaming 'This place is nothing but a dirty pothouse!' But the aggrieved tenant in question was Swinburne, far more often drunk and in need of help from his neighbours than in a position to complain about them.

Less boisterous company came through one of his Devon connections (which recur throughout his life). The two sons of the rector of West Putford—the clergyman who had married Lane's parents—had both settled in London, one a solicitor (also a collector of books and prints), the other a doctor, practising in Finsbury; there especially Lane was a frequent visitor, and, in due course, employer of the doctor's son, J. Lewis May, indefatigable reader, editor, translator and all-round hack.

The Railway Clearing House, despite its Dickensian ring and its denizens' partiality to chess, in fact carried work of a complexity which might seem to tax the powers of a Senior Wrangler. At a time when Britain was criss-crossed by scores of separately owned and run railway lines, it had by the 1870s become clear that there had to be many overlaps, the trains of one company running at times over the tracks of another; every such overlap had to be paid for; among other things the Railway Clearing House became famous for the maps and junction-plans it produced for its own calculations of borrowed use—those calculations in turn working out the sums due to be paid by one railway line to another. Though its work was simplified by amalgamations in the 1920s, this office continued its complex operations until nationalisation after the Second World War.

It was indeed not a scene likely to contain, or even hold for a moment, the interests and energies of the boy from Devon. He soon became a transplanted Autolycus, a spare-time dealer in books and antiques: and that spare time had extended to a point where he paid other clerks in the Railway Clearing House to do for him the mechanical tasks involved. He lived and learnt to some purpose. He made the acquaintance of Hodgkin, a quite celebrated bibliophile, at that time specialising in Pepys and Pepysiana. For ten years this dapper little clerk from the Railway Clearing Office went every Sunday to lunch at the Hodgkins' house in Richmond and, according to Hodgkin's son (in a letter to Lewis May), spent the afternoons in the library, going over catalogues with Hodgkin senior, who

'sent Lane off in search of various items, on the look-out for anything that caught his fancy. And every Thursday Lane arrived back in Richmond with whatever he had found, and was shown straight into the library. Sundays and Thursdays were known as "John

(13)

Lane's days" all through my boyhood . . . He used to say that my father had laid the foundation of his knowledge, as I'm sure he did. But Lane had an extraordinary flair.'

Nor were his uses confined to the older and more earnest side of the Hodgkin family.

'He had a special "way" with him. Certainly my mother liked him . . . Later, when he found I was so fond of dancing, many were the invitations he somehow wangled for me.'

Including, mysteriously, to Lady Palmer's at Reading, where he was a frequent visitor—evidently he quite took the biscuit. He was a deft and accomplished dancer, despite having no ear for music, on at least one occasion setting off boldly to 'God Save the Queen' until restrained. One way and another, what with carousing with bohemian friends, dancing stylishly (if at times inappropriately), putting in at least an occasional appearance at his place of employment, he might seem to have little time left for building up his assorted knowledge of, particularly, books and bookselling. Yet they came to occupy more and more of his attention; and his interest was perhaps fanned in one particular direction when he found that one of his fellow-clerks in the Railway Clearing House had a brother who was running, none too successfully, an antiquarian bookseller's shop in (Devon again) the Cathedral Yard, Exeter.

Charles Elkin Mathews (1851–1921) was the son of a refugee from a shipbuilding and ship-owning family long established in Gravesend. His father, however, declaring, it is said, that he could not 'bear the smell of tar' removed himself and his wife (much given to reading Shakespeare, and later of a mystical disposition) to Codford St Mary, a village near Salisbury; between them they produced nine children, educated largely by his family. His interest in literature began, as with so many, in the writing of poems about nature, but soon took a bibliographical turn, not least in connection with angling books. He began working with an antiquarian bookseller, C. J.

Stewart at Charing Cross, then went to several other establishments, including, as manager, the library in Bath, returning to London to Sotheran's in Piccadilly; all this while writing notes in specialist publications on early editions of this or that, recording folklore from Somerset and Devon—and building up a stock of books in order to start up on his own.

This, with money lent by an uncle, he did in Exeter at the close of 1884. But it was while he was still in London that he met John Lane; with shared interests, they began to correspond. Lane offered market hints:

'My dear Mathews—a tip to begin with—buy all the copies of Marlowe's plays, Mermaid Series, that you can meet, having 431 p.p., as the first issue has been withdrawn in consequence of some blasphemous lines in a note of the appendix. They are certain to go up. I got one by a lucky stroke on Friday.'

Further to confirm that his interest in books was not wholly literary, he also asked advice: a seller wanted 30s. for a copy of *Fanny Hill*; he had offered £1, but should he perhaps go as far as 25s.? Or, how much should he offer for Shelley's *Queen Mab*, 1821, in whole morocco with untrimmed edges? 'Your replies', he wrote to Mathews, 'are teeming with information.'

Soon Lane was writing as though they were already in partnership:

'We must get a few more Tennysons—we are weak in him. We must try for a *Princess*; look out for one. We have nothing in Shelley or Keats in firsts.'

Meanwhile, Lane was deputed, or more likely undertook, to seek about London for suitable premises, and in July 1887 found them:

'In company with my friend Mr. R. W. Wilson of the British Museum [Deputy Superintendent of the Reading Room], I was one day at an exhibition in the Rembrandt Head Gallery in Vigo Street; and, casually asking the proprietor, Mr Dunthorne, if he knew of any cosy little corner where a book-shop would be in fit setting, he at once rejoined that the premises in the same street where he had originally hung up the sign of the Rembrandt Head, were vacant, and that he would be pleased to show them to me. I saw them, liked them and at once made up my mind that here was the spot I had been looking for.'

Seemingly he had little difficulty in making up Elkin Mathews's mind either; but as the arrangements for the new establishment developed the poor fellow clearly had many misgivings, and no wonder.

Not for nothing had John Lane spent his boyhood in a hard-bargaining farming community, and then adapted himself rapidly to the no less sharp, not to say devious, procedures of the metropolitan world of antique dealing and second-hand bookselling. Moreover, he had tremendous energy, and a powerful urge for self-advancement up to a point. He wanted to know and use the big world, but showed no particular inclination to join it—just as during his Devon boyhood he and his family were on pretty good terms with the local gentry, but had no pretensions to membership of that class. So it turned out to be in the world of books and bookselling.

Elkin Mathews, according to Lewis May, 'was a neat, dapper little man, rather fussy and old-maidish in his ways. He was clean-shaven, with a bald, globular head much too large for his body,' and had a round, flat face with 'a flat, socratic nose'. He was a genuine biblio-phile, and perhaps it was because he was loth to see any book depart that he charged such formidable prices for them. He had a conserva-tive and unenterprising spirit, and the four walls of his shop, and the books he dusted and arranged with such jealous care, were world enough for him.

At 33, Lane was also a dapper, balding little man, with a neat pointed beard, already portly, but 'forever bustling in and out—always somewhere to go, something to see'. Something to fix, too:

notably a deed of partnership, valid for seven years, into which Elkin Mathews entered with understandable reluctance. 'I don't quite see how a partnership would benefit me.' It didn't. Assorted 'misunderstandings' attended its preparation, though Lane did agree to pay half the remaining rental of the Exeter shop and half the cost of the removal to London of Mathews's stock. This, plus £50, and his own stock, which he had been building up for some time ('his extensive but peculiar library', as a young Hartland friend called it), appear to have been Lane's sole contributions to the enterprise, in which, in any case, he was supposed to be only a sleeping partner. Mathews was to be paid £10 per month for running the business, before division of the remaining profits—a matter which Mathews viewed with further foreboding:

'I have an invincible dislike for accounts, and a partnership seems to involve never-ending book-keeping.'

To which Lane replied:

'The book-keeping clause is just so much red tapism over which I don't think you will find me unreasonable, as I have just as much dislike of looking thru' a/cs as you have in keeping them.'

Nor did Lane much sympathise with Mathews's anxious enquiries about the street number of their Vigo Street premises—'I believe it is No. 6B, but why a number at all?'

He thought they did not need a number because their sign would be sufficient address. As indeed it was—but who thought of it first? When the print-seller Dunthorne at the Rembrandt Head had first shown Lane their future premises:

' "It should have a sign," I mused. The inspiration waited on the wish: it should be *The Bodley Head*. Bodley, the most pious of founders! Who could so fittingly be enshrined as patron? Besides, Bodley was one of the most notable worthies of Devon, my native country . . . "It should have a sign," I said, "And I have thought *The Bodley Head* is what it should be."

' "The very same idea was in my own mind," answered my partner, fresh from Exeter, Sir Thomas Bodley's birthplace.' Very likely, since after opening his Exeter bookshop Mathews had become particularly interested in the life and works of the founder of the Bodleian Library; more, he had used that worthy's arms on the cover of what seems to have been his first Exeter catalogue in 1885.

In any case the sign ('We shall require a swinging sign later on, one that can be seen both from Bond Street and Regent Street') was duly made, though not to swing; at its centre the oval medallion portrait of Bodley which looked in the event very much like Lane himself. The shop fittings were installed, drawing from Lane a note of excitement, and a quick response from his collector's instinct: 'The bottom cases are in, and I must own they looked fine, they have such a wonderful polish in them that I first thought they were of walnut.' And, again, 'The letter-hole is cut, and the first letter to come oddly enough is from the Bodleian.'

Mixed with his pleasing excitement, Lane was still eager for advice:

'I offered a £1 last night for *Fanny Hill*. I dare say I may get it for that or 25s. Should I give 30s. for it, if I can't get it for less? Your customer ought to give 50s. at least for it, indeed I think I know where I could place it at that or more.'

Nor was he averse from giving what was perhaps intended as advice, but sounds more like instructions:

'You know Dunthorne has picture shows, private shows. Well of course we shall know of these events before they come off, so that we can make a show of art books for the first week—say, works by Ruskin —you must order a dozen copies of his new book. I can place at least six. In the season, the Fellows of the Society of Antiquaries meet once a week, at 7.30 I think, and I fancy they pass our door; we must keep open that night and dress our windows for them.'

Salesmanship: a new concept to Elkin Mathews. Hardly less try-ing, no doubt, than this application to trade was quite another sort of application—of which there were several: 'I am short of cash until pay-day. Could you send me a cheque for £10 or £15 until then?'

Nor was Lane one to withhold an encouraging word, as when pass-ing on the off-hand comment of a metropolitan acquaintance: 'Country booksellers never do in London: *they don't bring in the stock or taste*' (Lane's italics).

3

Setting up Shop

At the end of the 1880s bookselling in London was, as usual, in a state of flux. Nostalgia was rife:

'The famous old Chapter Coffee House in Paternoster Row is shortly to become a thing of the past. The house is rich in associations, and its very holes, corners and tatters seem to echo with the sounds of the *literate* of a century and more past. The spirits of a whole host of authors, hacks [*sic*] and booksellers seem to cling to the place.'

So lamented that long-lived organ of the trade, *The Bookseller* (with which is incorporated *Bent's Literary Advertiser*), in July 1887, the very month in which the firm of Elkin Mathews at The Bodley Head opened its doors at the other end of town. Not until October did it carry the first official notification of the new enterprise, under the all-embracing heading, Trade and Literary Gossip:

'Mr C. Elkin Mathews has removed his old book business from the Cathedral Close, Exeter, to The Bodley Head, Vigo Street, London. First editions and scarce books will continue, as formerly, to be his specialities.'

John Lane's name was not to be mentioned, ostensibly, perhaps actually, because he was extremely nervous that at the Railway Clearing House they would disapprove of his moonlighting; though he so quickly became the dominant partner that his activities can hardly have escaped notice.

Meanwhile, the 'country bookseller' held the fort while the firm gradually found its way into the London booksellers' world, a motley scene which still ranged from publishers at one end to newsagents and stationers at the other, rent with dissension on questions of copyrights and discounts:

'The spreading custom of giving 25% discount off the published price of books is fast ruining the bookselling business as an independent trade . . . the public expects a 6s. book for 4s.'

Confirming this gloomy picture, both *The Bookseller* and its rival *The Publishers' Circular* began every issue with a full page, or even a page and a half, of classified lists of Receiving Orders, Meetings of Creditors, Appointments of Trustees, Dissolution of Partnership, Winding-up of Public Companies and Distribution of Assets, with a very small section announcing dividends.

No wonder an article, cautiously signed A Looker-On was gloomily headlined:

BOOKSELLERS' DIFFICULTIES AND GRIEVANCES
Can Any Remedy Be Found to Meet Them?

The answer was, of course, and still is, No. But cheerfulness would keep breaking out. Occasional conviviality, too, was a help and was doubtless enthusiastically patronised by John Lane, by this time a diner-out of prodigious zest: as when, for example, he attended one of Murray's dinners 'for literary and trade friends', at which 'the venerable chief of the Albemarle Street house [there is still a venerable head of the Albemarle Street house] was . . . in excellent form; and undeterred by the chill November fog, had driven in from distant Wimbledon to give hospitable greetings to his guests.'

However hospitable his greetings, this same John Murray the Second was a little frowned upon in *The Bookseller*:

'Some reviewers of the recent work, *A Publisher and his Friends* have claimed for Mr. John Murray the honour of lifting the calling of a publisher above that of a bookseller. They speak as if one were a trade and the other a profession . . . they both have the same object—the gaining of wealth from the works of "authors".'

This was a subject which booksellers, and *The Bookseller* found hard to leave alone at the time (and even now the distinction has not wholly disappeared). Dr Johnson's Dictionary was called in aid. A publisher, it said, was 'one who puts out a book into the world'. A bookseller, on the other hand, is 'He whose profession it is to sell books'. These evasive definitions hardly conceal the fact that neither publisher nor bookseller was in Johnson's day likely to rank as a gentleman. But, even in the 1880s, to rub salt in the wound, private individuals were habitually addressed as Esquire, while booksellers had to make do with plain Mr, as another *Bookseller* correspondent complained.

Some attempt to achieve both status and professional coherence was made about this time with the formation of the London Booksellers' Society, at whose inaugural dinner 143 members were regaled 'at intervals throughout the evening by the members of The Greyfriars Quartet, who gave some excellent part-songs and solos; and the Society's Chairman, Mr David Stott, was effusively described in *The Bookseller*'s report as 'a good fellow all round, a man of kindly heart and wide experience, whose guidance might be trusted to lead the Society to prosperity and permanence, (loud acclamation).'

Let us hope Elkin Mathews and John Lane were present to join in. Yet perfectly genuine though the enthusiasm of both was, that enthusiasm only masked a wish in each man to develop into a publisher—in John Lane's case, doubtless, as much for social as for bookish reasons.

Mathews had in fact made an innocuous start, probably at the author's expense, and in association with five other booksellers, before he came to London, with an account of more travels with a donkey—*We Donkeys on the Devon Coast* by Maria Susannah Gibbons of Budleigh Salterton. He can hardly be said to have entered the big time with another work, published soon after his arrival in

London, the *Index* to Dr Oliver's *Lives of the Bishops of Exeter*, or even, in association with an Exeter man, *The Old Stone Crosses of the Dartmoor Borders*, and still less with another Index, to the same Dr Oliver's *Monasticon Diocesis Exoniensis*.

For the time being, however, selling books was the order of the day. Errors of judgment occasionally earned a sharp rebuke, as when one customer, returning a biography of the actress and royal mistress, Mrs Jordan, observed to Elkin Mathews that 'though it may appear strange to you, that class of literature has absolutely no appeal to me.' Other clients were perhaps less restrictive: just as John Lane was confident that he could easily find a purchaser for *Fanny Hill*, so he reported cheerfully to Mathews that he had just bought 'a curious little book called *Every Night Book, or Life after Dark, by the Author of The Cigar, 1827*'.

First steps towards publishing were taken by purchasing, and re-selling at an enhanced price, books privately printed by the Rev. C. H. O. Daniel, who, moving from Frome in Somerset to Oxford, had discovered, lying unused and indeed forgotten at the University Press, a quantity of eighteenth-century Fell type. With these he quickly made a name for his limited editions:

'*Ailes d'alouette* by F. W. Bourdillon, choicely printed in Fell's type, on Alton Mills handmade paper, by the Rev. C. H. Daniel at his Private Press; limited to 100 copies.'

Mathews himself showed an unexpected gambling spirit in these transactions—abetted, and surpassed, by Lane. It was a gamble that paid off.

The fashion, not to say craze, for limited edition books was already going strong, and the volumes from The Bodley Head caught the tide, being in their early years almost entirely limited edition books. In the case of those originating with the Daniel Press, The Bodley Head initially asked the same price as had Daniel (though having purchased them at a fifteen per cent discount). *Ailes d'alouette* was advertised by Daniel at 5s. in 1890, but in The Bodley Head catalogue later in the same year at 7s. and a little later still at £1.10s., with the enticing phrase 'very few remain' added. Although Bodley Head catalogues of the time were presented as Mr Elkin Mathews's list until 1892, a great many of them were in fact Daniel Press books, virtually whole editions from that source being taken over and sold at higher prices, on the strength of their steadily increasing rarity value. This ingenious though not original ploy was highly congenial to Lane. It was no less congenial to an altogether more rarefied spirit, the poet Robert Bridges (later Poet Laureate), one of the few contemporary Daniel Press poets. Of his slim volume *The Growth of Love* he wrote to Daniel:

'You ask about reserve copies of G. of L. I think that I do not want my nearer acquaintances to have any privilege. But I should think that if the book is certain to rise in price that you might withhold some copies for the advanced market.'

The 'advanced market' was of course an artificial higher price brought about by the retention of a number of copies by the seller, in this case the highminded poet himself—carefully excluding his 'nearer acquaintances' from the profits of the trick.

As time passed, this very book brought friction in train. This seems to have arisen from an over-eagerness on the part of Lane. The residual sharp-witted farmer's boy failed perhaps to grasp the borderline of those manoeuvres which could be glossed over—for example by gentlemanly phrases such as 'advanced market' and those which could not. Bridges wrote uneasily to Daniel in 1893:

'I see that Messrs. Elkin Mathews and John Lane have taken to putting "Growth of Love" among their own *publications*, to which statement there is no qualification except that at the head of the list they say "including some transfers from remainders from other publishers' or words to that effect."'

This upset Bridges on two counts: the first, an understandable

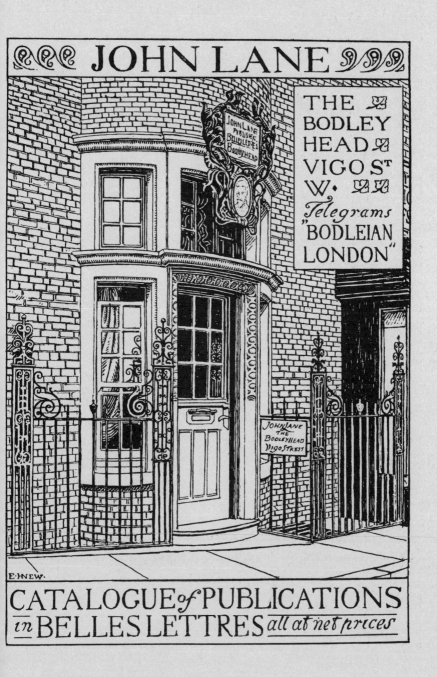

1. First premises of The Bodley Head in Albany, Vigo Street, after dissolving the partnership with Elkin Mathews in 1894. Drawing by Edmund H. New (see illustration IV).

· RICHARD · LE · GALLIENNE ·

11. *Volumes in Folio* by Richard le Gallienne, The Bodley Head's first book, appeared in 1887. Robert Bryden engraved on wood this portrait of the author.

dislike of the suggestion that his work had been remaindered; the second more practical if less comprehensible to the layman. So he wrote directly to Lane: 'The objection which I have is this—that the advertisement might be used as evidence that "The Growth of Love" was *published*, in which case it might cost me the American copyrights.' He thought a note to the effect that the book was privately printed might meet the case; adding in an ominous postscript:

'I also think that perhaps my publishers might have a sentimental, if not a businesslike objection to my name appearing in a list of your clients. You will know whether this would be so.'

Eventually Bridges, and the up-and-coming young poet Laurence Binyon, severed their connection with Lane and The Bodley Head; and indeed neither matched the image of stylish decadence which became the hallmark of The Bodley Head's new enterprise, which by commercial rather than artistic or aesthetic impulse shaped into a coherent voice, or rather chorus, of the Nineties. One who did fit that image, and can now be seen as by far the most important of them all, by a curious chance was greatly disliked by John Lane, a sentiment cordially reciprocated: Oscar Wilde. But his exciting and alarming shadow was not to fall across the blossoming young business until 1892—and to be cataclysmically resurrected in 1895.

4

Enter Le Gallienne

Meanwhile, the little bookshop in Vigo Street was doing well, in its way, though it was eighteen months after its opening that it launched into publishing on its own account—and that under the determined impulses of John Lane. It is usual to depict Elkin Mathews as an ineffectual duffer hovering nervously, and with some reason suspiciously, while Lane darted exuberantly in and out, bringing in potential buyers, potential poets, potential artists. Nor is the picture untrue; but though Mathews was willing to gamble on the 'advanced market' for existing limited editions (of 200–500 copies apiece), his temperament was not one for adventure. Lane's was; his excitement over the new was genuine, and though his own literary tastes were conventional, even old-fashioned, he was quite prepared to plunge into the business of boosting new young talent. Even so, he matched daring with caution, and regarded his discoveries with, on the whole, a sceptical eye—while they, for the most part, regarded him with amused contempt even as they revelled in his copious hospitality and gift for getting publicity for them.

The shop was tiny—some sixteen feet square, lined with books from floor to ceiling, divided by a wooden screen, behind which, on high stools, sat a one-eyed cashier, Roland Clarke, and J. Lewis May. Beneath their stools was a trap-door, leading to what May in *John Lane and the Nineties* called 'a dank, malodorous cellar' housing the lavatory, which many less adventurous folk would have regarded as an apt symbol. Round the epicentre paced Elkin Mathews, dusting and re-arranging the books, nursing his misgivings and bracing himself for Lane's next excursion from the Railway Clearing House.

Before long Lane had discovered, writing for *The Academy*, a quite distinguished London journal, Richard le Gallienne, a striking figure who personified the Nineties Poet, though his ultimate fate—more by luck than judgment—was less depressing than that of most of his fellows in this little flurry of poetasting, which is still, after a century, the subject of so much critical and academic scrutiny.

Le Gallienne's origins were hardly less removed from metropolitan Aestheticism than were John Lane's. He was born in 1866, in Liverpool, or rather in Everton, to John Gallienne (the Le was a romantic addition by his son), himself the son of a sea-captain from Guernsey. A deforming self-discipline enabled the father to escape from a vicious stepmother, to educate himself within grim biblical limits—he read the whole Bible through twenty-four times—and to raise himself very slowly to a position of modest prosperity on the management side of a local brewery. His son Richard himself grew up to be first the tyrant, then the adored cynosure, of his mother and a bevy of sisters, and to develop very early a consuming passion for anything in print, or in skirts, or in a glass. He did well enough at the Liverpool Collegiate Institution, though school reports spoke of his 'talking too much'. This did not stop him writing too much; at fourteen he produced, *Inter alia*, a poem on the modest theme of 'Eternity' which he hawked, price 1d., round the congregation of the Grange Road Baptist Chapel; and wrote an essay in which romanticism took a sociological turn as he described 'thousands out of work and starving, trade everywhere bad, and the country engaged in an unrighteous war, brought on by the cabinet ministers'.

Leaving school at fifteen, Richard was apprenticed for £100 to a firm of chartered accountants. He was quick and accurate at work; and lived, out of office hours, a sparkish life of youthful antiquarian cycle-rides and rapid acquaintance with local taverns. Two autobiographical novels, 'faction' rather than fiction, have described this phase of his life with remarkable accuracy and self-knowledge. He knew that on the one hand he was spoilt, and he also knew that he could not endure his father's apparent iron rule or the attrition of a clerk's life, however diversified by girls and fellow auto-didacts. He escaped not least through the companionship of his friend James

Welch, also a clerk, though in his own family business, and evidently a born actor. A bold assault on a famous touring actor, Wilson Barrett, in fact released them both—Welch to become a notable character-actor, not least in Shaw's early work; Le Gallienne to become, initially, Wilson Barrett's odd-job-man, or secretary, or, as would be said nowadays, personal assistant.

Before he left Liverpool, however, he had a book of poems, *My Lady's Sonnets*, privately printed on cream paper with rough edges, the expenses sportingly paid for by his fellow clerks; he had investigated several different religious systems, all rejected; he had numerous affairs, including one with the Galliennes' own housemaid, and had persuaded his father to pay the debts he had accumulated through his feverish book-buying. Bailing his son out was in fact a lifelong sideline for this supposed ogre, who also betrayed his feelings by keeping albums of press-cuttings—of which there were plenty—about his errant son. Richard had also founded a literary club, characteristically named 'The Squires and Dames of Books and Pens'; and—perhaps this was in the long run the major disaster of a life which knew many—attended a lecture given in Liverpool by Oscar Wilde, on 'Personal Impressions of America and its People'.

'Mark my words,' said Gallienne senior, who also attended, 'the man's no fool.' To young Richard, he was not only no fool, he was a celestial being, an inspiration and a model—not that homosexuality ever seems to have attracted him. But the broad-brimmed hat, the flowing cloak, the long and indolent posture became a familiar feature of the mercantile city. Not that his romantic idealism was absurdly proud. When a firm of Liverpool tobacco merchants printed a poem of his and then commissioned several more he was happy to oblige, as later he was to write what amounted to advertising copy for a firm of bedding manufacturers—organised by Holbrook Jackson, another chronicler of the bookman's Nineties, but then working in a Liverpool draper's shop.

He had also contracted one serious relationship—with a local girl, Mildred, who became his wife: a gallant girl, it is clear, putting up with poverty, drink, and infidelity both with other women and with what he would no doubt have called the Life Literary. No wonder she died young, leaving one daughter. True, he never ceased to love her, and was perhaps never the same again when she died, tending to pour out poems about her, even addressed to her, in a way which cannot really have gratified his two subsequent wives. Le Gallienne suffered most of his life from asthma as well as, later, overwork, under-nourishment, assorted humiliations, penury, alcoholism and phallomania. In the end he married money, and after a while, much of it spent keenly sailing in small boats, his hair short and neat, he came back to live in France, first in Paris, then in Menton, where he died, rather gallantly surviving the Second World War, in 1947, after 81 curious years.

He was in fact by no means the 'greenery-yallery' wisp of a poet his manner and his verses might suggest. A lout in Fleet Street one day, derisively knocking off his poetical hat, was rapidly cowed into picking it up and handing it back. It is true that he did visually resemble the poet Grosvenor in Gilbert and Sullivan's *Patience*. This derisive operetta had appeared in 1881, and seems to have acted as a spur, rather than a deterrent, to the affectations of Aestheticism; Le Gallienne embodied both aspects of Grosvenor—the simpering milksop and the 'steady-and-stolid-y, jolly bank holiday, everyday young man'. Shaw got it wrong when he wrote in 1891 a mocking review of *English Poems* (1890), mischievously sent him by *The Star*, for which they both wrote. Next day Le Gallienne published a pitiful lament, itself conspicuously tongue-in-cheek, as it could well afford to be, such was the 25-year-old's celebrity:

> 'A nightingale the Minotaur hath forn
> So seems my little murdered book this morn
> Bury it gently where no eye may see
> And for its epitaph write C. di B.'

Many were more upset than Le Gallienne himself at Corno di Bassetto's attack, to Shaw's irritation. Why all this fuss, he asked, about such a poor fellow: 'His fighting weight is not two and a half ounces: a rough wind would drive him to suicide.'

Nor, he added, would he have done the review at all 'if I had not thought he was getting spoiled.' Shaw was right about that; yet his spoiling at home, spoiling by his little wife, spoiling in the literary market place were as nothing to the way Le Gallienne spoilt himself. Long hair or no long hair, only a man physically tough (like many asthmatics) and mentally resilient could have survived the rough winds of his life—much rougher than those which did in fact drive several of The Bodley Head's poets to suicide. But if only it had been Shaw, and not Wilde, who had inspired his youthful fervour, he would surely have had an altogether more rewarding life.

Even Lane was perhaps a more suitable mentor. They met soon after Le Gallienne arrived, in Wilson Barrett's entourage, from Liverpool. Lane, himself by that time in his late thirties, always had an eye for a likely-seeming, good-looking young man; before long they went together on those expeditions in search of glass, or paintings, or old books, which were Lane's preoccupation. After one such outing, Lane had occasion to write to Le Gallienne, who replied, after thanking him for a letter 'in thy distingué (not to say "county family" hand) . . . I last saw thee [the second person singular presumably a reference to Lane's implausible Quaker leanings] rolling off like a nine-pin; or a wine-barrel, at Baker Street—you falstaffian seducer of youth':

> 'Beware the wine-cup's fatal hue
> Keep clear from every bloddy w——e'
> This was J.L's sweet last good-night,
> A voice replied 'You bet—all right.'

These warnings he did not heed. But he continued to pour out verse and prose, practically all of the former being in effect *vers d'occasion*—which like many such exercises occasionally struck a note of true poetry. It is worth remembering that when the publisher Grant Richards was in the 1930s sorting out the library of his friend

A. E. Housman, he was particularly enjoined not to weed out Le Gallienne—'He writes a great deal better than he's nowadays given credit for.' Well, yes—in even tinier fragments than is the case with most poets; reading his verse is like panning for gold—much rubbish, occasional delusive gleams, and very rare flecks of the real thing. His prose is on the whole much better, his critical insights into both life and letters often penetrating.

Nevertheless, in and especially in his association with John Lane, he touched one hungry strain of middle-class culture. His verse and prose alike almost all appeared in newspapers and periodicals; and when it was reprinted in book form it threw off the shoddy of newsprint and assumed the elegance of a style of book-making which greatly suited an age for which words like 'dainty' and 'winsome' were used as praise—used by writers as distinguished as Pater and Wilde. They were conceived by John Lane, who technically knew nothing about book production, but somehow, in choice of authors and artists-illustrators, showed undoubted flair: that word, vague though it is, was applied to him at the time by almost everyone, even hostile witnesses, who were not a few.

By applying it Lane quite suddenly, in his forties, created a nest of singing birds which made Vigo Street a household word—much, evidently, to Elkin Mathews's dismay. High pressure personal marketing, high pressure hospitality were Lane's stock-in-trade as a publisher, and he applied them gleefully to a disparate bunch of writers and artists, all of them rebelling, in their different ways, against materialism, the industrial revolution, a hypocritical religion and the ponderous late-Victorian philistinism of the Empire at its peak. Hoisting the flag of Beauty, of Art for Art's sake, they were minor figures all, and (except for Wilde) proud to see themselves as such, determined to escape the stifling shadow of those Great Victorians (though still admiring them, unlike the even feebler spirits of a generation later). Tennyson, Arnold, Browning, Landseer, Millais, Dickens, Thackeray, Trollope, Ruskin, Newman towered still.

The lesser talents of the day turned every which way for escape—some looked across the Channel, invoking second-hand *nostalgie de la boue*, worshippers with absinthe as their so daringly sacrilegious communion wine, opium their incense and the ludicrous tinsel of the music-halls their temples, amply stocked with accommodating vestals. These were proudly known as the Decadents, but in fact all the minor writers who made a mark of sorts in the world of, say, Kipling and Hardy and Henley were decadent. They lacked essential energy at best, substituting bluster. They were a symptom of a sick civilisation: not least those who, abjuring French fumes, conjured up an ideal Britain, all meadowsweet and roses and lush green pastures, into which the ghost of the great god Pan, not to mention Cuchulain and the leprechaun, had been wistfully translated. No less decadent (some became merely glum) were those who misread Whistler's vision of 'the time when the evening mist clothes the riverside with poetry, and the poor buildings lose themselves in the dim sky, and the tall chimneys become campanili, and the warehouses are palaces of the night'; and even, in their low-spirited way, the many who turned to the urban poor, to the wretched lives of those whom Le Gallienne rather finely spoke of as 'hopelessly buried in the back-streets and pawn-shops of life'.

Most of this motley crew were gathered in, came rushing in fact, towards Vigo Street; not to mention those to whom their subject-matter hardly registered, though it was, in contrast to later tastes, nice rather than nasty, those who rejected—Le Gallienne again—'dull sociological analysis', whose tastes were for:

'dreams and love and beautiful writing. Would the poet be a creature of passion and the novelist once more make you laugh and cry, and would there be essayists any more, whose phrases you would roll over and over again on your tongue?

'. . . That exquisite exaltation, that beautiful satisfaction of mind and spirit—even almost, one might say, of body—which for the lover of literature nothing in the world like a fine passage can bring.'

His hero—that is, himself—in *Young Lives* hoped 'to be too good a writer to expect to make money—except when it wasn't literature'.

His own failure is all too easily explained by this infantile romantic-ism, offset as it is by attempts at lightness of touch, as when he directs his readers' attention to his fiancée, 'if you want to know how fairies look when they are making hot-pot.' Or, again, the alarming corrup-tion of Pater shows him up, and the generation (including A. E. Housman) which so much admired him, when he depicts a young man of depressing sensitivity contemplating a painting with his innocent eye:

'. . . It was the terrible meeting of Youth and Love and Death in one tremendous moment of infinite loss. Infinite passion and infinite loss were here pictured, in a medium which combined all that was spiritual and all that was sensual, in a harmony of beauty that was in the same moment delirium and peace. The irresistible cry of the colour to the senses, the spheral call of the theme and its agony to the soul! . . . All Passion and all Loss, all Youth, all Love and all Death, meet together in an everlasting requiem of tragic colour.'

And yet this is the man capable of observing, of a matter on which he was a considerable expert, 'No lover will long be successful unless he is a humorist too, and able to keep the heart of love amused,' and of many highly cultivated women, 'Their very culture, while it may seem to broaden, really narrows them, limits them to a caste [*sic*] of mind, and for an infinite suggestiveness substitutes a few finite accomplishments.'

Such verbal flatulence and such sharp observation informed the mind of John Lane's right-hand-man as soon as the latter bustled into Vigo Street and woke up the little shop.

Entering, it would seem, into a conspiracy with Lane against Mathews, who, he was telling Lane with 24-year-old confidence, 'knows as much about the *modus operandi* of book production as a sucking-pig' . . . 'vacillating, procrastinating, old-maidish'—he added tartly that Lane's own proof corrections and emendations were both involved and indecipherable. Until he finally came to London, married, and fetched up in a villa in what was then the

(33)

tranquil suburb of Hanwell, he took to staying with Lane at the latter's rooms. These were ample and inexpensive; the landlord, an ebullient Welsh doctor, Owen Pritchard, was also a keen collector, a man after Lane's heart, who never put up the 10s. a week rent. Here Lane began his extensive entertaining with the evening parties which became such a feature of his life and work within a few years.

5

Odd Volumes
and Cheshire Cheese

While Le Gallienne was, still in his middle twenties, playing the Literary Adviser to some purpose, Lane in his early forties was busily expanding his personal and professional world. For one thing, he began getting himself elected to clubs. To the Hogarth Club in Down Street for one, haunt of painters and writers of all kinds—breakfasting with Whistler, arguing with Gosse—and, through a book-collecting patient of his Devonshire connection Dr May, had joined the dining-club named, in a way characteristic of the time, the Sette of Odd Volumes. Founded in 1878 (and still going strong), it originally had a membership of twenty-one, for no better reason than 'that this was the number of volumes in the 1821 Variorum Edition of Shakespeare.'

There existed a whimsical book of rules ('Rule 16: There shall be no Rule 16') and more or less appropriate ceremonial names and seals for its members. Lane became the Bibliographer—which he was, having already compiled one such list of Meredith's works to accompany Le Gallienne's study; he was to do the same for Hardy, not to mention a genial burlesque solemnly chronicling the Works of the stripling Beerbohm.

Buzzing as usual with enthusiastic energy, Lane in 1890 became Secretary of the Sette of Odd Volumes, and in 1891 its Master of Ceremonies. His interest in book design was catered for, as well as his greed for acquaintance, food and drink. The meetings were good for getting to know people of middling distinction and for buttering up useful people by inviting them as guests. Moreover, at each meeting a paper was read, and reprinted as 'Opuscula' in 133 numbered copies, with elaborate typography in red and black. The subjects of these papers were, to say the least, diverse: 'The Early History of the Royal Society', say, or 'Chinese Snuff Bottles of Stone, Porcelain and Glass Utilised to Appear a Fabric of Fantasies concerning China and the Chinese', or 'Harmonies in Japanese Music'. Two other talks, on 'Music in the Reign of Queen Elizabeth' and 'Richard Wagner and *The Ring of the Nibelungen*' are announced as 'Presented by John Lane'—rather strangely, in view of his antipathy to music.

It is no wonder that throughout his life Lane was subject to intermittent nervous exhaustion; apart from eating, drinking, socialising, collecting, organising, he was a voracious reader in many different fields, and eyestrain, doubtless genuine, was also a useful excuse for his habit, prompted alike by overwork, indifference and caution, of not answering letters. Not that *he* was above impatience. Once, spurring Le Gallienne on, he provoked the latter to cast aside his ultra-poetical robe and reply: 'My dear J.L., I beseech you—think of your trousers! There is really no need to . . . yourself.'

In 1888 Lane announced, in the Finsbury house of Dr May, that he was about to become a publisher—using much the same excited tone as another man might have used to proclaim that he was about to become a father. He reappeared early in 1889 with his first literary child, *Volumes in Folio*, by the poet whom he described as 'a young man of undoubted genius, who is bound to set the Thames on fire, and who has the face of a Greek god': Le Gallienne, of course.

Though *Volumes in Folio* was not in itself particularly distinguished in appearance (and still less in its contents) it inaugurated the extraordinary flowering of Bodley Head books which made the firm famous, credit for which must, on all available evidence, be given to the energy of the self-educated Devonshire farmer's son, John Lane. He was not quite the first to produce volumes which were a marked contrast to the general run of Victorian books considered as physical objects: these tended to have been graceless, ponderous and, if ornamented at all, then swamped in a congestion of gold. William Morris was improving matters a little, but only on a sumptuous scale which contrasted oddly with his socialist principles. Among commercial publishers J. M. Dent had made a few forays in the direction of stylishness at a reasonable price; but The Bodley Head, in its search for the affordably exquisite, opened the door to a whole galaxy of largely young (and therefore cheap) practitioners all of whom were at one in their search for assorted freedoms, and who gave the Nineties the character which itself lasted for a very short time, and on a very small scale, but which brightened the sky for a readership itself ready for refreshment—or for elegant triviality, according to one's point of view.

Praise, for the appearance of Bodley Head books at least, was almost universal on both sides of the Atlantic:

'To Messrs Elkin Mathews and John Lane, almost more than to any other, we take it, are the thanks of the grateful authors especially due; for it is they who have managed, by means of limited editions and charming workmanship, to impress bookbuyers with the belief that a volume may have an aesthetic and a commercial value.'

But their 'beautiful editions of *belles lettres*' were soon to prove an inspiration copiously acknowledged. The new Boston publishers Stone and Kimball announced in the American *Publisher's Weekly*— with an initial and necessary proviso—that its first aim,

'. . . after the worth and truth of a book is assumed, is to give it a beautiful setting . . . They are using the best papers in the market— Dutch, English and American—are decorating their books with designs by the best artists in this country and in England, and are printing and binding their books at the leading establishments in the country . . . The ambition of this new firm is, in short, to attain to the ideal realised by Messrs. Elkin Mathews and John Lane in London.'

Between the publication of that first book, Le Gallienne's *Volumes in Folio*, in March 1889, and the dissolution of the partnership of Mathews and Lane in October 1894, the firm published some ninety books. Almost all were books of verse or of that ill-defined and now discredited genre, *belles lettres*—as publishers of which, indeed, the firm proudly announced itself. For all its soaring reputation it ventured upon very small ordinary, small-paper first editions mostly ranging between 50 and 850 copies, and often with even smaller large-paper or luxury versions. Some achieved larger second editions, a few were favoured with ambitious initial printings, among them Sir Herbert Beerbohm Tree's essay on *The Imaginative Faculty*, 1050 copies (1893); William Watson's *The Eloping Angels*, 2025, and his *Excursions in Criticism*, 1000 (both 1893); Norman Gale's *Orchard Songs*, 2080 (1893); G. A. Greene's *Italian Lyrists of Today*, 1000 (1893); Florence Farr's *The Dancing Faun*, 1100 (1894); Dostoevsky's *Poor Folk*, 1100 (1894); Le Gallienne's *Prose Fancies*, 1112 (1894) and his *The Religion of a Literary Man*, 3000 (1893).

Others achieved rapid expansion, notably George Egerton's *Keynotes* (1893). This became the first and eponymous book of a once daring and celebrated series, but initially only 500 copies were issued of the 1100 printed; fourteen months later its sensational success had achieved a total printing of 6071 copies. On the other hand Walter Crane's *Renascence, a Book of Verse* was thought worth risking only to the extent of 215 copies for both England and the United States, and William Strang's Burnsian, powerful, and powerfully self-illustrated, *The Earth Fiend*, only 175, albeit on Japanese paper and with another 100 large-paper folio copies on old handmade paper. As for a reissue of Oscar Wilde's poems, taken over from another publisher in 1892, 220 copies were thought enough, it seems rightly since they were not reprinted; no doubt The Bodley Head felt uncommonly bold in putting out 600 copies of *Salomé* in French, even if *Lady Windermere's Fan* rated only 550 copies, as indeed did, in 1893, the fanciful baroque of Francis Thompson's *Poems*.

Among the prose *belles lettres* little to claim posterity's attention appeared. Buxton Forman's *Three Essays on Keats* peeped out in a mere 50 copies printed by the Chiswick Press in 1890. *Dante: Six Sermons*, by Philip Wicksteed, on the other hand, was thought in the same year to call for 1000 copies in three printings. Charles Jacobi's *On the Making and Issuing of Books* (1891), a landmark for bibliophiles, rated 450 copies in 1891. Alice Meynell's *The Rhythm of Life and Other Essays* (1893) quite quickly achieved two ordinary editions of 500 copies each. John Addington Symonds's alluring work entitled *In the Key of Blue*, an aesthetic's essential text (1893), climbed in assorted editions to 1927 copies. *The Poems of Arthur Henry Hallam, together with his Essay on the Lyrical Poems of Alfred Tennyson* ran to 860 copies (1893).

John Davidson's plays having passed without much notice in 1893 (his *Fleet Street Eclogues* achieved two quick printings, in all of 702 copies, in the same year), his journalism in *A Random Itinerary* was given an instant printing of 755 copies, followed by another shot at launching his plays in 1894 with a bold 760 copies, plus a few more bound in white buckram. 'I am so glad', the unhappy and often splendid poet wrote to Elkin Mathews in uncharacteristically Falstaffian tones, 'you have found it in your heart to give me buckram: I would have fought a whole hour by Shrewsbury clock over that buckram suit'—and added a more typical 'P.S. I have a swollen eyelid.' Temperamentally, this turbulent Scottish dominie had more than a swollen eyelid to contend with, and eventually drowned himself, like the subject of his fine poem 'A Runnable Stag' in 1909.

Another forgotten but by no means contemptible poet, Roden Noel, showed in a letter to Elkin Mathews another side of the literary flowering of the day—one not at all harassed by the thought of commercial struggle. He wishes, he says, to come to The Bodley Head from Kegan Paul, who have published his poems for many years, but

'. . . have now become a limited company . . . I confess I would like some human being to "publish" me, rather than a limited company! Especially someone with an interest in Literature as such and not *merely* as so much marketable and common retail "stuff"!—and having met you, I felt as if you *were* a human being of the kind.'

'But,' he added ominously, 'I see you have a partner now.'
Equally untouched by the cold necessity of commerce was John Leicester Warren, Lord de Tabley. His *Guide to the Study of Book Plates*, published elsewhere in 1890, had fallen flat. Perhaps owing

to Lane's enthusiasm for book-plates, The Bodley Head reissued the book in 1892, and was, on its own scale, highly successful. This led de Tabley to comment that 'It is like the irony of life that the only thing I should have succeeded in, is what I look upon as a complete trifle'. 'I have failed', he went on in terms which recall Eeyore, A. A. Milne's lugubrious donkey, 'in literature, I have failed in politics, I have failed in such a miserable thing as being a landlord, which any fool can manage. Nothing remains except those contemptible book-plates.'

This turned out not to be true, for he had written, years before, some by no means contemptible verse, and plays, in a classical and elegiac manner. Theodore Watts-Dunton, Swinburne's nurse and himself a man of letters, proposed that a selection should be made. Lane welcomed the idea, and at his own risk at that. Not so de Tabley, who contested the idea 'with his usual pessimistic vigour', said Watts-Dunton (or plain Watts as he was then, before the judicious addition to his name prompted the famous telegraphic enquiry: 'Theodore—What's Dunton?'). Nevertheless, de Tabley was talked into making a selection, partly with Le Gallienne's help. He made the book's production as difficult as possible, not least by his dithering over the choice, and by the addition of much new material:

'I may tell you that I do not think above 120 [pages] are up to the level which make them worth reprinting. 80 pages seem to me under that level. . . . the longer pieces have worked out rather worse than I expected . . .'

As for the new material—'I fully expect them to be much worse than the old.' Perhaps they were, for soon he wrote again about the new poems: 'My original material had proved so bad that it struck me that these could not be much worse.'

The text agreed upon, de Tabley wanted, but was not allowed, as glum a binding as possible. Nor did he care for Ricketts' cover. He wanted *Verse*, not *Poems*, in the title: this modesty was denied him too. At a late stage he wanted to abandon the book. Talked out of that, he riposted: 'It will be a failure, most assuredly . . . my only doubt is whether it will be a moderate failure, or a resounding one.'

In the event, it was, in its own terms, a resounding success, all 600 copies being sold out immediately, fully justifying Lane's astonishing refusal of de Tabley's offer to pay the costs of production. Unfortunately, neither partner actually informed him ('Not one word have I heard from the publishers'), and he was left to glean the information from the newspapers.

Perhaps the firm's indifference to the author's feelings was, at least in this case, due to the fact that when he was not groaning de Tabley was apt to lapse into a tone of voice which may have been one of the reasons why he had failed even, as he had put it, 'in such a miserable thing as being a landlord':

'If used for the book it [the book-plate] must be printed on the same kind of paper as the text and illustrations; a trial impression should be struck off at once; a good printer of engravings should be employed or the plate will be spoiled.'

These brisk instructions must have jarred on both Elkin Mathews and Lane, since their reputation had been largely built on just such production niceties. But the command that 'a trial impression should be struck off at once' must have gone especially against the grain, since (with rare exceptions such as had stung Le Gallienne and his Liverpool printer) the idea of doing anything *at once* was deeply uncongenial to both—it was perhaps one of the few things they had in common.

Another, however, was a care for the appearance of their books, shown also by Le Gallienne. Many more tributes than those already quoted appeared. Some signs had indeed already appeared of relatively inexpensive publications (before their 'advanced prices')—in Whistler's books and catalogues, for example, and indeed in those already mentioned from the Rev. C. H. O. Daniel, from George Over of Rugby, and the fancifully named Bibliothèque de Carabas, notably with Andrew Lang's edition of Apuleius's *The Marriage of*

Cupid and Psyche, all very 'dainty'. What came to be known as the Bodley Head book was not so much dainty as divided. Its general layout, and often (especially when its authors had a strong influence) its covers were attractively austere; its title-pages and decorations tended to what to a later eye might seem flowery, and to contemporary eyes suspiciously or insidiously curvaceous, subliminally sexual.

Art Nouveau here came on a tiny scale into its sickly—or Blakean—prime; and though the books were slight in both form and substance, they made so great a contrast to most of what had gone before that they became the talk of the town. In this curious flowering the role of the printer was considerable and has received little recognition: especially that of the Chiswick Press and of T. & A. Constable of Edinburgh. Since neither Mathews nor Lane knew anything about the technicalities of book production, they must certainly be given credit for employing men of such outstanding visual sense. Perhaps they did not always achieve, or try to achieve, Constable's golden rule in book design: 'Entire plainness and simplicity, with no ornament that is not absolutely required'—even Charles Ricketts, at the Vale Press, would hardly go as far as that. But it is no wonder that, for instance, in reviewing the Arts and Crafts Exhibition of 1893, *The Studio* should have commented that several Bodley Head books were 'a revelation to those who see them here for the first time'. In particular, the work of Charles Ricketts and C. H. Shannon, beavering away in Chelsea in snug impoverishment, and never inviting the menacing shadow of a Marquess of Queensberry:

'The work of these two artists already has influenced our younger designers to an unusual extent, and if they are not household words to the outside public, one may doubt if the work of any of their contemporaries is more eagerly studied by their fellow-artists.'

One aspect of their influence was to focus attention on the printed book, or more broadly on art intended for reproduction, especially in black and white. The Bodley Head rapidly became the prime channel for their work, and formed the stable of artist-designers and illustrators for which as much as for their literary content, or perhaps more so, the firm's books of the Nineties are remembered.

Prime among them, until the threat of ruin to The Bodley Head displaced him, was the youthful, not to say juvenile, genius, and Lane's special enthusiasm, Aubrey Beardsley. He did the bindings, title-pages, frontispieces for eleven Bodley Head works: including, with nine full-page illustrations, Oscar Wilde's *Salomé*, and Kenneth Grahame's first book, *Pagan Papers*. Ricketts and Shannon together in fact did only two books, Longus's *Daphnis and Chloe* and the Marlowe-Chapman *Hero and Leander*. Ricketts alone designed the binding for Wilde's *Poems* (the first book to appear, in 1892, under the joint imprint of Elkin Mathews and John Lane at The Bodley Head) and for *The Sphinx*; for John Addington Symonds's *In the Key of Blue*: for an elaborate edition of Lord de Tabley's *Poems Dramatic and Lyrical*, with six full-page illustrations, and for *Silverpoints*, another highly regarded graphic work to poems by Oscar Wilde's curious friend John Gray, often mooted, not least by himself, as the origin of Dorian Gray. Shannon weighed in with binding designs for Wilde's *Lady Windermere's Fan*.

In a small world and although not yet a playwright, much more famous than his brother the poet, Laurence Housman was entrusted with the binding designs, cover, frontispiece and title-page of Francis Thompson's *Poems*, John Davidson's *A Random Itinerary*, and Katherine Tynan's *Cuckoo Songs*. Another favoured artist, Selwyn Image, has vanished from general memory, but at least did the cover and title-page for *A London Rose*, by Ernest Rhys, who should certainly never be forgotten as the founder (though for J. M. Dent, not for The Bodley Head) of the Everyman Library.

He was also one of the founders of the so-called Rhymers' Club, at which indeed Elkin Mathews was a frequent guest—but never John Lane. It was formed in 1890 by this Welsh-speaking former mining engineer and by one of his authors, W. B. Yeats, who had written:

'I am growing jealous of other poets and we will all grow jealous of one another unless we know each other and so feel a share in each other's triumphs.'

This seems an optimistic conclusion to draw from the chances of acquaintance. And Yeats warned against the idea that the group was:

'a school of poets in the French sense, for the writers who belong to it resemble each other in but one thing: they all believe that the deluge of triolets and rondeaus has passed away, and that we must look once more upon the world with serious eyes and set to music—each according to his lights—the deep soul of humanity.'

Their lights were indeed very different, their serious eyes made their meetings, mostly in a gloomy, panelled room in the Cheshire Cheese, a Fleet Street public house, associated with Samuel Johnson (though Ben Jonson would have been more suitable) into occasions of extreme solemnity and, evidently, extreme boredom for the assorted poets.

Nevertheless, every now and again some member's verse made a tremendous impact, not least on Yeats, whose idea it was to produce an anthology of members' work. Since Le Gallienne was on the editorial committee, it was doubtless he who brought the book to The Bodley Head, who already published many of the likely contributors; but it was the indefatigable Yeats who made the necessary arrangements with Elkin Mathews. Each contributor was limited to six poems, and made, in theory, a small contribution to the expense in proportion to the space he occupied.

Though intended to be in time for Christmas, *The Book of the Rhymers' Club* was actually published, in a pale orange cover, in February 1892, 450 copies of the ordinary edition being printed, 350 of them for sale, and 50 copies in a large-paper format. They were all sold at once; and another volume of new poems was put together and published in June 1894, in an edition of 450 copies for Britain, 150 for the USA, in the small-paper edition, and 50 copies for Britain, 20 for the USA of the large-paper version.

These minute figures represented a considerable success. The two volumes, in fact, constituted the peak of achievement for the Nineties poets. Their works continued to appear in dainty volumes, but their short high noon was past; perhaps two poems from the two anthologies are still widely remembered—'Non sum qualis . . .', by Ernest Dowson, better known by its refrain, 'I have been faithful to thee, Cynara, in my fashion', and Yeats's 'The Lake Isle of Innisfree'. The former, with its cumbrous Latin title, has continued to offer the suggestion of sharing in a superior culture, a sense of mystery, an elegiac melody—and, of course, a useful, if unconvincing, excuse for infidelity. The latter offers an invaluable combination of the implausibly simple, the romantic and the escapist, with a hint of a celibate sacrifice.

But it is a sad irony that the finest Nineties poet of them all, so much finer than the rest that he is never thought of as a Nineties poet at all, A. E. Housman, gave the whole group an unfair, if private, *coup de grâce* when, in 1928, he was asked for permission to include some of his poems in another Nineties anthology being prepared by A. J. A. Symons. Housman declined in an agreeably characteristic manner: 'To include me in an anthology of the Nineties would be just as technically correct, and just as essentially inappropriate, as to include Lot in a book on the Sodomites.'

6

The Loyal and the Louche

If John Lane played little part in the activities of the Rhymers' Club
—'not an energetic institution', said Le Gallienne of what Arthur
Symons called its 'desperate and ineffectual attempt to get into key
with the Latin Quarter'—or of most of its poets, it was because he
had other fish to fry. True, he still retained a warm interest in some
of the Club's poets—particularly William Watson, in fact an absentee
member, and Le Gallienne—although the latter was already beginning to nurse misgivings about what he optimistically called 'Lane's
loyalty'—a volatile quality at best. Le Gallienne was not the first,
and certainly not the last, to suffer unease at the businessman's preoccupations, of which the creative artist's hopes and fears were but
one element. 'To be quite candid,' said Lane to him, à propos of *The
Romance of Zion Chapel*—a novel very well received in England—'I
want the book because I cannot afford to have you take it elsewhere—
indeed I don't think it would be good for either of us.' So, commented
Le Gallienne, 'one weapon he very fully placed into my hand in
mid-contest'; and for once Lane really was candid, and stumped up
the substantial £400 advance demanded.

But their relationship was never too seriously damaged until Le
Gallienne went off for seven years to the United States, in 1900. A
few years later Le Gallienne was writing of Lane:

'He has so flagrantly broken his contracts with me, in failing to
deliver accounts, that I think I would be legally supported in taking
the line that his failure in so important a matter exempted me from
keeping a contract so evidently precarious. There is no doubt at all

that his business is in a very bad way, and though he may show fight, he is in no position to keep it up.'

More basically truthful perhaps, is the fact that Lane was groomsman at Le Gallienne's first marriage, in St Andrew's, Holborn; or this pleasing glimpse recorded by Grant Richards from a Shelley celebration in Sussex in 1892:

'Le Gallienne, looking more like a poet than any man has ever looked, before or since; and John Lane in a straw "boater" decorated with the ribbon of the Railway Clearing House or something of the sort, proudly strutting along at his side, like an aircraft carrier in the wake of a racing yacht ... And if, on that occasion Richard Le Gallienne looked like a poet he talked like one, not with the calculated affectation of that other poet of those *Fin de siècle* days, nor with those curled epigrams, but with friendly disarming simplicities that won almost too many hearts.'

And Lane, notorious for caution, or what some would call cowardice, certainly stood by Le Gallienne when the poet found himself attacked on all sides over a matter of religion. Like Wilde before him, Le Gallienne made a considerable name for himself as a lecturer, with a taste for confronting his audiences: e.g. on 'The Entire Modern Revolt of Woman against the Immemorial and Absurd Domination of Men' or treating Liverpool nonconformists to a harangue on 'The World, the Flesh and the ... Puritans'. Out of this arose a newspaper controversy in London which drew sermons in Westminster Abbey and St Paul's, even newspaper posters trumpeting 'Mr Buchanan's Latest Reply, by Mr Le Gallienne'. The theme of this rumpus was, broadly, the heading of one of his articles in *The Daily Chronicle*: 'Is Christianity Played Out?' Le Gallienne's answer to this question was in effect an indeterminate set of the sort of views which would probably have gone down well with certain Anglican churchmen in the 1960s. From the series of articles in *The Daily Chronicle* he made a book, rendered especially absurd when published in a special edition, got up with double rules around the text, and annotations as rubrics printed in red. This he called the *Confessio Poetae Minoris*, though wisely retaining English for its main title: *The Religion of a Literary Man*. All religions, he said, were only forms of arbitrary symbolism; the notion of free will was nonsensical, there were only different strengths of will; sins were a kind of disease; Christianity has never been tried, and organised Christianity has corrupted the ideals of its founder; Whitman's *Leaves of Grass* is worth more than the New Testament; the Artist is the priest of today; 'We can do without the hereafter.'

All this and more, vigorously expressed, brought attack from three sides. Believing Christians were dismayed at this bizarre championship; unbelievers were cross that he had so muddied the waters; and other literary folk shrank in embarrassment—or, in the case of Henley's *National Observer*, exploded in predictable contempt.

'The tea-tables of the suburbs have been crying out for a Moses ... As a conjunction of pretentiousness and cheapness, affectation and simplicity, shallowness and foppery, it is all that the Heart of Woman could desire.'

Having disposed of women, the *National Observer* went on to deride a large slice of the population: 'It is the religion of a clerk ... with the sheerest inability to comprehend the difference between exact thought and floundering sentiment.'

And, added the review in a final sneer: 'Why does his very name sound ungrammatical?'

The pulpits thundered, the printing presses screamed. Not for the last time, one of John Lane's authors caused the fur to fly; and John, not averse to publicity, stood by him. At the end of his long life, all passion spent, Le Gallienne was to reflect truly, in a letter to Lewis May, that,

'... if "Johnny" did no little to make me, it is a mere matter of history that I helped considerably to make him—as his first reader, and a reviewer in various newspapers ... Indeed, we made each other, and the fact that I have had no accounts from his firm for thirty years—the Society of Authors is at the present moment investigating them on my behalf—makes no difference in my appreciating what you rightly call his genius as a publisher. I like him, too, as a companion. He was a real lover of books, with a remarkable flair.'

That word again. But the flair was leading him into fresh woods, even more storm-wracked than had been the case so far. And in 1892 a new, if deceptively diffident, voice was heard in the counsels of Vigo Street. Not that of the flamboyant poet with the face of a Greek god, but of the quiet, unassertive, widely read and practically competent Frederic Chapman. Throughout what follows in this chronicle, until his death in 1918, the presence of Chapman should be remembered in all Lane's transactions—as often as not, no doubt, as a counsellor or calm commonsense, by no means always heeded.

This extraordinary man was born in 1863 in Soho, the son of a publican's daughter married to a journeyman leather-cutter who set up in business as a coach-hirer and currier ('one who dresses and colours tanned leather') first in Kennington Park Road, then back in Soho—the business was still there in 1931.

The source of Frederic's education, though clearly admirable, is unknown: but apart from an almost donnish literacy, and a vast knowledge of English literature, it also included a useful grasp of French and Italian. He is next heard of in Leicester in his mid-twenties. The city was then a centre of the printing industry; the young Chapman joined the firm of J. & T. Spence, and formed a circulating library. In 1892 Lane discovered him; if nothing else, shared antiquarian interests would have brought them inevitably together—as they were to remain for the next twenty-six years. He came to London, first living in Smith Square, Grays Inn, and still in 1893 editing for his old firm *Spencer's Almanac*, and reviewing such particularities as, in *Leicestershire and Rutland Notes and Queries*, 'How to Study and Decipher Old Documents' or 'The History of Wyggeston's Hospital'. Soon he and a brother bought two houses in Sinclair Road, Hammersmith, though this move hardly seems to have pointed to any alliance with Elkin Mathews and the Bedford Park circle. Next he set up in Twickenham, renaming Sion Cottage as Sion House and installing there his whole family, father, mother and sister. Family, literature and The Bodley Head seem thereafter to have constituted his whole life. Certainly he played no significant part in Lane's socialising world, though later, after the flurry of the Nineties had died down, he wrote the text for drawings by T. R. Way of *Ancient Royal Palaces in and near London*, and edited several small series such as *The Lover's Library*, and such elegant titles as *Proverbs Improved* and *The Poets' Year Birthday Book* and *The Sacred Treasury*. He wrote a grave introduction to a new edition of Fitzgerald's *Euphranor*: his prose itself reflects that laborious cultural aspiration which was the other side of the Decadent's coin:

'Many of us have at times desired that it might be our lot, some day, with that delight which the recognition literary treatment of a noble subject ever brings in its train, to welcome a book on *Youth* which, with due regard to the fitness of things, we could shelve by the side of Cicero's *De Senectute*. Few of us have known that for upwards of fifty years a book has been procurable that, as nearly as any attained thing does fulfil a desire, corresponds in essential features with the treatment longed for.'

Few of us knew it then; alas, few of us know it now; Fitzgerald's *Dialogue*, such a joy when discovered by one ageing bachelor in the work of another, remains a closed book today despite Chapman's championship. He was, at least for some decades, more successful in his service to Anatole France, of whose English translations there were in the end forty-two volumes published by The Bodley Head—again, after the flurry of the Nineties had died, not to say been extinguished by events.

Meanwhile there was much for Chapman to manage, and as manager he joined the firm: keeping straight, for example, the various arrangements by which books were published: On commission, the author paying all costs, the publisher taking whatever commission he could get away with on copies sold (not on review or presentation copies, but with that mysterious book-trade incantation, 13 to count as 12, or 25 to count as 24, according to the value of the books); on a 'half-profit basis', presumably sharing costs; or buying the copyright for a lump sum, though sometimes adding a small royalty as well. In fact, though it seems improbable, Lane is credited with introducing the publishing principle that *all* authors should *always* get a royalty. If this improvement did begin with The Bodley Head, it must surely have been Chapman who with quiet persuasiveness sold it to both Elkin Mathews and Lane.

He was, said Grant Richards:

'a seeming-shy, unpushing sort of chap, but he had taste and fore-sight to an unusual degree. He must have been worth his weight in gold, but I doubt whether he ever had his proper reward.'

In material terms, almost certainly not: such invaluable executive workhorses never do get their proper rewards, and are presumably satisfied by having a dynamic figure to follow, the more erratic the better. Not that Chapman was a man to be put upon by outsiders, however eminent. Oscar Wilde, addressing him loftily one day as 'Chapman', received the chilling response, 'Would you like me publicly to address you as "Wilde"?'

Wilde! The very name is like a knell, and well before the events which were to follow in 1895. Nothing but trouble from the start, and complicated by a curious personal matter in which Lane can be hardly said to shine. In 1890 the firm had taken on, as a very junior dogsbody, a 17-year-old boy, Edward Shelley. He was the son of a blacksmith in Fulham, in whom mental instability was all too clear; nevertheless, he had social and cultural aspirations, much helped by his presence in the Vigo Street bookshop, though in the long run this was to do him no good at all. Very soon, in fact, he assumed a role which did neither him nor Lane any credit. He became in fact Lane's spy in the shop, and his letters to his master make sad reading, begin-ning in the autumn of 1890: 'I asked Mr. M. this afternoon for a day's leave on Monday, and he flatly refused it . . . will you use your influence, on my behalf?'

Shelley then reports that he has failed to obtain *The Whirlwind* for Lane:

'The newsagents are aware of it, and will not sell it, except for a price which is quite prohibitive—some are asking as much as 5s. for it . . . I would advise you to obtain your copies of "Meredith" *at once* if you want them all 1st editions. M. has forbidden me to give either you or Mr. le G. any more copies . . . He did not wish to see you or le G. this afternoon and went out purposely to avoid you. He was very quiet for the remainder of the afternoon— after that "little scene"—but remarked that "he was not going to let you two have all the say." '

The plot thickens:

'Dear Sir: I should like to have a few minutes conversation with you—nothing very important but I have some information, that can be used to advantage. If I see you, before I can receive a reply, make some sign to me, by which I shall know where to meet you. If you cannot do that with safety, please shut the door if I am to meet you at the coffee-house but leave the door open (as you come in) if you cannot meet me.'

In six weeks' time, in January 1891:

'Dear Sir: I enclose a copy of a letter of Mr. Julian M.'s, which Mr. Mathews received this morning. The copy was taken unknown to M. . . .'

In February, Shelley forebore to ask a favour of Mathews:

'. . . he was in such an ill-temper that I would not risk the possibility of a refusal. He did not at all like your borrowing that "Manchester

Quarterly" and was irritable the remainder of the day; however, I must not complain. You will be sure to write to me, to call either on Monday or Tuesday evening for the "Once a Weeks".'

By March he is reporting that Mathews is 'getting ready the accounts' and asking Lane to help him get an increase in wages; in April 'I have several things to tell you of, but am afraid to call at Southwick Street on account of le G.' And later in the same month, 'I enclose a list, & hope you will excuse delay in sending it—but I really could not make one out before now, because M. has been working in the shop all Saturday and Monday—it would not be safe to attempt it.'

In May Lane has, and no wonder, been ill and Shelley alerts him:

'I trust you have recovered your health, at Kingswood, and also preparing for the fray—M. is not losing time, I feel sure; he rarely goes into the warehouse, and sends me out on all kinds of trivial missions, and sometimes when I return I find him poring over the cash-book and pencilling down totals.'

And so the squalid letters go on. In July:

'Mr. M. has been telling me a great deal about your affairs, and asking numerous questions about matters concerning your relations to me . . .'

And Shelley is still pressing Lane to help him get an increase in salary, with a persistence that begins to seem strangely like black-mail. But a sudden silence falls for almost two years, until in July 1893 he writes to Lane asking for a reference when applying for the job of 'Secretary to the Secretary of the London Library'. Reference or no, he does not get the job. But evidently he has to leave The Bodley Head. Why?

The firm was preparing its own publication of *Salomé* in English:

'Mr. Wilde was in the habit of coming to the firm's place of business; he seemed to take notice of me, and he generally stopped and spoke to me for a few moments. As Mr. Wilde was leaving Vigo Street one day he invited me to dine with him at the Albemarle Hotel. I kept the appointment. I was proud of the invitation. We dined together in a public room. Mr. Wilde was very kind and attentive, and pressed me to drink. I had champagne with dinner, and after had whisky and soda and smoked cigarettes in Mr. Wilde's sitting-room.

Counsel: What happened afterwards?

Shelley: I do not like to say.'

So the wretched boy, faltering in the witness-box at Wilde's second trial, had his deposition read over. 'Will you come into my bedroom,' said Wilde, and as they went into the room 'Mr. Wilde kissed me. He also put his arms round me.' Shelley claimed to have objected 'vigorously', but in fact stayed the night and shared Wilde's bed. And so it went on, until, his father objecting, young Shelley set about in a rage, was arrested and sent to Wilde to bail him out. Worse, life at The Bodley Head became unendurable. 'People employed there, my fellow-clerks, chaffed me about my acquaintance with Wilde . . . They implied scandalous things. They called me "Mrs. Wilde" and "Miss Oscar".'

And having left the firm for a job with a tea-broker, he wrote to Wilde saying that he could not manage on a salary of £50. He asked Wilde for money, adding that he would accept nothing from 'that viper Lane'—who had in fact promised him help on condition that he broke off his association with Wilde. Why, he was asked, did he call Lane a viper? 'I think my mind must have been disordered.'

Indeed it was. In the spring of 1894 Lane, still apparently well-disposed, sent him a copy of *The Yellow Book* and one of Le Gallienne's. To this Shelley replied:

'Dear Sir: I regret that I am unable to retain "The Yellow Book" and Mr. Le Gallienne's book as gifts, but will send the cost of them

(54)

. . . I feel unable to accept anything of you. I prefer to trust to Time and Truth, rather than surrender to petty circumstances. You will not fail to understand my meaning; do not reply, Yours Truly.'

A few days later this was followed by a note grovelling apology for a letter written 'during a moment of what I can only call mental aberration'—and going on to offer to return to work for Lane: 'I would ten times sooner work for you than for any other house in the trade . . . I am only twenty, and have my youth and vigour still; I thank God that I had the courage to live down the terrible blunder of the past at all costs and completely sever my connection with those men, and I only regret that I did not follow your own and Mr. Le Gallienne's advise [sic] sooner.'

Alas, within a year the young man was stumbling through his humiliating evidence at Wilde's trial. And needless to say his offer to come back and work for Lane was not taken up.

Meanwhile, however annoying the business of one's office being used as a pick-up point for homosexuals, there was the matter of dealing with the famous and potentially profitable Oscar Wilde. It was not easy. Conciliatory gestures were made on both sides—Wilde, for instance, when Lane was going on what turned out to be an up-setting trip to Paris (where he was not at all at home), gave him an introduction to Pierre Louys, 'the young poet to whom I have dedicated *Salomé*. Pray introduce yourself to him. He is a perfect English scholar.'

'Dear Mr. Lane: I return the agreement signed and witnessed, I have made some alterations in it. The maker of a poem is a "poet", not an "author": author is misleading.'

Then again, a careful selection of publications likely to provide favourable reviews was a concern of all authors, or poets, at the time. Davidson, for example, had expressed horror at the thought of the *Athenaeum*, 'that supercilious journal'. Wilde was no less adamant, and clearly did not trust his publishers in their search for publicity. The work

'. . . must not be thrown in the gutter of English journalism. No book of mine, for instance, ever goes to the *National Observer*. I wrote to Henley to tell him so, two years ago. He is too coarse, too offensive, too personal to be sent any work of mine.'

'I hope', he uncommercially concluded, 'as few as possible will be sent for review.' However, he also managed to give a commercial defeat an air of magnanimity:

'I did not contemplate assigning to you the copyright of so important a poem for so small an honorarium as ten per cent, but will do so, it being clearly understood that no new edition is to be brought out without my sanction: I mean no such thing as a popular or cheap edition is to be brought out.'

More trouble arose over *The Sphinx*, on lines familiar to all John Lane's authors:

'You see now, I feel sure, how right I was in continually pressing you for a written agreement, and I cannot understand why you would not do so . . . I wrote to you endless letters—a task most wearisome to me—on this plain business matter. I received [. . .] excuses, apologies, but no agreement. This has been going on for three months, and the fact of your name being on the title-page was an act of pure courtesy and compliment on my part. As you are interested in literature and curious works I was ready to oblige.'

Then again, he objected, perhaps understandably, to *Salomé* being advertised as 'banned by the Lord Chamberlain'. When Lane does send a cheque it turns out to be too small. On the brink of ruin, Wilde has occasion to write stiffly to the firm about *Mr. W.H.*:

'I am informed by Mr. Lane that Mr. Mathews declines to publish my story on Shakespeare's sonnets "at any price" and that he himself will not publish it (at any price, I presume) unless he "approves" of it!'

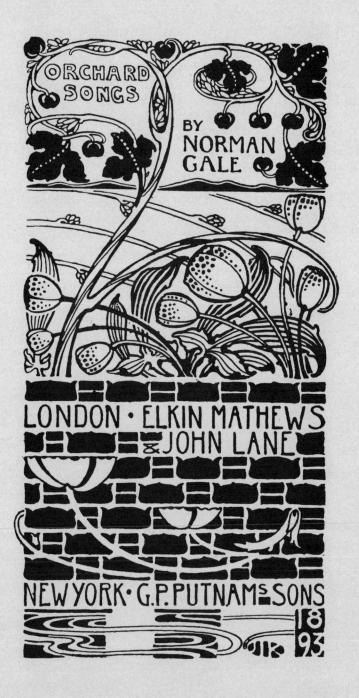

III. Title-page by J. Illingworth Kay with art nouveau influence leaving much to be desired for the lettering and layout.

IV. Self-portrait of Edmund H. New, illustrator of many books for
John Lane including White's *Selborne* and Walton's *Compleat Angler*.

But, he points out, he has an agreement signed and sealed eighteen months ago, and the work had been advertised as 'in rapid preparation' for sixteen months. Eventually Lane, by then on his own, agrees (as well he might) to 'accept the responsibility assumed by the firm', and Wilde accepts for £25. By this time he has come to the conclusion that while 'there is no objection to publishers reading the works they produce . . . It is never pleasant to deal with a publisher who is not really interested in one's work at the moment.'

Most trying of all for The Bodley Head, Wilde was, even more than most poets of the day, interested in and highly knowledgeable about book design. One trade journal notes that,

'in the case of new books, details of the binding are now very frequently advertised along with the particulars of size, price, etc. usually given. This is an innovation for which Mr. Oscar Wilde is mainly responsible.'

Particularly galling, then, to have him weighing in with hostile comments on matters for which everybody else agrees that The Bodley Head has a special flair: 'Dear Mr. Lane: The cover of *Salomé* is quite dreadful. Don't spoil a lovely book.'

Presumably he referred to the ordinary edition, bound in blue canvas, which Wilde called 'horrid Irish stuff'; the de-luxe edition, at any rate, was given a cover of green silk.

All this and Edward Shelley too. Even Le Gallienne had perhaps begun to go off his erstwhile hero, despite free tickets for *Lady Windermere's Fan* (at which the former acolyte sat next to the young Delius), in the face of letters claiming that:

'. . . friendship and love like ours need not meetings, but they are delightful . . . I hope the laurels are not too thick across your brow for me to kiss your eyelids.'

No wonder Le Gallienne joined with Lane in trying to warn off young Shelley. But Wilde was before long to deliver his worst blow to The Bodley Head only in the course of his own total downfall, and by giving one of its most famous, or notorious, publications publicity which it had not earned and which Wilde would have been the last man to wish it.

7

The Yellow Book

From the moment Lane left the Railway Clearing House in 1889 he was evidently looking ahead to 1894, when his partnership with Elkin Mathews would reach its natural term. The quest for new authors, new capital, new premises, was always in the background, increasingly in the foreground, of his mind.

The two men were almost absurdly incompatible, and getting more so every month. Elkin Mathews was and remained until his death in 1921 an antiquarian bookseller with scholarly attributes and a penchant for publishing tasteful editions, for the most part, of verse, though with occasional excursions into prose *belles lettres*— including, in 1894, Edmund Gosse's *The Letters of Thomas Lovell Beddoes*, resurrecting the author of that maverick masterpiece *Death's Jest-Book*.

Lane, on the other hand, was a lively lad, exuding an air of well-groomed prosperity, a 'card' in the sense used by Arnold Bennett (first published, indeed, by The Bodley Head on the recommendation of one of his readers, the youthful John Buchan). Many liked him, enjoyed his company as well as his hospitality, though often betraying reservations in jocular asides, such as William Watson's genial reference to 'that villain Lane', or the youthful Le Gallienne saying, 'Forgive my bantering, but you are such a *fraud*, you know.' His assorted interests kept him going at a feverish pace, but books, and their writers, were at the centre of his world. He often, he said, bought and sold *objets d'art* in order to put the profits into publishing —indeed he needed to.

Above all, as Lewis May correctly noted, 'He was ambitious, as it were, *for the fun of the thing.*'

Apart from subjecting his system as a whole to considerable nervous strain, and his digestion to herculean efforts as lunches and dinners succeeded each other in relentless excess, the fun of the thing sometimes got out of hand, leading him into deviousness which, when uncovered, led to distrust, though by no means always to dislike. His use of Edward Shelley was not agreeable, and his behaviour towards his partner over the establishment of the firm's most famous publication, *The Yellow Book*, seems inexcusable (though far from uncommon in publishing or any other business). It consisted simply in keeping Elkin Mathews as much in the dark as possible and for as long as possible.

The Yellow Book was by no means the first periodical to be published by The Bodley Head; but it was the first it originated. In 1893 the firm had distributed a new series of *The Hobby Horse*, arts-and-crafts based but publishing, as *The Yellow Book* was to do, many Rhymers' Club poets; for the same editor-patron, H. P. Horne, it produced the first issues of the short-lived and (even for its day) bizarrely titled *Diversi Colores*. At irregular intervals from 1889 to 1897 it produced four issues of the Ricketts-and-Shannon inspired, and very Wildean, *The Dial*—from which The Bodley Head's imprint disappeared after the alarming homosexual excitements of 1895. Respectability was maintained by the bulletins of the Ruskin Reading Guild, whose publication initially bore the impenetrable (save to students of Scandinavian inclination) title *Igdrasil*, soon changed, wisely if hardly less discouragingly, to *World Literature*. It offered 'a face-to-face, heart-to-heart inspection of Human Existence'. So did *The Pioneer*, official organ of the Pioneer Club: its text was to be Human Life, and it craftily, if not artily announced to its readership, 'It will be printed on hand-made paper.'

The Yellow Book did not burden itself with quite so dizzying a manifesto. It was to be, announced Arthur Waugh (father of Alec and Evelyn, and indefatigable man about letters), an illustrated quarterly,

'. . . representative of the most cultured work which was then being done in England, prose and poetry, criticism, fiction and art, the oldest school and the newest side by side, with no hallmark except that of excellence and no prejudice against anything but dullness and incapacity.'

Accounts of its actual conception vary. Did D. S. MacColl, as he claimed, put the idea into Henry Harland's head? Did the idea steal unbidden, as Harland claimed, into his head and Beardsley's as (both tubercular) they sat before a bright fire in the Harlands' flat in the Cromwell Road, itself murky in the dense fog with which London was blanketed? But then, Lewis May says that one day in the Hogarth Club, after a dinner given by Waldorf Astor for Bill Nye, an American humorist, Lane found himself with a literary group including Harland, George Moore, Frank Harris and Beardsley. Harris claimed that literary criticism did not exist in England. Lane demurred, standing up for the discursive and humane approach of, he suggested, Richard Garreth, Andrew Lang, George Saintsbury, William Archer and Arthur Waugh—of whom he published in book form only Archer; unmentioned, at least in May's report of the occasion, were two who would certainly have claimed to be, *inter alia*, literary critics whom Lane did publish: Le Gallienne and William Watson. Beardsley then broadened the discussion by claiming (as most artists would at any time) that in England there were no art critics of any worth either.

Why not start a critical-creative periodical to give them a local habitation and name, somebody suggested to Lane. Speaking, he said later, 'more in jest than earnest', he allowed his impulsive rather than his cautious side to take charge, agreed on the spot, and appointed Harland, aged 31, as Literary Editor, and Beardsley, aged 22, as Art Editor.

Harland was almost as strange a young man as Beardsley—more so as far as the outer circumstances of his life were concerned. He was born in New York, son of an Admiral from an established Suffolk family who left the Navy, went to New Orleans and made a fortune as a silversmith.

As a very young man Henry Harland had achieved some success with four novels, published under the name of Sidney Luska, about Russian-Jewish immigrants in New York. He then actually went to Russia, though afterwards, far from identifying with those immigrants, hinted, or more than hinted, at mysterious and elevated Russian origins. From Russia he moved to Paris, then settled in London, and established himself as a lively, at times frenetic, personality. Having acquired an equally lively wife, Aline, he lived with her, apparently on air, and in their flat entertained extensively if frugally. Occasionally the company was favoured with a song recital by Aline. Sometimes, along with earnest *Yellow Book* groupies such as Ella d'Arcy or Charlotte Mew, a magisterially affable Henry James appeared. He was himself a contributor to *The Yellow Book*, though not for long since he found the remuneration inadequate, and said so, in terms more of sorrow than of anger: What, only £75 for a complete long short story? Across the Atlantic he was offered more than that for the American rights alone of a story of similar length. But Harland was supposed to produce the whole issue on contributors' fees of only £200, though occasionally this could be stretched overall: 'Rather than injure the list,' wrote Lane, about the second volume, 'you had better risk another £50.' Meanwhile William Watson got £3.3s. For a one-page poem, Austin Dobson £2.12s.6d. Harland himself for some time, not then being a contributor, plaintively observed that he was getting nothing, and had paid so far for much postage out of his own pocket.

In fact *The Yellow Book*—the 7,000 copies of the first volume being reduced to 5,000 for the second—for all its *réclame*, was never within sight of fulfilling Beerbohm's no doubt ironical prediction (reflecting its publisher's ebullience) that with his new magazine Lane 'is going to make all our fortunes'. It was not for want of enthusiasm. A literary clergyman, Canon Ainger, wrote to Edmund Gosse to point out gleefully that The Bodley Head had announced that their edition of the Beddoes Letters was edited by Edmund Gosse; he added a reference to *The Yellow Book*:

> Heed not this last bêtise
> > Of John's
> We know that all his geese
> > Are swans.

Lane's, and perhaps Harland's, wish to get the best of both worlds, solidly established and avant-garde, and no doubt to placate all parties in the process, was only a partial success. It was all very well for that same Arthur Waugh to contribute to the first number a careful caveat in the shape of an essay on 'Reticence in Literature', attempting as he put it 'To establish a standard of taste, regulated by the normal judgment of the hale and cultured men of its age . . . steering a middle course between the prudery of the manse' and 'the effrontery of the pothouse'. Such attempts are always vain. It did, however, do Arthur Waugh much good; his article was picked out by almost all hostile critics of *The Yellow Book*, and attracted a great deal of work to him for years to come.

That first issue appeared in April 1894, the young Lewis May and the tutelary Frederic Chapman having with great care filled the entire window of the little Vigo Street shop with the black, white and yellow volumes, for in appearance it was more like a paperbound book than it was like a magazine, even a quarterly, as the word is used today.

The sensation was considerable; huffing and puffing was rife. *The Times* singled out Henry James and Waugh for praise, and for disparagement, if that is not too mild a word. It also commiserated with Sir Frederick (later Lord) Leighton for having to appear 'Cheek-by-jowl with such advanced and riotous representatives of the new art as Mr. Aubrey Beardsley and Mr. Walter Sickert,' but summed up its response by declaring that *The Yellow Book*'s note 'appears to be a combination of English rowdyism with French lubricity.'

The Westminster Gazette, after noting Beardsley's skill as a line draughtsman, and his capacity for refined and delicate work, shook its head over subject-matter and treatment, adding, presumably tongue-in-cheek: 'We do not know that anything would meet the case except a short Act of Parliament to make this kind of thing illegal.' Even the youthful, not to say juvenile Max Beerbohm felt the welcome lash of hostile pain. His essay in defence of cosmetics, a laboriously affected undergraduate diversion, may possibly be described, as it was, also by *The Westminster Gazette*, as 'triumphantly silly', but 'pernicious' it surely was not. Henley's *National Observer*, needless to say, denounced this harmless trifle's affectations (an easy target), while the *St James's Gazette* dismissed it as 'Detestable in matter and unreadable in style'.

On the day of *The Yellow Book*'s first appearance on 16 April, 1894, another wave washed over the crumbling sandcastle of Lane's relationship with Elkin Mathews. At the Hotel d'Italie in Old Compton Street, Soho, a dinner was held to celebrate the occasion. Henry James was abroad (perhaps diplomatically), so were Arthur Symons and Hubert Crackenthorpe; Le Gallienne was lecturing in Liverpool, as his youthful idol, Wilde, had so magnetically done before and to him. Edmund Gosse was ill, but sent verses in greeting. Harland was of course there, 'radiating good humour,' according to Arthur Waugh; so was Beardsley. Richard Garnett lurked, George Moore sparkled, not least with Mrs Pearl Craigie, the witty lady who wrote as John Oliver Hobbes. Poets abounded, all members of the Rhymers' Club—Yeats, Lionel Johnson, John Davidson, Ernest Dowson. Sickert amused the company with a speech in which he looked forward to the time when authors should be put in their place, and made to write their stories and poems around pictures, supplied to them by the artists. All was merry as a marriage bell—except that two divorces were impending.

Among those conspicuously not present was Elkin Mathews. It seems he was not asked, or even told about the occasion, though things were already at such a pitch of tension between him and Lane that he might well in any case have declined, even if his name did appear as part of the publishers' imprint. The other absentee, who was certainly not asked, was Oscar Wilde. Lane disliked him, although well aware of him as a valuable publishing property, and already the publisher of his *Poems*, of *Salomé*, and of *Lady Winder-mere's Fan*. More important, Beardsley disliked him too, in spite of having drawn the sensational illustrations to *Salomé* (in two pictures, 'The Woman in the Moon' and 'The Eyes of Herod', actually cari-caturing Wilde); it was on Beardsley's insistence that Lane made it a condition that nothing by Wilde should be published in *The Yellow Book*. This went down not at all well. Wilde did write to Lord Alfred Douglas in praise of Max Beerbohm's essay on cosmetics. It was, he said,

'. . . wonderful: enough style for a large school, and all very precious and thought out: quite delightfully wrong and fascinating.'

But elsewhere he was reduced to common abuse. To Ricketts he wrote of it:

'My Dear Boy: I bought it at the station, but before I had cut all the pages I threw it out of the window.'

And to Lord Alfred Douglas, despite his warm words for Beer-bohm, he wrote, 'It is dull and loathsome: a great failure—I am so glad.' In a year's time he was caught up in his own downfall, and he was to have his inadvertent revenge on Lane, Beardsley, and indeed the whole 'Nineties' spirit.

After the initial excitement and denunciation had died down, the flood of parody which was already widespread on account of Vigo Street, The Bodley Head, and the Nineties poets redoubled, no doubt much to Lane's satisfaction. The standard of visual parody, especially of Beardsley, was much higher than that of the prose and verse—the latter in particular, rather letting down the very high nineteenth-century standard so evident from Thomas Hood on-wards. One of the better short jokes in fact referred to Thomas Hood's elegy for a lost girl's suicide. It was by one of the Nineties poets themselves, a Rugby schoolmaster, Norman Gale, whose *Orchard Songs* were not in the suicidal mode, but beneath their arcadian surface concealed an eroticism which must have interested his pupils:

> 'One more unfortunate
> Volume ungodly
> Rashly importunate
> Gone to the Bodley.'

Visually Linley Sambourne, though perhaps a little cluttered by the standards of its original, excellently parodied a *Yellow Book* cover in *Punch*. *Punch* indeed was indefatigable in parodying, and so publicising, both *The Yellow Book* and The Bodley Head nest of singing birds in general. Owen Seaman, who became its editor, wrote parodies of many Vigo Street poets, on the whole neatly turned enough to imitate some of their subjects; but not Lane, who instantly invited Seaman to join his list, which he did with *The Battle of the Bays*, a collection arising out of the long hiatus in appointing another Poet Laureate after Tennyson's death in 1892. *Punch*, too, coined the pretty phrase, 'Uncleanliness is next to Bodliness' (which was—though not by the Bodley Head—resurrected with glee when in 1985 the firm moved to a house in Bedford Square next door to Jonathan Cape). This little joke particularly outraged Kenneth Grahame ('Not enough impropriety to cover a sixpence'), who urged Lane to sue; Lane knew better than that, and was in any case delighted by it. As Seaman wrote later, reflecting on his surprise at having been applauded at a grand party by many of the literary men he had lampooned:

> 'Much gratified, he drank their toast
> And subsequently laid
> The naked facts before his host
> Who understood the trade

' "The Publisher", said he, "Regards
 Your work as mainly sent
To serve the heavy-hanging bands
 For cheap advertisement." '

Then again, back in 1894,

  'How doth the little busy Lane
   Improve the Bodley Head
  He gathers round him, Day by Day,
   The authors who are read.

  'How rapidly editions sell
   How neat the pages too;
  He labours hard to bind them well
   In pink and buff and blue.

  'With works by poets let us fill
   Our shelves, and none deny;
  Trust Lane to find some new ones still
   For idle cash to buy . . .'

Verse parodies abounded. In *The World* Lewis Carroll was
ponderously called in aid:

  '. . . Beware the Yallerbock, my son!
  The aims that rile, the art that racks.
  Beware the Aub-Aub bird, and shun
  The stumious Beerbohmax.

  '. . . Then, as veep Vigo's marge he trod,
  The Yallerbock, with tongues of blue,
  Came piffling through the Headley Bod,
  And flippered as it flew . . .'

(67)

Lane was not a man to shrink from so much free publicity—free at least to the tune of an occasional invitation of a hack to a party; in fact in due course Lane gathered many of them together in 1897 and printed them in *Accepted Addresses* on hand-made paper in a grey wrapper with a particularly fine reproduction of the head of Sir Thomas Bodley, and dedicated the little book to the lady who was just about to become his wife.

With a handful of exceptions—Anatole France was first introduced to British readers in *The Yellow Book* by Maurice Baring, or rather 'The Hon. Maurice Baring'—Henry James, Kenneth Grahame, Wells, Buchan and Beerbohm among them, the very names of the letterpress contributors have sunk into near oblivion, remembered if at all as contributors to the magazine and to The Bodley Head list in general. The artists are another matter. Prime among them, then and now, was Aubrey Beardsley. John Lane later maintained that Beardsley made *The Yellow Book*, and that when he left it, it became 'just another good magazine', or, as *The Times* put it, 'showing a general tone of striving towards healthiness not hitherto noticeable'.

It is difficult now to grasp the impact of this publication when it first appeared, both for its aesthetic qualities and for what now seems naughtiness, but then seemed, and in Beardsley's and Ricketts's case often was, wickedness. Even Beardsley's drawing for the prospectus had to contemporary eyes a distinct aura of the *outré*, its sensually undulating figure in black gloves leaning over a book-box outside the Vigo Street shop while a caricature of Elkin Mathews, a puzzled Pierrot, glowered from the doorway. Lane can hardly have been surprised, and Mathews, still a partner, can hardly have been gratified. This emaciated boy from a well-off Brighton family, already affected (in mind as in body, some would say) by his wasting disease, had while working as a City clerk—significantly, for an architect— early made a mark as a more or less normal caricaturist, largely of theatre people. Then he was taken up by J. M. Dent to illustrate Malory's *Morte d'Arthur*. Snapped up by Lane—not that he ever worked exclusively for The Bodley Head—he rapidly showed his capacity for mischief and for dismaying respectability in the drawings he made for a handsome edition of Wilde's *Salomé*. Even as preparations for the first *Yellow Book* got under way Beardsley was writing:

'Yes my Dear Lane I shall most assuredly commit suicide if the fat woman does not appear in No. 1 of the Yellow Book. I have shown it to all sorts and conditions of men—and women. All agree that it is one of my very best efforts and extremely witty. Really I am sure you have nothing to fear. I shouldn't press the matter a second if I thought it would give offence. The block is such a capital one, too, and looks so distinguished. The picture shall be called "*A Study in Major Lines*". It cannot possibly hurt anybodies sensibilities. Do say yes. I shall hold demonstrations in Trafalgar Square if you don't brandish a device banner bearing a device "England Expects every publisher to do his duty". Now don't drive me into the depths of despair . . .'

As the fat woman was all too clearly a caricature of Mrs Whistler, Lane was not keen on stirring up a wasps' nest from that quarter; but—eventually a version of the drawing was used. Beardsley caused him much worry throughout their association. He was to be seen poring over Beardsley's designs with a magnifying glass, anxious to spot (if not eager to see) the neat little obscenities lurking within exquisite frond and graceful curlicue, and persuade the wicked youth to modify them.

Again, it is difficult today to grasp what the quite advanced Grant Richards called 'the distress—yes, the real distress', as opposed to mere shock or even outrage, that Beardsley's drawings caused: a visually more or less uninformed readership easily grasped what cognoscenti either welcomed or overlooked (and still overlook)—the viciousness underlying the skill, the sensuousness, the sheer poetry of line. Had that general public been able to read his unfinished fantasy *Under the Hill*, their eyes would no doubt have been opened to what they saw by what they read: the fantasy of a corrupted adolescent, a compendium, written in a tone of wretchedly florid facetiousness, of phallic frenzy, transvestism, sadism, child molesting ('Ah the little ducks . . . the children cried out, I can tell you'), an ejaculating unicorn, a coprophile youth, a designer called Le Con, an actor called Les Fesses, Tannhauser (the hill *is* Venusberg) masturbating in front of a picture of a woman 'Offering her warm *fesses* to a panting poodle', satyrs displaying 'Interminable vigour and hairy breasts' . . . and so on, and on.

Beardsley had worked on this sad stuff, which outdoes the dreariest fantasies of nineteenth-century underground pornography, for two years, leaving it unfinished at his death in 1898 at the age of 28. The contrast between the external manner of this charming young egotist and the seething sleaziness of his subconscious is extreme. Both Leonard Smithers, publisher of *The Yellow Book*'s short-lived successor, *The Savoy*, and Lane both kept trying to publish what they could of the text of *Under the Hill* for some years. Lane waited more than ten years before in 1904 The Bodley Head published extracts ('The whole being deemed unprintable by the editors') in *Under the Hill, and Other Essays in Prose and Verse, including Table Talk*, though he had advertised the work in his 1894 prospectus as 'The Story of Venus and Tannhauser'. An illustration to the work 'Venus between Terminal Gods', was planned for the ill-fated *Yellow Book* No. 5, and actually appeared in *Aubrey Beardsley*, by Robert Ross, with an iconography by Aylmer Vallance, which The Bodley Head published in 1909. Smithers, meanwhile, had published privately a transcript of the complete existing text; but it was left to the enterprising Olympia Press in Paris to put out a full commercial edition in 1959, in the Traveller's Companion Series, which also included *Lolita*, Genet's *Thief's Journal* and *Our Lady of the Flowers*, William Burroughs's *The Naked Lunch*, and other tasty morsels (but including, out of place in this titillatory company, Beckett's *Watt* and *Molloy*).

Apart from *The Yellow Book*, Beardsley's contribution as designer and illustrator of Bodley Head books is unequalled; he was responsible for binding designs, frontispieces, title-pages and, in two cases, illustrations to eleven books in five years. Next in distinction was Charles Ricketts, usually less severely classical than Beardsley, and at times even more creepy, often moving closer to the heavy ornamentation of William Morris's Kelmscott Press, which began operations in 1891, producing books which by and large were not designed for reading but as display objects. His partner Shannon did Wilde's *Lady Windermere's Fan* for The Bodley Head, and the two together did the woodcuts (themselves, unlike almost all the other artists, being skilled engravers) for Longus's *Daphnis and Chloe* (luxuriant) and Marlowe's *Hero and Leander* (erotic text, sober designs).

Ricketts's living authors were, in this *galère*, a distinguished group. A very elaborate production of Wilde's *The Sphinx* was bound as Wilde wished in ivory vellum, printed entirely in capitals, a title-page placed on the left with Gothic-Celtic tendrils, two inscrutable figures and the word Melancolia broken up among the curves. John Addington Symonds's *In the Key of Blue*, an aesthetic pre-echo of Corvo's *Stories Toto Told Me*, evoked an extremely florid cover design, a sinuous combination of laurel and hyacinth stamped in gold on cream (originally blue, but Ricketts protested that reviewers would make jokes about that then prevalent laundry aid, Reckitt's Blue). On the other hand this dizzyingly eclectic designer produced for John Gray's *Silverpoints* (1893) a most simple design of vertical lines and single willow-leaves on a long, thin book of real elegance—as befitted, no doubt, the supposed original of Dorian Gray.

A singular figure, John Gray, like many Bodley Head writers, came of a modest working-class, or lower middle-class, background: he was the eldest of nine children of a journeyman-carpenter working mostly in Thames dockyards. He left school at thirteen, worked first in Woolwich Arsenal, then in the General Post Office, then as a librarian in the Foreign Office, in the meantime, it seems, learning to draw, play the violin and to read and speak French fluently, although he did not visit France until his mid-twenties. This last talent was very strongly expressed in his own verse, quite apart from translations of Verlaine and Mallarmé. The latter he knew, as well as other French Symbolist poets, whom he met in the Paris family home of a young Jewish Anglo-French-Russian, André Raffalovitch, and he often contributed to French periodicals, including *La Revue Blanche*. He became extremely well-known in literary London as both poet and dandy, though Ernest Dowson thought him 'Incurably given over to social things'. At the age of thirty he had, according to Lionel Johnson, the face of a boy of fifteen. He first made his mark in 1891 with a lecture, first given to the Playgoers' Club. He repeated it in connection with a performance by the Independent Theatre of his translation of Théodore de Banville's play *Le Baiser*; this time the lecture was attended by, among others, Henry James, J. M. Barrie, George Moore—and Oscar Wilde, accompanied, according to *The Star*, 'by a suite of young gentlemen, all wearing the vivid dyed carnation which has superseded the lily and the sunflower'.

Gray wanted Lane to publish this translation, but the idea seems not to have appealed—any more, one suspects, than did its author. Nor would Lane have been much gratified when ten years later Gray was ordained a priest of the Roman Catholic Church, and spent the rest of his life working among the poor in Edinburgh. Lane disapproved of Roman Catholicism; it is a curious irony that so many of the writers on his list, if not already in it, joined the Roman Church, G. K. Chesterton towards the end of his life, Wilde only in the nick of time. At any rate Lane accepted Gray's poems for publication, demanding in his cautious way the excision of two on the grounds that they were obscene, a step Gray accepted with equanimity. Lane, who refused Wilde's offer to pay for the production of *Silverpoints*, with his usual mixture of boldness and caution, had after all not blenched at (in 'The Barber'):

> 'I moulded with my hands
> The mobile breast, the valley; and the waist
> I touched; and pigments reverently placed
> Upon their thighs in sapient spots and stains,
> Beryls and crysolites and diaphanes,
> And gems whose hot harsh names are never said.
> I was a masseur, and my fingers bled

With wonder as I touched their awful limbs . . .
. . . The throat, the shoulders, swelled and were uncouth,
The breasts rose up and offered each a mouth.
And on the belly pallid blushes crept
That maddened me, until I laughed and wept.'

No wonder Ricketts decided that discretion was the better part of valour, and (as with Marlowe's *Hero and Leander*) subdued his own deviant hand not to what it worked in but to a chaste simplicity, perhaps taking his tone from his poet, who in another mood, speaking of a poet in a garden, notes that:

'He does not sing, he only wonders why
He is sitting there. The sparrows sing. And I
Yield to the straight allure of simple things.'

Undeterred by Lane's growing reputation as a slow and paltry payer, Shannon and Ricketts were no less hopeful than other young artists and poets in regarding Lane as a potential milch-cow. Shannon writes to Lane:

'Is it true that you are going away on Monday? We should like to know when you can send us our cheques, we are of course immensely hard up. Ricketts has borrowed the dummy of the Sphinx from Leighton to show Oscar. Do you require it for your journey?'

The tranquil Shannon hands over the dunning to the more mercurial Ricketts, who writes (both these letters are undated, and Ricketts's on National Liberal Club writing paper):

'My Dear Lane: Will you think me a bloody bore if I throw myself on your tender mercies to advance me the price of Le Gallienne's head? I am not always thus but my pictures at the New English Art Club have not sold, and I am starving. If it is in any way inconvenient

I shall not be hurt if you say, and I will beg, borrow or steal else-where.'

Whether Lane was softened by these modest appeals or whether he was himself in any position to answer them, is open to question.

The next most interesting artist to work for The Bodley Head at this time, Laurence Housman, who designed the binding, frontis-piece and title-page for Francis Thompson's *Poems* (1893), certainly got money out of Lane. With some ingenuity he wrote saying that his beast of a publisher (i.e. John Lane) simply wouldn't pay up, and could he, Lane, as a friend lend the sum owing. Much amused by this dodge, Lane did send £5, but, according to Housman, in repeat-ing the incident with appreciative chuckles, multiplied the sum in question by ten. Later, again according to the artist-poet, author of those mild and agreeable playlets, *Victoria Regina*, Lane wrote to him saying in woebegone tones that by some mischance all the drawings Housman had done for The Bodley Head had been disposed of (i.e. sold), and would the artist do one especially for him, Lane. Certainly, replied the artist, but of course he would have to charge the going market rate. And heard no more.

Reflecting an age of singular diversion, of conscious revolt against materialism in the outside world, against psychological barriers in the inner world of individuals, in quaint contortions under the grave shadows of the literary and artistic forest giants, Lane's little patch grew, and mostly withered, like flowers in a desert; and his was the rain, or rather the soon emptied watering-can, that germinated them.

8

The Partners Split Up

Yeats in his old age bestowed the tribute that The Bodley Head (which, at the time spoken of, included Elkin Mathews) 'offered whatever was original, inventive and new in the way of poetry, illustration, and book design, irrespective of its particular point of view' (*Autobiographies*, 1955). But already, in the words of one commentator, the 'first edition mania' had 'reached its extremest form of childishness', or, as *Fortnightly Review* put it: 'First editions of Dickens and Thackeray are no longer the rage of the collecting public . . . every ephemeral and often rubbishy tract by living authors is being eagerly bought.' Attacks multiplied, as in 'Literary Notes' of the *Pall Mall Gazette*:

'[Mathews and Lane] issue nearly all their books on the principle that rarity, not excellence, involves a speedy rise in price.'

This sort of thing genuinely upset Le Gallienne, who riposted with an essay on 'The Philosophy of Limited Editions'. All very well, though, to point out that small was beautiful, and that The Bodley Head turned away much inferior stuff which subsequently got published elsewhere: it hardly answered the point that if the poems were as good as all that, they could be sold in the same format in numbers large enough to cover the lack of income from what Robert Bridges had discreetly called 'advanced prices'.

But then Lane, at least, was in it 'for the fun of the thing'. Advanced prices were all part of the game, as long as he could make *some* money out of it—and after all, he was giving great opportunities to young writers and artists, who flocked to his door. Still, the writing here was on the wall, his partnership was in disrepair, and clearly doomed to end as soon as the formal arrangement expired in 1894.

In search of new (preferably young and inexpensive) talent Lane foraged far and wide. *The Yellow Book*'s fame, as well as that of The Bodley Head poets, had made Vigo Street a magnet to many different sorts of writers; and many, if not most of them, were not of a kind to please the cultured, fastidious taste of Elkin Mathews. One of them, William Rothenstein, son of a well-to-do manufacturer, had come south from Bradford in 1888 at the age of sixteen to study at the Slade School, well-equipped with talent, vivacity, humour and a determination to know everybody who was anybody. In this resolve he succeeded pretty well. He was, thought the hardly older Beerbohm, 'rather nice to look at, with his huge spectacles and thick raven hair combed into his forehead. He looks like a creature of another world. I wonder if he will succeed. He ought to. Such utter self-confidence I have never seen;' and Beerbohm added, in a note-book found after his death: 'Full of gaiety and self-importance—a mascot, inspiring and helping. Strong sense of humour, cerebrative power'. The beginnings of success soon beckoned when in 1893 Lane offered him £120 for 24 portrait drawings of Oxford notables to be issued in lithographic parts by The Bodley Head.

Alas, the rapprochement was fragile, partly because of Rothenstein's drawings, partly because of Lane's brashness. To begin with, Rothenstein insisted, 'much against Lane's will', he claimed, on including a few undergraduates. Then, though perhaps not quite so hysterically as Beerbohm described the moment in his story *Enoch Soames*, the elderly dons who were to be his subjects got in quite a flutter, and some of them were appalled by results—notably Walter Pater and Henry Acland. The former (who in any case, according to Grant Richards, looked less like an aesthetician than 'a gambling major, and whisky-sodden at that') called his sisters' disapproval in support of his own dismay; the latter felt that he appeared a helpless dotard (which, according to Beerbohm, he did). Lane, anxious not to offend, was appalled, perhaps not understanding why, if artists of the past produced great works of art which are unquestionably flattering, Rothenstein couldn't do the same. The boy artist was obedient and persuaded his old gentlemen to sit again for milder images. Nevertheless, the drawings being published, in five parts, at 200 printings a part (1893–94), he swallowed his pride, and remained on reasonably affable terms with his patron, for example in usefully socialising hours, evoked by Rothenstein when he writes of the craggy John Davidson and Lane together: 'I often met them together at the Hogarth Club when Lane was entertaining his authors, and I wanted to draw them together.'

Both were active together in organising a visit to Oxford and London by Paul Verlaine, with whom Rothenstein had become remarkably, and loyally, close in Paris. The poet lectured to tiny audiences in both places, but looking after him was an uphill task, as is suggested by a letter from Lane to Rothenstein:

'. . . Verlaine was a great success last night . . . He called at The Bodley Head this afternoon, but I was out. Meredith sent a message to me that he would like to have Verlaine down to his place for the day, and this morn, he wired in reply to me that he would be delighted to have him on Sunday night if I would take him down, but Verlaine is not feeling very well.'

And the projected publication by The Bodley Head of Verlaine's poems, with an Introduction by York Powell, never came off.

Friends of Rothenstein were eager to make use of the connection too, as when the Australian artist Charles Conder, to whom and whose drunken ways Rothenstein was also most loyal, wrote from Paris: 'Ask Lane to give me a book cover to do and you will be a very good boy;' and repeated the plea a few weeks later. Beerbohm, on a visit to Broadstairs, of all curious places, wrote in an unconvincingly off-hand fashion: 'By the way, did you remember when you saw that poor fly in the amber of modernity, John Lane, to speak of my caricatures?'

Of his description of Lane as a 'poor fly in the amber of modernity' Beerbohm seems to have been uncommonly proud, since he used it several times in correspondence with others. In 1893 Lane had taken up with all three young lions—Rothenstein, Beerbohm and Beardsley. And all three delighted in mocking him, at least to each other. Beardsley wrote:

'. . . have you had a satisfactory explanation with Jean de Bodley? Or are you ready to join the newly-formed anti-Lane Society?'

And Beerbohm:

'Why do I write on this odd piece of paper? Because it was wrapped up with two very lovely drawings which J. Lane has just given me. They lie before me as I write: I am enamoured of them. So is John Lane: he said "How lucky I am to have got hold of this young Beardsley: look at the technique of his drawings! What workmanship! *He never goes over the edges!*" '

At this point Beerbohm must have felt a spasm of guilt, for he went on:

'He never said anything of the kind, but the criticism is suggestive, dear Will? And characteristic of Art's middleman, the Publisher—for of such is the Chamber of Horrors. How brilliant I am!'

Beerbohm indeed was not above mocking his friend Rothenstein as well as John Lane, in a straightfaced joke which can have done nothing to warm the other pair to each other:

'John Lane has consented to publish a series of caricatures of Oxford celebrities by me: they are to appear concurrently with yours in order to make the running. I am sending you the proofs of the first number. Very satisfactory, I think. Do not think harshly of John Lane for publishing these things without consulting you—there is a taint of treachery in the veins of every publisher.'

(78)

In a moment of truce, or at least an attempted armistice, Rothenstein invited Lane to spend a few days with him in Paris—disastrously, as it turned out. In deference to his supposedly conventional tastes, as well as his status as a source of money and reputation, Rothenstein seems not to have subjected him to the loose-limbed rigours at *La vie de Bohème*. But Lane managed to irritate the arrogant young painter at every turn: he confused St Sulpice with Notre Dame, he fell asleep in a Brahms concert. Worst of all was their visit to the Louvre. Beerbohm described Rothenstein's account of it, in a letter to his dégagé friend Reggie Turner:

'It seems that John Lane is furious with Will Rothenstein, whose guest he has been for a few days in Paris. After conducting the publisher to the Louvre, taking him into every room and listening with great attention to his detailed opinions of all the pictures, he suddenly turned upon him with pent-up fury and insolence and told him never to mention Art again: in as much as he knew nothing about it and probably cared less. John Lane is extremely bitter about him now in consequence and is probably going to get someone else to design a book-plate instead of one for which he has already paid Will Rothenstein. Isn't it rather sad?'

The story naturally went the rounds, calling from Beardsley a pleasing caricature and the heartless comment: 'I am sure you must have had a very funny time with John Lane, who by the way is behaving (I think) very treacherously both to you and myself.'

A letter of apology of sorts from Rothenstein later in the year attempted to patch things up:

'I quite admit that I have not been grateful enough to you of late, but my dear Lane, we are all human and youth, as the saying goes, is hot-blooded, and I am sure you will admit that you can understand a person like myself being occasionally a little quick-tempered.'

But the scars still showed, and itched. Early in 1894 Beerbohm was again regaling his friend Turner with an unfortunate encounter in his rooms:

'Enter upon Bosie, Will and me, John Lane, gentleman. Will, who has heard that John Lane, gentleman, has said various things against him, bowed very stiffly and relapsed Byronically into an arm-chair . . . Bosie attacked the Publisher about the awful quarrels and so forth there have been. Imagine me! Walking swiftly and suavely up and down the room talking about anything that came into my head while John Lane sat very red and uncomfortable on a high chair. Figure him moreover in very new doeskin gloves, a citron-coloured bowler and a very small covert-coat beneath which fell the tails of a braided black coat. Poor me. What a position.'

In effect, the Rothenstein-Lane relationship was at an end, though the artist was later to find a good moral excuse for his part in discontinuing it. Still, writing some forty years later, he had the grace to add a final comment: 'Lane certainly produced his books extremely well, and he had the courage to publish unknown or unpopular authors. He was above all a poet's publisher.'

The remaining member of this trio of mischievous young men remained on good terms with, and published by, Lane, until the end of the century. If Rothenstein had come to a London of a peculiarly English bohemianism, of rigid ladies and their daughters, and of Jack the Ripper, Beerbohm had come down from Oxford—('What!', said Henry Harland in dismay, 'an undergraduate!' But Lane insisted)—already notorious for his 'pernicious nonsense' about cosmetics in *The Yellow Book*, to a world, as he recalled in a broadcast talk in 1935, in which 'Hampstead upon its hill was a little old remote village, and so was Chelsea, down yonder by the river, where the milkmaids milked their cows, and sold their milk, in St James's Park.' And hard by Vigo Street:

'. . . nor did the Piccadilly goat seem more than a little odd in Piccadilly. He lived in a large mews in a side street . . . about ten o'clock in the morning he would come treading forth with a delicately clumsy gait . . . He would pause at the corner of Piccadilly and flop down there against the railings of the nearest house. He would remain there until luncheon-time and return in the early afternoon.'

Beerbohm always, he confessed, liked to have his 'set' around him—'I can only stand life when it is made pleasant for me. Usually it *is* made pleasant for me. I have been pampered rather than otherwise'. So, from his comfortable Kensington home, he wrote a little here and there, published caricatures here and there, politely refused (because it would not pay well enough) to have that pleasing fable *The Happy Hypocrite* published in *The Yellow Book*, but accepted Lane's proposal to issue it as a Bodley Head booklet: he quietly nurtured his obsession with our grosser royalty and with masks and became languidly engaged to two actresses before eventually marrying a third, Florence Kahn.

A very different figure was cut by another of Lane's captures—one by whom, on the whole, he stood loyally through trying times. William Watson was Yorkshire-born in 1858 and harped on the fact, though he grew up, like Le Gallienne, in Liverpool; like Le Gallienne, too, he had little formal education, was supported by his father, and simultaneously developed two sides to his nature—a deadly serious, rhetorical poet, aiming high, and a lively-minded spinner of jocular verse and even self-mockery. The serious poet allowed himself a taste for epigrams as well as much extended hot air; but, his father dying inconveniently early, the Poet (a capital letter seems essential) descended to journalism, 'consciously stooping to work that is beneath me . . . I would rather measure tape or weigh sugar.' But he didn't, and in due course made his mark, though never much steady money. Recommended by Edward Dowden, Shakespearean scholar and professor of English at Trinity College, Dublin, to try Kegan Paul, he also tried Macmillan and Fisher Unwin before reaching a safe harbour with John Lane, who thought him an excellent fellow, though Le Gallienne remained suspicious of the hot air, which he politely called 'vowelisation'.

Friends collected a sum of money which produced £5 a week, doled out by Lane, and when this source was exhausted Lane—most people would think uncharacteristically—continued to pay it to him, nominally as an advance for odes and sonnets for *The Yellow Book*.

Not that Watson was a natural *Yellow Book* man, though he contributed to five issues. Like Le Gallienne again, he was passionately anti-decadent and anti-French, or at any rate Frenchified English: 'Such rubbish and such filth as appears in every number'. This, too, Lane liked; it offset the fancier contributors, of whom he was likely to speak with a contempt which quite equalled anything they could say about him. Always a Rabelaisian letter-writer to the right recipient, Watson was apt to favour Lane with accounts of his 'fiddling around with Mrs. Watson's twat', and was by no means shy of announcing that he was setting off for a visit to the Isle of Man with a pocketful of French letters, having made rapid progress from the slightly built, pale, modest and reticent youth he was at eighteen. Soon he was laying about him with his pen, writing regularly from Liverpool for the *National Review*, satirising 'The Fall of Fiction' and, surprisingly, launching a scornful attack on Rider Haggard. He became engaged to a sixteen-year-old, though scarcely older himself, but broke it off in order to philander with the wife of a local doctor. He had finally moved to London in 1890, got engaged again to a bluestocking charmer, Marian Roalfe Cox, whom he soon regarded as Delilah to his Samson, and broke that off. Yeats thought him by no means negligible, but essentially critical not creative. Lane welcomed him—'an excellent fellow'—for his anti-aestheticism: Watson spoke of the Decadents as 'such rubbish and such filth'.

Among the women on The Bodley Head list the one who has achieved lasting fame did so under a different imprint: E. Nesbit, who at the end of the century, forced by the collapse of her husband Hubert Bland's career as a Fabian philanderer (by no means the only one), turned out assorted pot-boilers and—what she thought of as also pot-boilers—the children's books which still keep her name alive, *The Wouldbegoods*, *The Treasure Seekers*, *The New Treasure Seekers* and *The Railway Children*. She came to The Bodley Head as early as 1889 with a collection of her own verse and translations of Heine, both of which Elkin Mathews declined. She then turned her attention to Lane, and made a little headway: he commissioned a book on Meredith, which she undertook to do with her husband for £50 down and a royalty. In fact, of course, Le Gallienne did it instead. However, Lane took them both to the Sette of Odd Volumes, and it seems as though she, at any rate, returned his hospitality: 'The next Fabian meeting will be an interesting discussion, I think. Will you come?' Or, more promisingly (perhaps she contemplated a little philandering on her own account): 'Next time you come to see me please remind me that I have long proposed to ask you to take away two little pencil china mugs belonging to a set presented to my grandfather by the late King of Sweden.'

But evidently her proposals fell on increasingly stony ground, although Lane did publish *A Pomander of Verse* and a volume of Kentish stories, *In Homespun*. Evidently invitations to visit the Bland home in Lee, a dispiriting South London suburb, did not appeal, especially when accompanied by plaintive notes disclosing in true Fabian style that 'My maid, scenting extra work, with the unnerving instinct of her kind, took herself off at the first alarum.' Nor, it seems, in spite, or perhaps because of Lane's fondness for dancing, was he drawn by a jollification at Lee, consisting 'mostly of country dances, polkas, etc.' Eventually she was given to note that 'I perceive that you don't mean to come and see me *here*.' She came to his office to ask his help in getting a poem into *The Yellow Book*. After that, there seems to have been a long silence until she is heard from again, in 1910, and in a tone echoed a hundred times in the Bodley Head archive: 'It is a very long time since I have had any accounts from you, and longer still since I had any money.'

Perhaps Lane could hardly have been expected to foresee those children's books. He was, however, alert to the rise of feminism, though it was Le Gallienne whose enthusiasm first set The Bodley Head off on a temporarily very profitable track. Early in 1893 a manuscript arrived which excited him greatly. It contained eight short stories. Unfortunately, as Lewis May reports:

'The author had forgotten to leave an address . . . Weeks, or it may have been months went by, when at last, one summer morning, the door opened and admitted, together with a flood of sunlight, a very attractive young woman [she was 34], slim, dark-haired, and dressed all in white. She spoke with vivacity and charm . . . She had come, she said, to know if we had anything to tell her about a collection of short stories which she had left with us some time ago.'

The tantalising mystery was solved. She had sent them under her pen-name, George Egerton.

She had been born Mary Chavelita Dunne, in Australia, of a Welsh mother and an Irish father—the latter so very Irish as to match the general impression of a stage Irishman, or to have stepped straight from one of Charles Lern's more extravagant pages: he had been cashiered from the Army, in Australia, dismissed from a prison governorship, in New Zealand had served as a mercenary in the Maori wars; he was an enthusiast for Irish Home Rule, he drew, sang, acted, rode and was an expert fisherman, as well as being a born liar (who published some picturesque reminiscences in 1896 with Fisher Unwin). As for his daughter, her mother died when she was sixteen, and she was bundled off to Germany to teach English to small girls, returning two years later to look after her younger siblings, their Catholic relatives being indifferent to all of them. Next she nursed in a London hospital—fairly horrific, no doubt, in the early 1880s—then tried New York, without success.

At this point a most remarkable man took charge of her. The widow of a forgotten writer, Whyte Melville, invited young Miss Dunne to accompany her and her own companion, one Henry Higginson, on their travels. She did so, and ran off with Higginson. He appears to have worked variously as a customs clerk, a bank clerk, a fishmonger's agent, a traveller for 'gay checks' (whatever they are) and rubber stamps, to have been an Anglican monk, a missionary, and 'Domestic chaplain' to Mrs Whyte Melville, a role which apparently required him to change his own name to Whyte Melville; and he had a divorced wife in the United States.

(84)

Somehow he seems to have amassed a good deal of money, with which he went with his new woman to Norway, there building a house at Langesund and setting up as the Norwegian equivalent of a squire. On the strength of three stories in *Keynotes*, as her book is overall entitled, their relationship seems to have been a tempestuous one, engendering a condition in her combining hypnotised fascination and self-contained revulsion. He died in 1889; back in Britain, she married in 1891 George Egerton Clairmonte, originally from Newfoundland: 'Tall, bearded, idle and penniless' according to her great-nephew, the Irish novelist Terence de Vere White. They settled in Cork, and clearly shared a low opinion of the natives.

Role reversal now took place. Her husband pottered about; she, in intervals of repaying loans from her father-in-law by sending him pawn-tickets, set about writing stories, taking her husband's first name as pseudonym. These she sent to T. P. O'Connor's *Weekly Sun*. An assistant editor suggested that she should try Henley's *National Observer* and *The Speaker*. Under the impression that the author was a man (though when the stories were published, few others thought so for a moment) Henley wrote back in terms which embarrassed him when he discovered his mistake:

'. . . a particularly warm description of rounded limbs and the rest . . . of its effect on a young fellow . . . It puts him in a state that he either goes off and has a woman or it is hard for his health (and possibly worse for his morals) if he doesn't.'

It seems not to have occurred to him that, *mutatis mutandis*, it might have the same effect on a woman. But, he went on, if a writer feels obliged to introduce physiological detail, 'Why then let him write a scientific book in scientific terminology and not a spurious thing decked out in the allurement of art.'

Still, Henley continued to think well of her writing, and after another young firm, Heinemann, had turned the book down with the wounding comment that 'We are not interested in mediocre short stories', he suggested that she might try Elkin Mathews and John

Lane—'You may mention me to Mr. Lane.' Not a warm recommendation; and when, later, Lane took her to the Sette of Odd Volumes, 'The d—d Odd Volumes' Henley called them, advising her that 'They are a third-rate crowd' and above all that she should not 'Make yourself one of that horrible world of penny-a-liners and guinea-a-verse and city shopkeepers. And above all don't be led about the world with that little man Lane for a bear-leader.'

He was to ask her, two years later ('Always affectionately') to examine herself and decide whether she had 'the large creative faculty of achieving by *imagination*, independent of *experience*'. She had not, it transpired. But with the publication in 1893 of *Keynotes* she was an instant success, not only in Britain, but in the United States, in Germany and in Scandinavia. There was in her stories considerable power and sensuality, not to mention the first mention in England of Nietzsche's name. Praise was almost universal, the word 'genius' being a good deal bandied about. Not quite universal: J. A. Spender, for example, in the *Pall Mall Gazette*, finding these studies of strains between men and women, produced and resolvable only by sex, 'a set of stories written with the least amount of literary skill and in the worst possible taste'.

One disappointment: the book sold splendidly—more than 6,000 copies in less than six months; but the libraries jibbed at the projected binding in rough, stiff paper covers, in light blue with gold lettering and a Beardsley design in dark blue. It had to be a cloth. Its titillating reputation having preceded it, it is odd that the libraries accepted it at all in view of other works they were wary of. In the event, Beardsley's elegant if fairly standard title-page survived, with its dark lady, clown and harlequin—and his extravagantly baroque key, subsequently attached to all the books in what became a series of short novels and stories intended to be in tune with the times. Earlier volumes included *The Dancing Faun*, a pointed and lively exercise by Florence Farr, a briefly celebrated actress, friend of Shaw and even more briefly fiancée of Max Beerbohm; full of Wildean epigrams and with a hero diffusing an air of wickedness and 'charming languor'. To this extent it was indeed in tune with the times to the point of parody.

Parody came—from another house in the shape of Robert Hichens's *The Green Carnation*, Davidson's *Earl Lavender* and from The Bodley Head itself in *The Autobiography of a Boy*, by G. S. Street. This sheaf of mockery was originally published piecemeal in the *National Observer*, which never tired of lambasting the Decadents; it is agreeable to find Street, a friend of Henley's as well as a contributor, taking his jibes to The Bodley Head, and to find Le Gallienne, one of the *National Observer*'s most savaged targets, reporting on it as 'extremely well done . . . makes one laugh'; but then Le Gallienne was no fonder of the French kind of decadence than Henley. The Boy in question is a fat little fool, whose intolerable nature is widely rebuffed without being in any way dented, even when he is banished to Canada, announcing absurdly that 'I shall make straight for the forests, or the mountains or whatever they are, and try to forget. I believe people shoot one another there. I have never killed a man, and it may be an experience—that lust for slaughter.' At times these little pieces might be thought to mock not so much Wilde or Huysmans as the instantly famous Max Beerbohm: come to that, it could be considered a precursor of *Zuleika Dobson*, and Saki's *The Unbearable Bassington*, not to mention a disastrously similar 1920s frolic by Raymond Mortimer and Hamish Miles, *The Oxford Circus*, and, far ahead, the world of Anthony Blanch in Evelyn Waugh's *Brideshead Revisited*.

Le Gallienne also said of Street's book that it was 'worth doing as a sort of companion to *Pagan Papers*'; an ill-assorted companion, it must seem, just as Kenneth Grahame's career, climbing steadily and indifferently up towards the Secretaryship of the Bank of England, was by no means of a piece with his writings. Born in 1859 into an upper-class Scottish family to an idle, witty and popular father, the boy Kenneth was removed first to Loch Fyne on Scotland's west coast, lost his mother when he was five years old, himself suffered scarlet fever, was left bronchial for life, and removed to grandparents in the Thames Valley, going to school at St Edward's, Oxford;

(87)

steered away from the University, he was put to work first in an Uncle's office, then in the Bank of England—not at all the sedate establishment normally envisaged, but a lively, rowdy place, with much drunkenness in evidence. There remained with him from early childhood what he called 'the Shadow of Scotch-Calvinist devil-worship'. Not surprisingly he shared a fellow-Scot's taste for vagabondage, and called his earlier pieces Stevensonettes rather than, shall we say, Borrovian. Hatred of Puritanism powered him—hence his rage at attacks on *The Yellow Book*—and he sought also the ecstasy of fatigue, found after prolonged exertion in the open air: especially walking, which particularly encouraged his imagination.

He was in line with Keats, Arnold, Elizabeth Barrett Browning, Richard Jeffries, Saki, Kipling, Buchan, Rupert Brooke and E. M. Forster. The appearances of goat-footed Pan are sometimes seen as welcome animistic malevolence, but also as the source of that elusive 'purity of soul' for which Grahame describes himself as praying to the feral spirit, as he cast back all the time to that 'Golden' Age (1895), those 'Dream' Days (1898), which were by no means the cosy nostalgia for childhood of a whimsical city gent—and which made his private life, his bearing as husband and father, a tightly controlled disaster. Quite why The Bodley Head actually turned down *The Wind in the Reeds* (as it was then called) is not clear; Lane had already begun to envisage a children's book list, and, farmer's son though he was, he is hardly likely to have felt as dismissive as the reviewer in *The Times* who opined that 'as a contribution to natural history the work is negligible'. No doubt he thought it would not sell, and he was not alone in holding this view. Even Methuen, who eventually took it on, were by no means enthusiastic.

By 1893 the natural term of the ill-starred partnership with Elkin Mathews was drawing to its close. Not so Lane's ambitions. He was the moving spirit behind the success of the firm. He was the untiring salesman and the ubiquitous maker of contacts. He was the real, effective herald of Beardsley's success, with *The Yellow Book*. He seized the chance to make a series of what was thought to be significant fiction out of George Egerton's title, *Keynotes*—and it was

Keynotes

by

George Egerton

London : John Lane
Boston : Roberts Brothers
1895

v. Title-page to the first book in the Keynotes Series of novels and short stories. Aubrey Beardsley made the drawings which also appeared on the front boards of the bindings. This title was first published in 1893.

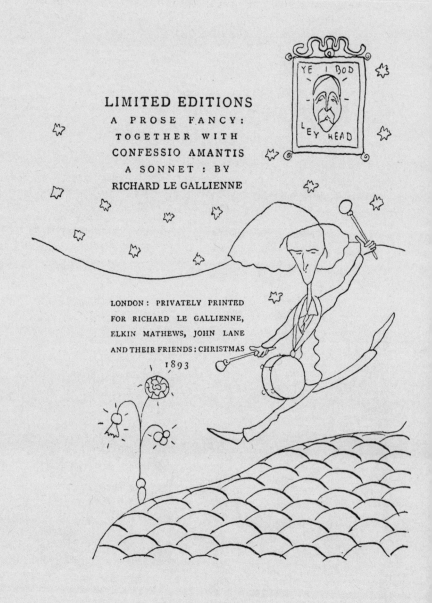

LIMITED EDITIONS
A PROSE FANCY:
TOGETHER WITH
CONFESSIO AMANTIS
A SONNET : BY
RICHARD LE GALLIENNE

YE BOD
LEY HEAD

LONDON : PRIVATELY PRINTED
FOR RICHARD LE GALLIENNE,
ELKIN MATHEWS, JOHN LANE
AND THEIR FRIENDS : CHRISTMAS
1893

VI. Max Beerbohm's caricatures of le Gallienne and John Lane on the cover of a gift booklet, Christmas 1893.

surely he who acquired for it so out-of-the-way a work as Dostoievsky's *Poor Folk*, and got George Moore to write a preface for it; the publication, in June 1894, was in an edition of 1100 copies. It is not too much to suppose that he felt in his bones the nearing end of the age of the exquisite and the decadent, or at the very least that he himself was heartily tired of it, *Yellow Book* or no *Yellow Book*.

Not that he would cease publishing the exquisite and the decadent; but the time was passing when they would be the talk of the town, and exquisite production with it. Perhaps he felt the Empire flexing its already tiring muscles in anticipation of its decline—surely it was he who approved the publication in August 1894 of so uncharacteristic a book as *The Land and Wealth of New South Wales*. He was certainly aware of that tide of feminism which invigorated the Nineties and after in all the arts. This sort of thing was hardly to Elkin Mathews's taste; no wonder Lane was increasingly apt to meet his authors, and transact his business, outside the Vigo Street office, in his rooms in Southwick Street or in the Hogarth Club.

When the time for dissolution arrived in September 1894, the matter of dividing up the firm's authorial assets caused more trouble, as might have been expected. It is hardly possible not to sympathise with Mathews for the assorted humiliations he had had to put up with; hardly possible not to respond to the enterprise and energy of Lane, while necessarily turning a blind eye to his diligent deviousness.

The Rhymers' Club was divided, several members fiercely proclaiming that if a third volume of its anthology were to be published by Lane rather than by Mathews, they would certainly resign from the Club. Wilde was left in a state of courteous but understandably irritated confusion. Having been told that Lane would be taking over his works, he replied that:

'I think it should be left to me to decide with which partner I will place my work ... There is after all no reason why I should not be treated with the same courtesy that is extended to obscure and humble beginners in the difficult art of Literature.'

He therefore proposed entrusting his plays to Mathews, 'Whose literary enthusiasm has much gratified me' and to leave to Lane 'the incomparable privilege of publishing *The Sphinx*, *Salomé*, and my beautiful story on Shakespeare's sonnets'. In the event, Mathews did not want any part of 'Mr. W.H.' and nor did Lane, though in fact he did take over all the rest of Wilde's work up to 1895. Even Mathews did a good deal of lobbying on his own behalf. When what would now be called an opinion poll was taken, the result, as far as the poets were concerned, were on the whole favourable to Mathews; but Lord de Tabley, John Davidson, Norman Gale, Richard Garnett, Le Gallienne, Alice Meynell, Ernest Rhys, Francis Thompson and William Watson preferred to go with Lane. This list Lane promptly made public in the *Publishers' Circular* and the *Daily Chronicle*, although the circular about its compilation was marked 'Confidential'. It included among the prose writers going with Lane Edmund Gosse, Kenneth Grahame, Grant Allen, Allan Monkhouse, as well as *The Yellow Book* and the *Keynotes* series; against which Mathews could claim only H. P. Horne's *Hobby Horse* and *Diversi Colores*.

Stephen Phillips, the briefly famous verse dramatist, who at one point, like Somerset Maugham, had four plays running simultaneously in the West End, most notably *Paolo and Francesca*, was another writer, surprisingly not mentioned in the published list, who wrote a sorry letter to Elkin Mathews on hearing of his fate in this imbroglio:

'Lane has communicated with me the contents of an Agreement with him of which I was unaware during my illness and when I made the Agreement with you, and from which it would appear that I inadvertently offered you a volume of my work, which is certainly covered by the Agreement I have with him. Rather than have any friction with him, and you know what he is from long experience, I am writing to know if you will allow me or my agent to return the advance of £10 you gave me some years ago and at the same time return me the MS of Poems. I shall be willing of course to allow you 5% interest for the use of the money.'

Lionel Johnson struck a pitiful note in his letter to Elkin Mathews:

'I have finally, after much consideration of the matter, decided to leave it to be decided by yourself and Lane. Of course, as you both know, I would greatly prefer you to publish the book but I cannot stand the wear and tear of Lane's arguments and claims.'

Perhaps not. But this did not prevent Johnson from offering Lane a second volume of poems, writing to Mathews that:

'I have told him that if he declines to publish for anyone who also publishes with you, I don't understand or sympathise with that state of mind, and shall offer everything to you exclusively.'

Trying to secure John Davidson, Mathews received a discouraging reply:

'I have elected to allow him [Lane] to have my stock, and to read for him what MSs he sends me. I shall also in all probability offer him my next book. It is therefore impossible for me to accept the confidential post with which you have proposed to honour me.'

Still, in the end Mathews emerged honourably, with a fine record of publishing young and far from established poets, including Yeats, Masefield, Binyon, W. W. Gibson, H. H. Munro, James Elroy Flecker and Ezra Pound.

What particularly upset his friends was his decision to give Lane the name and the actual sign of The Bodley Head, apparently on the grounds that as it was he, Mathews, who was retaining the premises (which he did for another eight years) it was only fair that Lane should have the name. It is likely that Mathews simply did not care for the sort of books the firm had been publishing since (in Le Gallienne's phrase) 'the soul of John Lane entered into The Bodley Head': vulgar modern Bohemia had defeated the aesthetic niceties of Norman

Shaw's redbrick arcadia in Bedford Park. He washed his hands of it, and more particularly of Lane's artistic rake's progress.

Lane indeed was broadening his publishing horizons. By the autumn of 1894 the time had come for him to set sail. As John Davidson's poem aptly if unwittingly put it:

> 'The boat is chafing at our long delay
> And we must leave too soon
> The spicy seapinks and the inborne spray
> The tawny sands, the moon
>
> Keep us, O Thetis, in our Westward flight
> Watch from thy pearly throne
> Our vessel, plunging deeper into night
> To reach a land unknown'

The vessel plunged indeed and the night got alarmingly dark. Luckily Thetis, in the guise of a rich American widow, was just over the horizon; but Lane was not to know that when, too soon indeed in terms of the financial backing he had found, he set out.

Characteristically, mischievously and ambitiously, he had not far to go. Just across the road, in fact.

9

A Trial

Immediately opposite the little shop in Vigo Street there stretched, and still stretches, that curious enclosure, the Albany—or Albany *tout court* as it has been thought correct to call it since the end of the last century. T. P. O'Connor called it 'that relic of an ancient day which hides its dark rooms and its semi-monastic gloom in a passage between Piccadilly and Burlington Gardens'. The 'passage' in fact is wide; flanked by shrubs, a central path—the 'Rope Walk'—is roofed, and blocks of chambers rise severely on either side.

It had been built on the site of Melbourne House and its gardens in 1804, and took its name from George IV's brother, the brave old Duke of York and Albany, first of its residents; it was a masculine fastness, women being allowed to own property there only in 1883; though there had been nothing in the rules to exclude them, the very idea had entered nobody's head until a widow took over her late husband's tenure.

It had a ring about it of aristocracy and the arts: Byron, for instance, Bulwer Lytton, Admiral of the Fleet Sir Harry Keppel, Brougham, the architect Robert Smythe, Gladstone, Macaulay, Monckton Milnes, the Marquess of Clanricarde, eccentric and most appalling of Irish landlords, Arthur Henry Hallam, Montague Corry, Disraeli's secretary, better known as Lord Rowton of the Rowton Houses, Sir Squire Bancroft, most polished of actor-managers, and for almost forty years *The Saturday Review*.

Here, evidently, was the very place for Lane. His rooms in the doctor's house in Southwick Street were all very well; the landlord was a congenial fellow, and moreover one who never put up the rent. But Southwick Street, even so, could hardly match the *cachet*, let alone the convenience, of the Albany. By 1893 he had been at pains to get to know many of those connected with this desirable residence. In January, 1894, he took over *Saturday Review*'s old set of chambers, G.1, at the extreme end of the eastern block, its north side actually facing Vigo Street. He did so initially in conjunction with Edmund Trelawny Backhouse, eccentric scion of a frequently eccentric family; but almost immediately the latter (perhaps persuaded by Lane to act as a guarantor of respectability) withdrew, his health having given way.

Lane was living there, and doing most of his work there, by the time the partnership with Mathews was dissolved in October, 1894. He was apt to describe the parting of the ways as 'of a perfectly cordial character'. But of course it was not. Mathews understandably seethed with bitterness, in his quiet way:

'Of course as Lane took it upon himself to run after the authors *presumably* for the firm, but as it now appears from his own avowal, *really* for himself, many of them therefore feel they ought to offer themselves to Lane, and those who have no such compunction Lane tries to *worry* over to his side. Lionel Johnson for instance is a case in point.'

Nor, probably, was he much comforted by well-meant letters telling him that 'the fact that you are too modest gives the enemy an advantage—at the same time it endears you to your friends.' No man, surely, likes to be commiserated with for being feeble. Still less to be told by another supporter that 'I don't think Lane should climb up over you in an unfair way:' to which Mathews replied by making a point which had evidently not worried his friends:

'Lane misrepresents and falsifies matters as is his custom . . . but The Bodley Head is fast becoming identified with fiction of a very modern character—made up of emotion and no morals; probably I shall in time get reconciled to its loss.'

A process made no easier by the fact that the two men were in effect face to face across the narrow street: especially since Lane evidently had no difficulty in persuading the Trustees of the Albany to allow the installation of a handsome street doorway to G.1, opening onto what had been his dining-room, and crowned by the equally handsome sign which Mathews had so readily abandoned to him. The result of these alterations, along with the removal of the pillars which had closed the street to traffic, and a handsome pair of gates at the north end of the Albany (to allay Lane's fears of inadequate security) were generally felt to be a great improvement, and to Lane's gratification were favourably commented on in the Press.

They also rather dwarfed the firm's original premises. Yet Lane, a sentimental man, must have glanced across the road from time to time to remember his excitement over finding and fitting up the premises back in 1887, the mahogany bookshelves so highly polished that they might have been walnut, the very first order to be delivered by post coming by a lucky chance from the Bodleian Library; and the growing success of the publishing side of the firm, which required them to hire the upper rooms over a neighbouring tailor's shop. (The tailor, whose name confusingly, was Sadler, hated noise, one of the conditions of The Bodley Head's taking the rooms being that there should be no talking on the stairs.)

Such stirring times must have left their memories, many triumphant, not a few rather guilty. But here now he stood, king of his own tiny domain in the Albany (cock on his own dunghill, some would have said, bearing in mind some of his shabbier tricks, and *The Yellow Book*). Business was booming. All those minor poets were still going strong, even if he felt in his bones that their star was waning; and now, having made his mark, indeed his name, on this small scale, he could be a real publisher, and issue books which really caught his own fancy.

Although he was no great traveller on a large scale, he delighted in whirling about England, he delighted in London and books about London; and from his armchair, or his desk, the call of Empire stirred not only his blood but his sense of the saleable; he greatly enjoyed the theatre, and could expand the publication of plays. Then there were the ladies—not for nothing was he sometimes called 'Petticoat Lane'—whether for his pleasure in women's company, and theirs in him, or for his bargaining powers.

And, perhaps above all, there were furniture, paintings, glass, book-plates; among other things he was acquiring an encyclopedic knowledge of the whereabouts of paintings in country houses up and down the land. Those were the sort of subjects he would like to make a name for, and in notably well produced books at that, if not in such exquisite little objects as those he had so far marketed so successfully.

At this heady moment in his career as a publisher perhaps he did not dwell too much upon economic aspects. After all, for all his notorious closefistedness with his authors, he was, as he had made clear to Elkin Mathews even before they set up shop together, never much of a businessman. Even the journal of the Railway Clearing House, in a friendly notice at the time of his death nearly forty years after he had left it, observed that 'he was never very brilliant at our complicated work'. Now, he had found some backing. There was a detached figure, one H. H. Robinson, partner in a firm in Long Acre. There was Francis Money-Coutts, soon to be Lord Latymer, himself a rather peppery minor poet in search of a publisher, with whose wife Lane seems to have got on exceptionally well. And there was Miss Emma Chamberlagne.

This lively lady lived principally in Atherstone, Yorkshire, but was often to be found at various less than shabby areas of London, notably in Lowndes Square or Chesham Place. With her Lane formed an advantageous but evidently real friendship which lasted well into the next century: they shared, this farmer's son from Devon and this county lady from Yorkshire, a passion for the work of Beardsley. At an early stage in their acquaintance, however, Lane was far from reticent. In March 1894, even before Lane and Elkin Mathews had separated, she was writing to Lane:

'What I wanted to mention to you when I saw you last (only there were so many people) was, that when we were talking over your future affairs you said, that if you did not take another partner you would have to "raise money" and it occurred to me whether I could be of some use to you . . . I am fascinated by Beardsley's Salome—I should like to learn how he arrives at that state of mind.'

In August she writes:

'I am very glad to hear you have come to so satisfactory an agreement with Mr. Mathews; as far as I understand it, you seem to have obtained all you want . . . I will send you a cheque for £500 tomorrow . . . I have always had full confidence in you and your career, and am very pleased to be able to be of a little service to you.'

And then, after signalling this mutually agreeable bargain, she writes again on the very next day:

'. . . I suppose Mr. Elkin Mathews could not make up his mind to descend from the publishing house to the bookseller only, but from what you have told me of his characteristics, I am afraid his publishing will not be likely to flourish.'

As things turned out, of course, in spite of his having escaped from the squalor of trade into the elegance of a profession, it was proving none too easy for Lane to make his own publishing flourish. By November 1895 Miss Chamberlagne is desolated: 'I quite understand how much easier you would be with more capital and only regret that I am at this time so placed that I cannot assist you. My property is in trust and I cannot meddle with it.' She does, she explains, accumulate some interest on a deposit account, but she has just now given it to her eldest brother—'In these miserable times for landowners, gentlemen so often have to farm their own land.'

Never mind. Despite this disappointment, Lane sends her some Beardsley drawings, and Miss Chamberlagne is delighted with them: 'There is no-one like him in knowing what he wants to say,' she writes from Yorkshire. Alas, 'I cannot bring them back myself as my coachman is ill and I have not been out since Saturday.' And, Eureka! on December 31: 'I am very glad to be able to send you the cheque for £320 . . . a growing concern like yours may put you in transient difficulties:' and another for £350 in March 1896.

The difficulties were not quite as transient as Miss Chamberlagne hoped. Lane's optimism bore her up, perhaps, more than it did him. Nine months later she writes to him, before one of his most important trans-Atlantic trips, in a positively lyrical vein:

'I am very pleased that you have been able to arrange your monetary affairs so satisfactorily and I hope all will go on and prosper now, and that a calm voyage will give you a thorough rest and rejuvenate you.'

It did; it is possible to detect a hint of relief in this friendly note. But Lane paid her the agreed interest as it fell due, it seems, which is more than he ever did his authors' royalties. Not that he was in any hurry to pay off his debts, regarding them perhaps as more of an investment. By 1902 she has with Lane's agreement shown to her brother a business letter. He thinks 'It will be well to reduce the capital of the loan by your offer of notes of hand for £500 payable in two, three and four years time, and the remainder in five years . . . the interest to be at $3\frac{1}{2}$%;' but her faith is still calm, unlike her brother's: 'I do not look at it quite in his light, and my mind is not uneasy . . . Remember I have just the same confidence in you that I have always had.'

His own confidence in himself, as he set out on his new adventure, was also firm, despite the financial tightrope he was walking. After all, the Keynotes Series was continuing to do well, not least with its standard-bearer George Egerton, who followed up *Keynotes* with *Discords* (1894 and more than living up to its name), over which Lane's efforts to publicise her and her books suffered a sharp rebuff:

'Interviews I bar—also portraits in ladies' papers. I would burn every exclusively woman's paper in England . . . I suppose in my way I am an irritable little person, but I can't stand cant of any kind, and not too much flattery. I am suspicious of it. You are a genius in your own way.'

But she wisely retained warm, not to say fulsome, feelings for Lane. These survived even his asking her to tone down some of the stories in her next book, *Symphonies* (1896); this she agreed to do, as a concession to 'the new Bodley Head policy'. They survived even Lane's keeping Knut Hamsun's bleak *Hunger*, in her translation from the Norwegian, after rejecting it. Hamsun was another of George Egerton's lovers, from an earlier stage in her life, witness her dedication of *Keynotes*: 'To KNUT HAMSUN, In memory of a day when the west wind and the rainbow met'; and Lane did publish it in the end. Despite his notorious closeness with his authors, moreover, he guaranteed her up to £20 at the bank, and offered her £10 a month in a sticky patch. Meanwhile fame brought other rewards. She met Shaw. She was, he said:

'Good natured and well-meaning, but so intolerably loquacious that she talked herself off the stage after she had won her way to the centre of it by her literary talent. It was incessant gabble-gabble without any grace of address or charm of speech. Many sought to meet her once, but not twice.'

She did not develop as a writer. Her second husband gave her not only a pen-name but a much-loved son (killed in the First World War), and her demeanour as mother moved John Lane to tears as he described her to others; her husband did, however, prove increasingly unsatisfactory. In due course he was packed off to South Africa, made a nuisance of himself to her relatives there, came home, made their housemaid pregnant, and departed for America and divorce. With all her experience to draw on, though, she could not hold the interest of the public. Book after book took her further down hill, despite a long and apparently successful marriage to a man fifteen years younger than herself—Golding Bright, a friend of Shaw, and theatrical agent.

In 1922 she did not take up Lane's suggestion of a book of memoirs; in 1931 *Toss of the Cup* was turned down by thirteen publishers, and she gave up, not least perhaps because her husband gave her no encouragement: 'George Egerton is merged in "Mrs. Golding" ... G is not interested in me as a writer.' So taking refuge in Irish genealogy and the Savoy Grill, her husbands dead, her son killed, her market gone, she survived until 1945.

But with *Keynotes* she had sounded not so much a feminist as a feminine note—independence of vision and submission of body seem to have been her dominant themes. Her men are for the most part insensitive sex-objects. In any case sexual freedom, that is to say freedom of sex, was, so to speak, the root of the matter, and eagerly unearthed by others; not least by an industrious journeyman-writer, Grant Allen, in another Keynotes book, *The Woman Who Did* (1895). Allen, Canadian-born in 1848, had been Professor of Mental Philosophy and Logic [sic] for a time in Jamaica, then, in England, a leader-writer with the *Daily News*, and a champion of the New Hedonism ('self-development is greater than self-sacrifice'). With its inviting title, his work was a notable, and notably successful, 'advanced' novel of the period. The period was one about which Grant Allen's nephew, Grant Richards, was given a stern warning by Walter Haddon, publisher of a *Winter Annual*:

'I don't want any contribution from Grant Allen on the lines of "The Woman Who Did", nor do I want one from Davidson on the lines of a recent contribution of his to the Yellow Book. Writing of that character may be literature, but it is not decency.'

In this light The Bodley Head could be compared to the deliciously notorious bars, such favourites of Vigo Street writers, to the Alhambra or the Empire music-halls, and Lane seen as a purveyor of moral iniquity or as a bold pioneer of literary freedom. He was indeed a pioneer of literary freedom, but a cautious, not a bold one. The 'woman who did' was a tiresome and wrong-headed woman, but stood firm against a good many widely held attitudes to women: 'developing every fibre of our natures. That's what nobody yet wants us women to do. They're trying hard enough to develop us intellectually; but morally and socially they want to mew us up just as close as ever.'

With this determined lady, Herminia, steady, sturdy Alan is at thirty falling in love for the first time, and she with him. Her heart gives 'a great bound', and in no time 'he folded her in his arms. Her bosom throbbed on his . . . she quickened to the finger-tips.'

Where else? Tribute should be paid here, with all respect to *Lady Chatterley's Lover*, to the ability of so many writers of this time to evoke a steamingly sensual atmosphere without committing to paper the slightest hint of the explicit. What Herminia does is to get her man to defy 'the abject hollowness of the conventional code which masquerades in our midst as a system of morals'. Unmarried, they go off to Italy. At this point Allen provides what must still strike a chord in many a woman's heart—the picture of a woman desperately trying to enjoy something on which the man she loves dotes (in this case Perugia) but which she greatly dislikes. Then, hardly is she pregnant before he dies of a fever.

Home again, an ostracised unmarried mother, she struggles to earn a living and bring up her daughter on her own absurdly independent lines. Alas, as must often be the case with high-principled unmarried mothers in the 1980s, the daughter revolts against her mother's standards and opts for convention and luxury. This twist to the plot neatly allows the reader to have it both ways: to thrill to Herminia's courage and independence, to sigh with relief when her daughter sticks to the proprieties.

Allen tried to achieve another best-seller with *The British Barbarians*, which, along with a good deal of anthropological enthusiasm, is a do-it-yourself manual on how to get an attractive woman away from a boring husband. This one didn't catch on, perhaps because he could not think of ending it except by turning the lover into a supernatural being who, having achieved his kidnap, disappeared in a puff of smoke when confronted by the injured party: thus presumably signalling to frustrated wives that such notions are but fantasies and sexual daydreams.

These two books were answered by a visitor to the Keynotes Series from another list, Victoria Cross, with an equally steamy novel, *A Woman Who Did Not*. Returning by boat from the East, on long leave, the male narrator meets an attractive mystery woman: the rest of the book retails the exploits of an accomplished tease working upon a man who supposed her to be a lady and is sadly put about by her stratagems. Here again, the title assures us that nothing dishonourable will occur, while the working out of the story keeps us, or kept readers of the Nineties, on a titillating knife-edge.

With the Celtic Twilight represented by 'Fiona Macleod' (in fact a busy novelist and literary biographer, the Scot William Sharp), and the supernatural by Arthur Machen (Welsh), who was a fellow-member with W. B. Yeats and Aleister Crowley of the sect known as The Order of the Golden Dawn, not all the volumes in the Keynotes Series were concerned with the more concrete problems of the day, but the imprint served as a sort of guarantee of social relevance or literary quality, and occasionally of both.

It was Elkin Mathews who had originated the firm's interest in publishing plays with his Bedford Park neighbours Dr John Todhunter and the aunt-and-niece team of 'Michael Field' (Katherine Bradley and Edith Cooper). Theatrical values were hardly their strong suit. The former's *A Sicilian Idyll*, anti-naturalistic and graceful, won the approval of anti-Ibsenite, anti-naturalistic playgoers, including Yeats, with its neo-pastoral simplicities. A reviewer in *The Academy* approved of its success in Todhunter's private theatre, with Florence Farr in the lead, in terms which might have been written at any time since the mid-1950s; a success welcome 'in days when art—and especially, perhaps, the dramatic art—tends so much to become a form of nervous excitement'. As for the ladies, the one burly and emphatic, the other sharp but in appearance deceptively wan and wistful, the Independent Theatre chose to put on *A Question of Memory*, transforming the stage, in William Archer's view, into a theatre where 'On s'ennuie.' They conceived, he thought, 'that style was the most dramatic which could boast the greatest number of metaphors to the square inch' expressed in the diction and versification of the 1590s, even if its subject were a young Hungarian patriot in 1848.

John Davidson's *Fleet Street Eclogues* having been accepted enthusiastically for The Bodley Head by Le Gallienne, its author set about getting his plays rescued from their stillborn publication; not without difficulty, he and Lane eventually succeeded, and five had appeared in *Plays*, with a striking illustration by Beardsley. His plays are altogether more interesting, not so much decadent as despairingly defiant, albeit drawing heavily on the Commedia dell'Arte. Elkin Mathews and the Bedford Park coterie could perhaps go along with them. Wilde's *Salomé*, on the other hand, put them in a fix, for Wilde was a firm supporter of Bedford Park's kind of drama. Bedford Park, however, could hardly have been expected to enthuse over *Salomé*, and still less when it was published by The Bodley Head with Beardsley's alarming illustrations. Still, Wilde's *Lady Windermere's Fan*, with its suggestion that even good women have the seeds of evil in them, had proved acceptable in 1893 (as, apparently, had an edition, introduced by Le Gallienne of Hazlitt's *Liber Amoris*, and even Longus's *Daphnis and Chloe*, with Ricketts/ Shannon woodcuts).

Lane, however, was looking ahead, and in 1892 approached the outrageous young George Bernard Shaw with a view to publishing *Widowers' Houses*, much to Shaw's surprise: 'Were you serious about publishing a play of mine? I am not sure that it would be a very gorgeous investment; but I suppose a limited edition at a high price would be bought by a certain number of idiots who would not buy anything of mine for a penny or a shilling.' Evidently Lane thought not, but in April 1894, Shaw seems to have approached him:

'Has your experience with *Lady Windermere's Fan* led you to suppose that publishing plays is worth while? Is there anything to be done with this play of mine [*Arms and the Man*], which is to be produced on Saturday evening by Miss Farr?'

As The Bodley Head was about to publish Miss Farr's lively

novel, *The Dancing Faun* in its Keynotes series, Lane might—should—have been interested, but apparently was not; and when, soon afterwards, he wanted to include a reprint of *Cashel Byron's Profession* in the Keynotes series, Shaw 'never had time to follow that up.'

Another young and forward-looking publishing house with whom Shaw had unfruitful dealings was Heinemann's, rather surprisingly linked with Lane, at that time, in a manner which came about as follows, according to Lewis May. One day, after Lane had set up shop on his own, William Heinemann dropped in for a chat. Lane had just seen Heinemann's autumn list, congratulated him, but added, 'There is one book on your list which ought to have come to me, and I feel rather resentful at seeing it among *your* books.' With his habitual slight stutter, Heinemann replied 'M-m-m-my dear Lane, I'm so sorry. Which one?' '*The First Step*, by William Heinemann, of course.' 'Oh,' said Heinemann modestly, '*You* wouldn't have taken it.' 'Of course I would,' said Lane. And so, according to this pleasing story, Heinemann transferred his book to Lane's list, along in due course with two more plays, *Summer Moths* and *War*. If their reported mutual admiration is true, both men would perhaps have been amused, in their bookmen's heaven, by a less amiable transfer of authorship which was to take place sixty-five years later.

The year 1895 dawned fair and promising for John Lane and The Bodley Head. Even if it were financially insecure, and decidedly under-capitalised, the minor poets were still on top of the world, the topical novels of social significance were selling like hot cakes, the fencing with authors and artists over fees only added a zest to life, and the firm's publishing horizons were indeed widening in Lane's exploratory eye. That eye was so busy, in fact, that it failed to notice that storm-clouds were gathering. He even took up golf in order to expand his range of contacts, though he proved no good at it. 'One can't know too many editors,' he cried. At the Sette of Odd Volumes he was a star member, bringing his interesting guests, printing their elegant booklets (called 'Opuscula') at his own expense, glorying in the jokes of which he was the constant butt.

The American market was doing splendidly, too. Every book thus far published by The Bodley Head had been placed with American publishers. Already the idea of setting up his own company in New York was beginning to form in Lane's mind. His salesmanship was quite as effective in New York or Boston as it was in Britain. On both sides of the Atlantic the name of The Bodley Head was on every lip, or so it seemed, and remained so for many years. As far ahead as 1902 the secret marriage of an eighteen-year-old heiress, Lena Head, to a young English estate manager, Frederic Bodley, did not for long escape attention. *The Tatler* celebrated the occasion in verse:

'. . . Behold the parson, meek and godly
Handing the long-lacked Head to Bodley!

Bound in the holy bond, the twain
Appeal to every heart; but where
Oh, where, we wonder, was John Lane?
He surely should have figured there.
How much we should have joyed in finding
Him sagely managing the binding.'

Lane was in fact in New York—as was Le Gallienne—when he heard, or rather saw, the fateful news of Oscar Wilde's arrest: 'Yellow Book Under His Arm' as the headline put it. Not, as it turned out, *The Yellow Book*, only a French novel with a yellow cover; but the damage was done. This, and Wilde's conviction on charges of homosexuality, gave the signal for a public outburst, long simmering, or rage against Decadence in general. Lane's world was turned upside down. He at once sent a cable to Chapman in London withdrawing the Wilde books on his list. Hardly had he despatched this message than he was told that William Watson had indicated that unless this was done he would withdraw all *his* books from The Bodley Head list. The same message came from Wilfred Meynell on behalf of his wife Alice and from several others.

Worse was to follow. The trial reports brought back to public view the debased figure of Edward Shelley and his shaming account of what had occurred between him and Wilde while the boy was employed at Vigo Street—and the suggestion that Shelley had been introduced to Wilde by John Lane himself.

It was also put about that another close friend of Wilde was Beardsley. This was untrue; but by that time any stick was good enough to beat Beardsley with, and with Beardsley *The Yellow Book*, of which, after all, he was Art Editor. Moreover, Lane maintained his admiration for the young artist, even if his proposed line of defence may be thought naïve or disingenuous:

'If Beardsley is attacked I hope someone will suggest that he has been the modern Hogarth in pointing out and, as it were, lampooning the period and its customs, *and chiefly in the Yellow Book.*'

He felt dreadfully cut off across the Atlantic, or so he claimed: 'I do not intend to remain in New York a day beyond the time I have done my business, as the Oscar case may make it desirable for me to return at once.'

It surely did, but he was not really in any hurry to return, being still in New York at the end of April, when he received a disquieting letter from a politician-journalist friend in London, a pillar of *The Daily Telegraph*, Henry Norman:

'Your friends here have been much exercised about your name cropping up in the Wilde-Queensberry trial. I was in court at the time, and did not consider that the reference appeared to be in any way unpleasant enough for any immediate action to be taken on your behalf... I think you have done well to withdraw Wilde's book, and in my opinion very well also to withhold Beardsley's illustrations from "The Yellow Book" ... it will need, however, to be carefully edited for some time to come, with a view to the newly-aroused and quite wholesome disapproval of the morbid.'

The removal of Beardsley from the fifth volume of *The Yellow Book*, indeed the suppression of the whole issue, was ordered by the unfortunate Chapman, who was left alone to cope with the crisis, with Lane and Le Gallienne in New York, Henry Harland in Paris, and a mob gathering outside the firm's Vigo Street offices, amusing itself by throwing bricks through the window. When he did return to London, Lane was indeed confronted by embattled hostility, regardless of the fact that Wilde had never had anything to do with the periodical. He saw his whole enterprise crumbling: not only *The Yellow Book*, but, as a result of guilt by association, his whole publishing enterprise. As a sop to baying public opinion, he decided that Beardsley must go—which he did, to emerge soon on the short-lived *Savoy*. Even Beardsley's name could no longer guarantee confident interest; nor the enterprise of its dazzling but self-destructive publisher, Leonard Smithers; his disreputable way of life may be said to have hastened the early death (in 1898 at 26) of the most remarkable artist to have emerged from the whole Nineties movement.

The Yellow Book itself staggered on for another eight issues; still an excellent magazine, it advanced a talented clutch of Glasgow-based artists—including Herbert MacNair and the Macdonald sisters, Margaret and Frances—and discovered, it may be said, Frederick Rolfe, self-styled Baron Corvo. But Lane ruefully remarked of the whole episode that 'It killed the *Yellow Book*, and it nearly killed me.'

Lane was certainly marked by this threat to his young business, and for years continued to see a homosexual, so to speak, under every bush. But, at least superficially, his resilience was unimpaired, and by August 1895, barely three months after the debacle, he had set off for another trip to the West Country, writing exuberantly to poor battered Chapman from Place House, Padstow, home of the Prideaux-Brune family:

'I am having a delightful time here. Oddly enough Lady Rosalind Northcote—a sister of Lord St. Gyres—joins the houseparty tomorrow. Yesterday I was out fishing all day.'

A little later he is writing from The Duke of Cornwall in Plymouth that once grandest of west country hotels, where stayed passengers disembarking from the Atlantic liners:

'Dear Chapman:
    I am feeling much better this morn: I am here till the night train for Exeter.
    Should there be any letters forwarded from Penzance, Padstow, or here for me, *please don't open them.*'

On with the motley.

10

An End to Decadence

In 1892 Alfred, Lord Tennyson, the Queen's Poet Laureate died. His successor was not appointed until 1896, and then turned out to be Alfred Austin, a wealthy barrister-turned-upmarket-journalist of staunchly imperialist views, who rather fancied himself as a country gentleman. He was a neat enough little versifier, but as Laureate became, and has remained, a national joke. Whether any of his rivals for the post, several of them from the Bodley Head stable, would have fared any better is open to question. All were capable of sensationally bathotic lines, not to mention suspect morals. These were seized upon by Owen Seaman, a young man born in London of a Suffolk family, who, after school at Shrewsbury and Clare College, Cambridge (where he read Classics and became Captain of Boats), became Professor of Literature at Durham College of Science, and a barrister of the Inner Temple. He also began publishing what were instantly felt to be not merely amusing but shrewd parodies.

John Davidson, Le Gallienne, Arthur Symons, and William Watson felt what was thought to be the lash; friends began to commiserate not only with them but with Lane for this untoward mockery of his singing-birds. He, on the other hand, thought them admirable, and saw the commercial possibilities of them in book form. According to Grant Richards:

'I remember sitting with Hind and John Lane one May day in the Old Hogarth Club . . . would I make some excuse for going into the Savile Club and inducing the porter, if, as Lane thought, Seaman was a member, to send a letter to him by special messenger. That interest in the man who was to be editor of "Punch" was to be profitable to Lane.'

It was indeed. Year after year, through knighthood and baronetcy, Seaman's books of satire and parody, beginning with *The Battle of the Bays* (1896), sold excellently; and year after year Seaman was deeply irritated by Lane's dilatory payment of royalties and failure to submit royalty accounts.

Nevertheless, as long as the Nineties Poets held public attention, Seaman's lines continued to publicise both Lane and The Bodley Head's

> . . . precious few, the hens of utter godlihead
> Who wear the yellow flower of blameless bodlihead.

Witness the distraught lady in 'A Ballad of a Bun' (after John Davidson), who found that 'songs and tales of pleasant cheer' were not wanted:

> A Decadent was dribbling by;
> 'Lady,' he said, 'You seem
> You need a panacea; try
> This sample of the Bodley bun.

> 'It is fulfilled of precious spice,
> Whereof I give the recipe;—
> Take common dripping; stew in rice,
> And serve with vertu; taste and see!'

But retribution followed:

> The seasons went and came again
> At length the languid Public cried;
> It is a sorry sort of Lane
> That hardly ever turns aside

> 'We want a little change of air;
> On that,' they said, 'We must insist;
> We cannot any longer bear
> The seedy sex-impressionist.'

Though some of the poets were not pleased, Lane himself was: Seaman (surely) in an anonymous piece which appeared in *Punch*, in March 1897, 'The Uses of Parody', described 'a man of modest wits, who dealt in vacant chaff [and] finds himself invited to dine with his publisher, and to his dismay seated between two of his parodic targets.' Become the object of fulsome praise:

> Much gratified, he drank their toast,
> And subsequently laid
> The naked facts before his host
> Who understood the trade.
>
> 'The Publisher,' said he, 'Regards
> Your work as mainly sent
> To serve the heavy-hanging bands
> For cheap advertisement . . .
>
> Already tasting better times
> He sells by twos and fours;
> *The Public has to buy his rhymes*
> *To see the point of yours.'*

William Watson was a particular target, on political as much as on literary grounds. When he was not writing popular lyrics such as 'April, April, laugh thy girlish laughter', writing to friends telling them that 'French letters were quite unknown in Glastonbury,' while assuring them that 'having a woman does one a heap of good', or attacking the Prince of Wales in Windsor Great Park, he was a political poet of the fiercest kind. He made the task of Lane and others championing his bid for the Laureateship virtually impossible by the virulence of his views. He was an Evolutionist, an agnostic anti-Christian, anti-imperialist (in due course pro-Boer), dismissing Kipling's 'Recessional' as 'merely barbarous and primitive'. He could hardly do less, having the year before published two works expressing his outrage at the British government's failure to intervene in the matter of the Turkish atrocities against the Armenians. Proceeds from *The Purple East* were given to the Armenian Relief Fund (headed by the Dukes of Argyll and Westminster, the Archbishop of York and four other bishops). Later came *The Year of Shame*:

'. . . a patriotic appeal, intended to provoke men to serious thought about national honour and duty . . . on behalf of those sufferers who, having endured long agony and sore bereavement, and horror that cannot be easily described, are now perishing in misery and want.'

And directed against those who:

'look upon international duty as something that is to be measured chiefly, if not entirely, by financial and material interests . . .'

and against:

'the demoralising influence of the financier, the bond-holder and the speculator.'

Never, he cried:

'Never, O craven England, never more Prate of thy generous effort, righteous aim!'

The Ottoman government he dubbed 'The Vice-Regency of Hell' and coined the popular title for the Turkish Sultan—Abdul the Damned.

At this point Owen Seaman's genial satire was sharpened. After mild mockery of Watson's self-educated classical pretensions came 'To Mr. William Watson, on his writing the first instalment of *The Purple East*:

> 'Dear Mr. Watson, we have heard with wonder
> Not all unruing with a sad regret
> That little penny blast of purple thunder
> You issued in the *Westminster Gazette* . . .
>
> *Never, O craven England, nevermore*
> *Prate thou of generous effort, righteous aim!*
> So ran the lines, and left me very sore,
> For you may guess my heart was hot with shame . . .
>
> It further seemed a work uncommon light
> For one like you, a casual civilian,
> To order half a hemisphere to fight
> And slaughter one another by the million,
> While you yourself, a paper Galahad,
> Spilt ink for blood upon a blotting-pad.'

Lane published both poets with aplomb. Nevertheless, Watson was angry at the prices charged for the fourteen Armenian sonnets, which had, he thought, achieved literary success—'But I have not reached the mass of the people.' All the same, their relations remained good, Lane frequently 'lent' Watson money, Watson joined Lane in trying to arrange a pension for John Davidson's widow. Undeterred by his friend's occasional attacks of temporary insanity, Lane did his best for the one poet, of all those in his nursery, that he liked the best and admired the most.

The Bodley Head was to all appearances establishing itself handsomely, despite the ultimate failure of *The Yellow Book*, and the knock-out blow to Decadence given by the Wilde trials. In New York, too, Le Gallienne found that willowy poets with long hair had become objects of suspicion; but Lane saw ample opportunities, and set about establishing his American company. It opened in November 1896 at 140 Fifth Avenue, publishing the parent firm's own books from London when the rights were available, and sometimes buying them back, and also *The Studio*. His first announcement in the *Publishers Weekly* was initially untrue:

'The American Bodley Head will be presided over by an American. Whether the customs of afternoon tea will be kept up, as in Vigo Street, is not known, but the Bodley Head without five o'clock tea would be an anomaly.'

These functions, for which Beardsley often designed suitably restrained invitations, were for mixed company; they were soon supplemented by the evening functions known as 'Smokes', all male gatherings which in turn gathered their share of publicity, as drawn by Beerbohm, or celebrated in verses such as those which appeared in *The Westminster Gazette*:

> 'There's a street that men call Vigo
> Whither scribblers such as I go . . .
> There's a sign we know as Bodley
> Whither wander folk ungodly;
> All the writers, all the scribblers,
> All the critics, all the quibblers
> Smoking pipes and drinking whisky
> Telling tales of matters risky—
> "This is business, this is commerce",
> Thinks their doughly host, Sir Thomas—
> Steers with skill the conversation
> Till to *him* it hath relation.
> An it please you he's the fellow
> Owns a certain Book that's Yellow—
> 'Neath the sign we know as Bodley
> Business greeteth friendship oddly.'

Nor were the firm's books neglected, if suitably near the knuckle. When The Bodley Head published H. T. Wharton's *Sappho*—'Memoir, Text, Selected Renderings and a literal Translation, with three Illustrations in photogravure and a cover designed by Aubrey Beardsley'—J. M. Bullock in *The Sketch* favoured the occasion with forty lines of verse in which the words 'Vigo Street' and 'Mr. Lane' recur gratifyingly. And when the New York office was opened, the magazine *Woman*, then edited by Arnold Bennett, whose first novel The Bodley Head was soon to publish, saluted the occasion with another thirty lines:

'Are you dead, O Bodley Head?
Or has Sir Thomas merely fled?
Fled across the great Atlantic,
With Bodley fervour, hot and frantic . . .
Has he fled, with sign and thread,
To swing them in New York instead?
It can't be true that there are two;
We never could think that of *you*,
You who stand supreme, unique,
With pointed beard, of cut antique,
We'd rather, frankly, give you credit
For making Bodley double-Headed . . .
Oh had you not enough to do,
But you must needs shock New York, too!'. . .

Had Lane realised what trouble the New York office was to give him over the next twenty-five years, his warily adventurous spirit might well have drawn back. At first managed briefly by Temple Scott, another ex-Liverpudlian, it soon passed into the hands of Mitchell Kennerley, a boy of under twenty, who found the New World so stimulating that he soon gave Lane the horrors by the way he laid out the firm's money, and then took to outside publishing adventures on a scale which left Lane little choice but to dismiss him —the first of several bright young Englishmen to disappoint him in

New York's heady atmosphere. Only then was his opening announcement, that the firm would be managed by an American, fulfilled: but this was to lead to even worse disasters.

In London itself The Bodley Head's expansion brought problems: for one thing, even the wise and patient Chapman was driven to protest about the amount of work required of the few members of the staff. More part-time assistants had to be taken on. Lewis May had left shortly before the Wilde upset for a marginally better wage in order to support a wife, but he loathed City life and returned to work in the Albany, in the servants' quarters at the very top of the building; whither, he says, Lane used to repair to take his mind off the turmoil below by reminiscing about the good old days in north Devon.

Many more readers had to be employed as the range of books increased. These, down the years, seem to have been of a high standard; among their reports there are no examples of books, or authors, rejected out of hand on submission, later achieving a reputation when issued by another house, though Lane did publish a number of books despite discouraging remarks by his readers.

Among these was the young John Buchan, who, having contributed to *The Yellow Book*, at once, at the age of twenty, began reading fiction for Lane, who paid him, though sometimes belatedly, £6 a week for several years, during which he won a First-class degree in Greats at Oxford, the Newdigate Poetry Prize and sat and won a Fellowship exam; and having already sold outright *Sir Quixote* to Fisher Unwin, published several not obviously saleable books of his own with The Bodley Head: *Scholar-Gypsies* in 1896, a fishing anthology, *Musa Piscatrix*, in 1897, *Grey Weather* and *John Burnet of Barns* in 1898. From this time the indefatigable young man has left behind 172 reader's reports, 29 of them proposing acceptances, and in eight of the latter suggesting revisions. Each runs to 300–400 words, well laid out in terms of plot, theme, quality and likely sale; occasional corrections suggest that these holograph notes are first drafts, written on Brasenose College, Oxford Union, Cocoa Tree Club and Vincent's paper; but such is their ordered fluency that hardly an alteration would need to be made in the unlikely event of their being reprinted.

Buchan's prize draw, out of his on the whole dispiriting survey of aspiring late nineteenth century novelists, was a book at that point called *In the Shadow*, a first novel by a young provincial, Enoch Arnold Bennett. 'The title is inadequate and must be changed,' correctly pronounced the 21-year-old reader. There was also 'a certain amount of journalistic detail which might be left out . . . I do not think it likely to be a striking success. Yet it is an honest and creditable piece of work, quite creditable to any firm.' The title was indeed changed, to *The Man from the North*.

The Scot in him purses his lips a good deal about sex. Edgar Jopson's *The Passion for Romance* is dismissed for its 'minute description of audacious vice . . . full of sickening descriptions of passion, and sickening paroxysms'. A novel called *Mortal Man* is 'utterly revolting, vulgar and prurient in the extreme . . . The cleverness of the book . . . lies in the analysis of animal passion . . . Anyone with a sufficiently unclean mind could do it to satisfy.' And as for another called *Two Sinners*, 'the descriptions of Passion—minute and realistic—which make up a large part of the story are vulgar and disgusting in the extreme.' To Chapman he writes that he is 'glad to hear that you intend to keep "sex" novels to the Keynotes Series;' but—throwing an illuminating sidelight on the undoubted success of those books in terms of attention—of another novel he writes that it is 'as good as any Keynotes novels you have published, but if you feel you are issuing such books at a loss, I am afraid I could not prophesy any difference in the case of this one.' In fact, 'I think you will agree with me that it would be well for your firm to undertake a few more solid and scholarly books, something as a change from belles-lettres.'

Though he didn't care for the worldly American novels of Gertrude Atherton, he saw possibilities in the stories of Charlotte Mew, but found them in urgent need of rewriting. His distinguished fellow-Scot, R. B. Cunninghame Graham, on the other hand, that autocratic socialist equestrian, is written off in his *Essays and Studies* as a 'vigorous, whimsical, ill-natured ragbag'. He is alert to the possibilities, too, of the various other series which The Bodley Head was busy spawning in an effort to disown, or at least modify, its *Yellow Book* image—'Lane's Library' of lighter fiction, the 'Lovers' Library' of agreeable little keepsake series, a projected shilling novel library.

He is full of suggestions. Lane's production of his own books delights him. Of *Scholar-Gypsies*, handsomely subtitled 'Essays and Studies in the Art of Life': 'I cannot praise too highly the *Format*; it is so simple and pretty that I do not know how to thank you for it;' and of the fishing anthology, 'You have made a very charming book of it.' All in all he remained for years on excellent terms both with the firm and with John Lane, who, himself by that time a busy clubman, put Buchan up for the Devonshire Club (he was elected on the spot). Frequently Buchan used G.1 Albany as his London *pied-à-terre*; and when he was reading for the bar at the Inner Temple, Lane stood surety for the young aspirant. No wonder that, in *Memory Hold-the-Door* (1940), Buchan spared a few lines in appreciation of the picturesque benefactor of his youth, who did not reap the benefit of the best of Buchan.

Not everyone remained on good terms. Maurice Hewlett, middling pretty writer, flounced off in a rage when Lane had not given him any answer about his *Pan* after six months. Arnold Bennett, after Buchan's warm recommendation, showed understandable signs of testiness in September 1897:

'Will you please let me know when my book is coming out. It is now eighteen months since you accepted it, and I am extremely tired of waiting.'

In November he was still waiting: 'You promised a long time ago to send me a contract, but it has not yet arrived.' The book, if not the contract, did appear in 1898. This does seem, however, a curious way to treat not merely a promising new author, but one who was writing a regular literary column for *Hearth and Home*, and was the editor of *Woman*, in which he had printed the generous puff-poem on Lane quoted above. But much the same series of events came about with Bennett's *Journalism for Women*. It is no wonder that he left, although evidently bearing no ill-will.

Nor, come to that, did Kenneth Grahame, while *Dream Days* (1895) and *The Golden Age* (1898) continued the adult-child's-eye view of the world first broached in *Pagan Papers* (1893). Nevertheless, Lane's off-hand way irritated him as it had irritated and was to irritate many others:

'You seem to imply that there is imposed on me some sort of restraint or qualified serfdom—not upon you, on me only, which entirely and for all time prevents me even doing freely what I may think best for myself.'

All the same, he duly offered *The Wind in the Willows* to Lane, who duly declined it; but even then Grahame merely relapsed into an amiable resignation, mildly enquiring, from Lane and his successors, about royalties on the continuing sales of *Dream Days* and *The Golden Age*, which might be anything up to two years late.

Lane's relations with his fellow-publishers, too, were variable. The great ones—Murray, Macmillan, and the like—looked with perhaps even greater suspicion at Lane than at other upstarts in their world—Dent, Methuen, Heinemann among them. He was of course on excellent terms with Heinemann—both men were sailing near the wind with many of their titles. With J. M. Dent, on the other hand, things were for a while less easy, but by 1897 the two men were swapping books from each other's catalogues.

For all the firm's expansion, or rather because of it, what is now known as the cash-flow problem remained acute. The alterations to the building were not cheap, though a stylish improvement. And Lane was never one to economise, except on his authors. E. H. New, a young artist according to Lane much admired by Whistler, was commissioned to illustrate not only White's *Selborne* and (Elkin Mathews's favourite) Walton's *Compleat Angler*, in 1895, but also to draw the new Bodley Head in all its glory; he stayed with Lane in

G.1 while he did so. He also kept a diary, giving a brisk impression of Lane's world:

'*July 25:* Introduced to R. Watson Gilder, editor of *Century* magazine. Began again drawing front of "Bodley Head" from opposite side of Vigo Street, for Catalogue cover . . . Tea at 5.0 in Lane's room. Met "Mrs. Devreux" again, Wilfred Ball, James Welch [the actor, and Le Gallienne's brother-in-law], who told us of the fall of Le Gallienne's mulberry tree at Brentford, Arthur Symons, Dr. and Mrs.—(very beautiful), Cunningham Grahame, Pauline Johnson, "Teka-Lionwake", the Canadian-Indian poet, Miss Gertrude Prideaux-Brune, etc. Dined with Lane and William Watson at the "Cheshire Cheese" . . . and then had a lovely walk along the Embankment to Watson's rooms at Westminster, under the Abbey.

'*July 26:* Beardsley to breakfast: brought wonderful design of Venus (proof), T. C. Gotch (very pleasant man), Professor Sylvanus Thompson (delightful person), Mr. Millard, of publishing firm of Chicago, and Laurence Housman, dined at the Hogarth Club with us. George Moore, Greiffenhagen, Bell, Professor Raleigh and H. G. Wells (it was their first meeting) returned with others for smoke and talk. Miss Netta Syrett (Grant Allen's niece) to tea. At Bodley Head drawing all day . . . Captain Dunne ["George Egerton's" father] took me to Fly Fisher's Club to see book on fishes, for "Walton". Couldn't sleep, either of us, so we

'*July 27:* . . . came down at 1.0 and I went on with drawing for Catalogue until 2.0 and finished it before breakfast next day. Lane off at 11.0 to Wilfrid Ball's wedding, Watson in.'

And so it went on, with interludes at the Sette of Odd Volumes, the Devonshire Club, the trips to the West Country or to Oxford, the lunches with potential lady authors (even if the 'champagne' was as often as not well-napkined Asti Spumante), those *tête-à-têtes* in the back room, those City dinners, those Book Trade Benevolent

KITWYK

by
Mʳˢ JOHN LANE

JOHN LANE
London and New York:
1903

VII. A title-page drawn by G. W. Edwards for *Kitwyk*, stories by
Annie Eichberg (Mrs John Lane). Curiously, the illustrations in this
book are by three artists—Sterner, Edwards and Pyle. Howard Pyle's
drawings are in a strikingly different style.

MR. JOHN LANE REQUESTS THE PLEASURE OF
THE COMPANY OF

....

TO MEET PROFESSOR AND MRS. STEPHEN
LEACOCK AT A BODLEY HEAD TEA ON
SATURDAY, JUNE 20TH, FROM 4 TO 6.

R.S.V.P. ·

PRIVATE ENTRANCE
G I THE ALBANY
    BURLINGTON GARDENS, W.

VIII. An invitation card, designed by Fish, to meet Stephen Leacock.
A great many guests attended including George Clausen, Ford
Madox Hueffer, Wyndham Lewis, Saki and Ezra Pound.

dinners, those mixed teas, those male Smokes in Albany . . . and Lane all the time exuding an air of genial prosperity, treating each guest as though for the moment he or she were the one person above all others that Lane was eager to see. No wonder his patient authors sometimes ground their teeth.

Nor was all his affability insincere. His enthusiasm for the work of a new discovery, artist, poet or novelist, was real enough, and persuasive enough, while it lasted—which sometimes it did in defiance of the realities of his position.

At this time the remarkable woman who called herself Vernon Lee joined his list, and stayed on it, though never a strong seller, until long after Lane's death. Born in 1856 near Boulogne to wildly eccentric cosmopolitan parents, Violet Paget grew up in Germany, then Nice, where she became, and remained, friendly with John Singer Sargent and his family, then Rome and finally near Florence. She was a never very happy Lesbian of restless mind, burning intelligence and excessively strong opinions. Her effect upon Max Beerbohm, as inscribed on his copy of her *Gospels of Anarchy*, was even worse than George Egerton's upon Shaw. 'Oh dear', scribbled Beerbohm:

'Poor dear dreadful little lady! Always having a [bone] to pick, ever so coyly, with Nietzsche, or a wee lance to break with Mr. Carlyle, or a sweet but sharp little warning to whisper in the ear of Mr. H. G. Wells, or Strindberg or Darwin or d'Annunzio! What a dreadful little bore and busybody! How awfully at this moment she must be button-holing Einstein! And Signor Croce—and Mr. James Joyce!'

Her books, all the same, have singular charm, in her microscopic listing of natural beauty at its most minutely Italian. Her historical fictions and fables are in line with, say, John Addington Symonds's *In the Key of Blue*, and for that matter with another briefly Bodley author, Frederick Rolfe, Baron Corvo, especially in their devotion to fantastical romance, ablaze with the singular fruits of scattered scholarship: no wonder Aldous Huxley admired her. She followed copiously both Ruskin and Pater, and yet was violently 'anti-fleshly', as she made all too clear in an early novel *Miss Brown* (1884), as well as in her unashamed enjoyment of Paterism. Her comments on writing in *The Handling of Words* were, though free of jargon, amazingly modern—she first introduced the word 'empathy' to English—despite her occasional relish for archaisms. In her youth (having first published in French, at 14), she described herself as 'a half-baked polyglot scribbler', and so in a sense she remained, pouring out fantastical tales or highly perceptive comments on 'Musical Expression and the Composers of the Eighteenth Century'. If her arrival on the Bodley Head list in the mid-Nineties was not extraordinary, her remaining there, reprinted doggedly, even anthologised, up to the late 1920s, was. Her *mondaine* wealth (from her mother's West Indian money) and her aristocratic pretensions, gave her an *entrée* which must have delighted John Lane, though she would have seen through his blandishments, and treated him as she would have treated an upper servant—none too kindly.

Her erudition, and indeed her romantic fantasising, she shared with Frederick Rolfe. He came to The Bodley Head by way of *The Yellow Book*, though possibly that was not quite his first encounter with Lane, for in October 1890 Elkin Mathews's list of 'new and forthcoming books from The Bodley Head' carried an impressive entry:

'Will be published shortly, medium 8vo, finely printed on hand-made paper, in a limited edition with Etchings. THE STORY OF S. WILLIAM: THE BOY MARTYR OF NORWICH. From forty contemporary Chronicles, all of which are given in full, with copious Notes and Translations, etc. etc. by THE REVEREND FREDERICK WILLIAM ROLFE, late Professor of English Literature and History at S. Marie's College of Oscott.'

This less than truthful statement was accompanied by a four-page prospectus stating that the edition would consist of 50 copies on hand-made paper, bound in parchment, at one guinea, and 250 copies on antique laid paper, bound in indigo linen or white buckram, at half a guinea. The book was never published, and very likely never written, like several other putatively 'lost' books by Rolfe—who was in any case writing much else, including shoals of newspaper articles under a variety of pseudonyms.

Among these were the first of a long line of florid and agreeable stories, more or less based on Italian folklore, which appeared in Volume VII of *The Yellow Book*. Harland had failed to pay for these by July after the stories had appeared in April—no time at all by The Bodley Head standards; Rolfe wrote direct to John Lane, who seems to have responded favourably, up to a point. Rolfe sent two more stories to *The Yellow Book* for Volume IX, and a further pair for Volume XI. Even so he was plaintively forced to ask why he had received only £7 for payment when he had been promised £10. He also suggested that Lane should employ him: 'Why not take me on your staff as a reader, or even as editor of *The Yellow Book*? . . . Won't you make some effort to get to know me for myself? Why not cultivate the admirable Baron Corvo, whose contributions to your seventh volume no pressman noticed and no reader snipped . . .?'

Wisely ignoring the first suggestion, rashly taking up the second, Lane saw him when, having published the six *Yellow Book* stories as a Bodley Booklet (an agreeable series in which Beerbohm's *The Happy Hypocrite* first appeared), he contemplated republishing them with 26 more stories of the same kind. For his pains he earned himself several years of bickering, and, along with Grant Richards, Temple Scott (soon to be Lane's New York manager), Kenneth Grahame and many others, a vindictive caricature in *Nicholas Crabbe*, the fantastically autobiographical novel Rolfe wrote about 1905, but which understandably failed to achieve publication until, in 1958, all concerned were dead. In this book Lane was called Slim Schelm:

'A tubby little pot-bellied bantam, scrupulously attired and looking as though he had been suckled on bad beer . . . both interested and afraid. Slim Schelm expressed in words his pleasure at the meeting;

and put on a mask which was intended to represent sympathetic commiseration. Crabbe brushed all veils aside. "I am come to see you about my new book," he began. "Don't think though that I wish unduly to occupy your time," he continued with an arctic highness which strangely contrasted with his frightfully shabby garb. He thought that he saw a spark of patronage in Schelm's watery china eyes; and made haste to quench it.'

Give or take the rude descriptions, which were second nature to Rolfe, his account of the interview has an undoubted ring of truth. Lane subsequently appears as 'a beery insect . . . a snivelling little swindler . . . a carrotty dwarf with a magenta face and puce pendulous lips, insinuatingly piggy as his rotund protuberance augmented'. Perhaps he thought Lane was a Jew; certainly other characters in the book are lashed with anti-semitic jibes.

Nevertheless The Bodley Head did publish the second book of Toto stories, as *In His Own Image*, and even, after Rolfe had gone off to be published by Grant Richards and Chatto & Windus, commissioned him to make a complete bilingual prose translation of J. B. Nicolas's French version of *The Rubaiyat of Omar Khaiyam* (his characteristically perverse spelling), which the firm published in 1903; it was received with indifference in both London and New York—not least because of a host of grotesque new-minted words for which Rolfe prepared a very necessary glossary, which Lane refused to include. He regarded the whole thing as a trivial nuisance and its author as a poet, attracting more abuse as he did his best to ignore it. The idea was not his, but Harland's and Temple Scott's, the latter seeming to think that the United States market would welcome it.

Rolfe's self-portrait in *Nicholas Crabbe* is not afraid of the truth:

'I had no kind of education to speak of: but I've picked up a little, and I have a natural gift for window-dressing . . . I have no fundamental knowledge of anything; and my polish is mere veneer.'

A self-portrait which might well have been written about himself by John Lane: perhaps it is not surprising that long after the self-educated son of a London musical-instrument maker died in 1913, all the self-educated Devonshire farmer's son could find to say was:

'He was the most ungrateful person I have ever met, and I have met many of that tribe. The first time I saw him he came into my office with a stick on his shoulder and all his worldly possessions in a coloured pocket handkerchief tied to his stick. I, like a fool, gave him a sovereign and afterwards took some of his books, on all of which I lost money, though I am bound to say he *could* write. *Stories Toto Told Me* are among the most charming things of the sort I ever read; but he was when he came to me . . . and proud to be such a liar, that I am afraid I have become prejudiced even against his work.'

He was not, it is fair to say, easily prejudiced in this way. Lewis May has a pleasing story of Lane closeted with one of his poets (presumably still alive when May told the story), when those outside became aware that the interview was becoming heated. A crash gave them the impression that some piece of furniture had been flung against the wall. The door flung open, the poet strode out. Then Lane appeared gathering up the fragments of a little occasional table. 'This', he is reported as saying, 'is one of the sacrifices that mediocrity must needs make to genius.'

Not all his authors were as difficult. There was, for example, the charming young lady, a Miss Evelyn Sharp, a schoolteacher from an ordinary middle-class background, who wrote at home in the evenings. Greatly daring, she sent a short story to *The Yellow Book* in 1894, and a novel to The Bodley Head. This was recommended by both Davidson and Le Gallienne, quickly published as *At the Relton Arms* (1895) in the Keynote series; and she, to her delight and with a sense of liberation, found herself at home at G.1, Albany, and at the Harlands's Cromwell Road flat, mixing on equal terms with all the *literati*. Soon she published another novel, *The Making of a Prig*, and a series of children's books about a group called the Wymps, highly successful on both sides of the Atlantic. 'Lane', she wrote affably, 'knew better than anybody how to push his authors into fame, but he had not the most elementary notion of the way to push them into matrimony.' She had no difficulty in seeing through his attempts to nudge her into the arms of William Watson, poor girl. But she always retained a great affection for him, even when, a few years later, he remaindered her novels without telling her. When she felt she was owed money, she wrote not to Lane but to Chapman, charmingly adding, 'I do not wish to embarrass Mr. Lane in any way if he is at a loss for ready money.' When he visited her home, 'He pleased everybody by his simplicity and appreciation of country life'—and remembered the names of her family 25 years later; and she credited him, as few others would have done, with 'the temperament that places generosity higher than justice'.

Staying one week-end at Selborne, Gilbert White's Hampshire paradise (and Lane's favourite village outside Devon), she found there also another of Lane's favourites of the moment, Max Beerbohm, putting up at the local inn and 'becoming the talk of the village by dining in a claret-coloured dress suit'. The mannered young man was, of necessity, interested in money: 'I am sorry to bother you—but would you let me have the promised Y.B. cheque today or tomorrow —as I have given several post-dated cheques (on the strength of it).' He was quite ready for *The Happy Hypocrite* to go in *The Yellow Book*, 'but,' he insisted, 'I really cannot let it go for less than £25— three times the length of "George IV"—for which I got £10 two years ago.'

The essay on King George the Fourth looms very rightly large in the collection of pieces by the young dandy which The Bodley Head was about to publish, Scribners issuing it in New York just before Lane had set up his own company: a partnership which inspired Beerbohm to one of his quaint pastimes—inscribing *graffiti* in his own, and other people's books. This time, his ear tickled by the rhythm, he expanded the information given at the foot of the title-page:

'Across the bottom of the page
The magic legend runs
London: JOHN LANE, *The Bodley Head*
New York: CHARLES SCRIBNER'S SONS'

'King George the Fourth' was the best piece in it, an exhilarating essay shot through with irony as it pretends to defend the excesses which Beerbohm apparently loathed as much as he was to loathe Edward VII. In the last piece of his in the decisively titled *Works*, he writes as an old, old man . . . 'Already I feel myself a trifle outmoded,' he says, and I 'crave no knighthood' . . . 'To be outmoded is to be a classic, if one has written well.' All this probably gave John Lane the idea for his well executed joke, the Bibliography with which he ends the little book, a parody of the Bibliographies of Meredith and Hardy he had already done to accompany studies of those two by Le Gallienne and Lionel Johnson respectively. It is neatly done (with Beerbohm's help?), noting with a flourish:

'That the same week should have seen the advent of two such notable reformers as Aubrey Beardsley and Max Beerbohm is a coincidence to which no antiquary has previously drawn attention. Is it possible to over-estimate the influence of these two men in the art and literature of the century?'

But these interesting people, though a credit to any publisher's list, were unlikely to make their own or any one else's fortune; or, indeed, to keep the firm afloat. In any case Lane, despite his enthusiasms—and all publishers, to be successful, need a powerful strain of self-deception—still did not himself much care for Decadence, and certainly did not intend to rely on it and its packaging, however relatively exquisite, and whatever the plaudits of the world of book collectors. True, his fiction list was broadening: on the one hand progressive, in an old-fashioned way, most of his novels used the formulae of the standard romantic novel to project the new sexual relationships in staunchly middlebrow daydreams; on the other hand pastoral, they invoked the verbal equivalents of say, Helen Allingham's paintings to conjure up a threatened Britain of roses-round-the-door. He even started the Arcady Library, under the supervision of that dogged and not unpleasing ruralist, J. S. Fletcher, whose own titles included *Life in Arcadia*, *In the Mayor's Parlour* and *The Wonderful Wappentake*.

Hardship and pathos were not excluded from books of this sort, or even satirical comment, but by and large their touch was light; their subjects might well have appealed to Hardy, but his generally low-spirited bleakness would not have appealed to their writers—or their readers. It may be assumed that a book such as *The History of the Ministry of the Royal Navy and of Merchant Navy*, a far cry from Decadence, as that word is usually understood, was subsidised. Poets still appeared: for example the Irish AE, with *The Earth Breath and Other Poems*, dedicated to Yeats; Dr Richard Garnett's translations of 124 sonnets from Dante, Petrarch and Camoens, and of course the unstoppable if injudicious William Watson ('I have published far too much,' he wrote to Chapman in 1897). Criticism too, with Lionel Johnson's *The Art of Thomas Hardy*, not to mention Elizabeth Rachel Chapman's *Marriage Questions in Modern Fiction and Other Kindred Topics*.

None of these could be called money-makers, but producing them required reserves, and reserves were not to hand, especially in view of Lane's extravagant life-style. Something had to be done, and something quite different from publishing those briefly famous minor poets. Were the assorted series the answer? Perhaps they were all too literary? How about tapping the do-it-yourself market? For example, gardening books? And so it was—beginning in suitably high-class style with the *Book of Asparagus*. The new note did not go unremarked. The ingenious Mostyn Piggott piped up with what he called an 'Ichabodleian Ode':

> Thy Head was once the habitat
> Of Ev'ry human lark and linnet,
> The marrow and the marrowfat
> Dared never hope to pass within it.

The briony and eglantine
   Made of thine ante-room a bower—
Shall it in future be the shrine
   Of carrot and of cauliflower?

... Oh can it be that o'er the beet
   And broccoli thy soul enthuses,
Making once flowery Vigo Street
   The kitchen garden of the Muses.

How sad our lot! The newsman tells
   And tells in very mournful numbers,
That hands which once framed vilanells
   Are now content to frame cucumbers!

Oh Charon, scull us far away!
   We long for nothing now but thee, Styx!
The radish routs the roundelay
   And pea-sticks banish anapaestics!

The times they were-a-changing. Le Gallienne, standard-bearer of the poet's army, was getting more restless than ever. The Bodley Head must expand, but John Lane also intended to continue publishing books on his own special interests—furniture, English painting, old glass. How to, so to speak, balance his books?

Deliverance was at hand. That Thetis of whom John Davidson sang, materialised, a goddess from over the sea to ensure that he himself was comfortable and safe, even as The Bodley Head teetered along its fraying high wire.

II

JOHN LANE
ALLEN LANE AND THE
UNWIN YEARS

II

Enter an Angel

In the summer of 1896, at a party in London, Lane met one of those saviours of the British middle and upper classes, a wealthy American widow. Two years later he married her. But it would be an injustice to both parties to gloss over their romance—for such it was—as a mere stroke of opportunism on his part, and gullibility on hers. That is how many regarded it; but she was anything but gullible, and he displayed qualities unexpected in this bearded, pot-bellied 43-year-old tightrope walker. Their relatively brief courtship was put under considerable strain by his candour, and survived owing to her confidence and, it is not too much to say, initial rapture. She remained at his side until his death twenty-seven years later, and played a modest role as one of his authors and a major role as confidante and adviser in the affairs of The Bodley Head.

The same age, and the same height (5 ft 4 in.) as he was, she had a striking appearance, though no beauty, and throughout her youth always considered herself too fat. She was born in Switzerland Anna Eichberg, only child of Julius Eichberg, who originally came from Düsseldorf, and of a musical family. Soon after Anna was born, he emigrated to the USA, where for seven years he conducted the orchestra of the Boston Museum, and established the Boston Conservatory, which soon enjoyed a high reputation in the United States.

Anna, who as a child in Boston soon became known as Annie, was very close to both parents, a lively pair; she was educated at one public and one private school in Boston and got excellent marks. In no hurry to leave her home, she was 29 when she married a counsellor-at-law, Tyler Batcheller King, of a very well-to-do family and himself, it seems, too hard-working for his own good, for all too soon he fell into a decline. Annie nursed him devotedly, accompanying him at the end to the Bahamas, where he died, leaving her and her own father, who was devoted to his son-in-law, numb. She was not numb for long, and, plain though she felt herself to be, lived a brisk and humorous existence. She also travelled a good deal, visiting her family in Düsseldorf, spending some time in Paris, and regularly taking rooms in London.

Thus it was that she met John Lane. Some strange chemistry was at work; besides, she had by this time made a small reputation as a writer of stories and sketches, which had been published in a number of East Coast magazines—but she had not found, or sought, a London publisher; and she had money. Yet it is not possible to account for their mutual attraction in middle age solely in terms of self-interest.

On the next of his in any case frequent visits to the United States he has, as usual, legitimate reasons for visiting Boston, and calls upon her, to their mutual satisfaction. At Christmas he has sent her 'a little Christmas book' and she, thanking him for it, takes the opportunity to boast of the Paris *Revue Britannique* 'with my stories most delightfully translated'. She hopes that 'the success of The Bodley Head will surpass your greatest expectations' and signs herself, warmly, 'With kindest regards'.

Early in February Lane is back in Boston again, and things are moving faster. He has praised her stories, and she asks him to dine en famille on Saturday evening, also suggesting that she should take him 'to stroll through Boston society Friday afternoon'. In no time, 'I have just received your dear letter . . . I want to be very proud of you and you know that what interests you is what interests me.'

What interested Lane was the stability of his young firm, and he lost no time in telling her so. They were already on intimate terms when they discussed ways of financing the business:

'When you spoke of needing money for your business [she wrote] I took accurate note of it . . . My instinctive desire would be to give you the $4000 dollars of which you spoke, but that is impossible . . .

cannot the money you require be borrowed by me and the interest paid by me?'

This in fact is what happens, though panic sets in while the transaction is going through because some telegraph clerk makes a mistake. Calm of a sort returns when this is rectified, and Annie reflects that:

'It would be nice if our income [from her money], which will be $7500 a year, would see us through, for then instead of taking money out of your business you could simply put it back in again . . . My dearest dear—I loved you last night more than ever.'

Just as well, since he 'frankly confessed need of capital . . . to turn the corner'. He did, later that year, with help, turn the corner. But meanwhile some ill-wisher in Britain had written to her man of affairs in Boston suggesting that on Mrs King's behalf Lane should be asked some pertinent questions: or, as Lane felt, impertinent questions. Needless to say, he refused to answer them, causing great anguish to poor Annie, who was reduced to tears on several occasions. Her faith in Lane seems not to have wavered, but the feasibility of standing by it seemed seriously threatened, especially since her mother's well-being was involved. Although the daughter was not always wholly candid with her mother, the old lady knew very well that something difficult was going on. She became ill, and when she picked up somewhat, Annie herself fell ill; as for John Lane, when the date of the wedding approached (the year was 1898), beset by a sea of troubles, he fell into a state of nervous prostration.

During the eighteen months of their engagement she wrote him scores of letters, larded with love; but also, when not disastrously concerned with his finances and his refusal to talk about them, larded with laughter, mockery and self-mockery, alarm at high-powered literary figures in London, gleeful accounts of enjoyable parties, delight in the New England scene, and speculation—'I do not know what kind of nature you have.' She well describes her own nature as part frivolous, part poetic and part severely practical. She plays down

Lane's expressed admiration of her business abilities, and in her constantly reaffirmed confidence in him attributes to him qualities which would have surprised most of his London associates:

'I am so glad *you* are not a poet, but you are a poet in your letters, very often, dear John, dear John Lane, do you know that you write the most charming letters?
You have the power to make my very soul vibrate by a word.
I love you so, my Beloved, you have mastered my heart, my soul, and my life!
You are a restless mortal . . . how often during these unhappy weeks I longed for you, longed to put my head on your shoulder and cry, cry as I did that night at the Bodley Head—you remember? There is something very comforting in you, dear. You have a fine and sensitive nature and your soul is upright.'

Having thus praised up the publisher, in her own mind, she made herself an assiduous promoter, in Boston bookshops, of his books, which were often available in two editions published in London and from his New York office, as like as not differently bound. She was not often grateful for the books Lane gave her to read, especially when he had a parcel sent off instead of writing her one of his charming letters, even if they were published by The Bodley Head. 'What a book! ! ! ! It has mildew on it and iron dust. And you leave me *that* as my entertainment over the Sabbath, and it's only 5.30 p.m. Saturday. Then you left, as a diversion, a gift book, and if there is anything I loathe it *is* a gift book.'

Both parties to this correspondence evidently thought it wise to arouse at least an occasional spark of jealousy in the other. There was, for instance, the matter of Lane's relationship with the wife of his versifying backer Francis Money-Coutts, by now Lord Latymer. 'Your affection and sympathy for her', writes Annie, 'are too strong to make you quite understand *my* position. *She* understands it, I am sure she does.' The lady clearly needed sympathy, since the poet seemed to think she had been a mistake, and—which outraged

Annie—was in the habit of giving dinner-parties which his wife was not encouraged to attend. Then again, in the line of shrug-it-off: 'You *dear* John—How you have made me laugh! *Is* it one of your duties to hold a girl's hand and pat her hair? O you naughty John—publishing must be a very pleasant occupation.' And then, of course, his mother has told her that there were plenty of girls he might have married.

But if it comes to that, she insists, she might have re-married many times. What is more, she admits, she is of a flirtatious disposition: there was the mysterious gentleman on board the S.S. *Pavonia*, for instance, not to mention the bicycling Colonel. Yet clearly this side of their relationship always dissolved in laughter—laughter on brisk orders from her to him. Orders which had to be repeated rather often. He must, for instance, book her a certain set of rooms for her summer visit to London. Has he done it? Hasn't he done it yet? Even more important, he must look about for a place for them to live after they are married. What about Whitehall Mansions? What about Queen Anne's Mansion? And why, when he is living alone in the Albany, does he want a woman housekeeper? Surely a manservant would be better? And as for his wife—like all men what he really wants his wife to be is a good comrade.

Once married, it is fair to say that, on all the evidence, the middle-aged lovers lived happily ever after, settling in no mansion flat but in what Frederick Rolfe unkindly referred to, after he had rashly been invited to visit them there, as 'Barbaric Bayswater', at 8 Lancaster Gate Terrace. Not for nothing had Wilde, in *The Importance of Being Earnest*, named *both* menservants, Lane and Mathews, after his old publishers. Lady Bracknell would have dismissed it as on the wrong side of the Park, never mind the square. Then a mere half-century old, its stucco canyons, crawling with housemaids, tweenies and other unfortunates, signalled from their painted, pillared porticos the aspirations of a newer middle class. Annie Lane compared it very unfavourably for comfort and convenience with American houses. There she was all the same able to hold her musical Sunday evenings; and as for John, much as those occasions distressed him, the house, not far from his old rooms in Southwick Street, was equally handy for Paddington Station and the railway to the West which he continued to take with unflagging delight, while the Vigo Street office continued its erratic course despite the dwindling role of long-haired poetasters in broad-brimmed hats.

12

Some Copious Authors

The year 1897 had been in every way more important to Lane than the old Queen's Diamond Jubilee. In March the ebullient publisher had gathered together a judicious selection from the innumerable squibs which had been, and still were, appearing about him. As *Accepted Addresses*, a handsomely produced little volume, it was dedicated to his future wife:

'To A.E.K.

the wonder of whose humour—and eyes—
proved such a revelation to him, the butt of
this collection of ribald rhymes humbly offers
them for her delectation.'

Thus neatly combining affection and advertisement, Lane enthusiastically set about widening the firm's range and changing its character—or at least changing the character of its books and book production, for its business methods remained as haphazard as ever.

It continued to publish verse, but by no means on the scale or in the style of its work in the recent heyday—which it had itself created —of the Decadents. Among what might be called the old regulars to be published in the first decade of the twentieth century, Lane's backer Francis Coutts, Lord Latymer, produced *The Heresy of Job*; it received a mixed reception, which in turn was itself peevishly received. Lord Alfred Douglas's *The City of the Soul* eventually involved Lane in a good deal of abusive and libellous correspondence, the latter mostly about Oscar Wilde's other friend, Robert Ross ('the biggest bugger in London', wrote Douglas with zestful venom).

Swinburne's friend Theodore Watts-Dunton ('a lively, confusing, muddled old bird', with failing sight and hearing, two secretaries and an enormous gramophone), who had appeared on the list with *The Coming of Love and Other Poems*, and a *Jubilee Greeting* for the Queen in 1897, sent in *Christmas at the Mermaid* for publication in 1902. That year Maurice Baring, who had met Lane through Edmund Gosse on one of the publisher's talent-spotting trips to Cambridge, produced *The Black Prince* (a verse play), and a mere eight years later remained confident enough to give Lane his *Collected Poems*. And, of course, the indefatigable William Watson, undeterred by his own earlier admission, 'I have published far too much' continued his erratic course; while poor, pallid, over-praised Stephen Phillips went fecklessly from triumph to destitution.

Lane's trips to America by no means diminished once his wife had settled in England; ever alert for sources of new talent or new sources of patronage he soon became friendly with the formidable Mrs Katrina Trask, of Yaddo, near Saratoga, and remained so for a decade or more, despite the usual ups and downs. In 1905 she was addressing him as 'Dear Friend and Publisher' and regaling him with lurid accounts of the difficulties she endured while preparing her book of poems, *Night and Morning*:

'Ah—against what odds I have worked! Blindness—faintness—and all kinds of physical complications, with which I will not bore you, but which would overtake me just as I was in full tide of enthusiasm.'

And having thus endured, alas she was 'terribly disappointed' in the book's 'mean appearance and tiny print, not at all what she had expected from him or from his other books. Her husband, indeed, had offered to pay for re-setting . . .' Somehow Lane scrambled out of this scrape—a familiar exercise for him, and was still on visiting terms five years later, in 1911. It was, though, foolish of him (perhaps Mrs Lane had a hand in it) to penny-pinch over the work of so promising, if unprofitable, a patron: a patron indeed of letters as a whole and American letters in particular, for she it was who established the Yaddo writers' retreat, which is still going strong.

One poet, the finest of them all, continued to elude Lane's English list, though he did manage to publish A. E. Housman in the United States. He even asked Housman's permission to do so, 'adding', wrote Housman to Grant Richards, 'that of course there was nothing to prevent him from reprinting the book there, but that he would not "commit this act of piracy".' To this, for the time, gentlemanly gesture Housman frigidly replied that it was all the same to him since in any case he refused royalties ('Vanity, not avarice, is my besetting sin'). In 1906 worse was to follow when Housman again wrote to Grant Richards to say that if *A Shropshire Lad* was to be republished either by McClure, Phillips and Company or by John Lane Company in New York he prefers McClure, adding that he particularly 'did not want to have anything to do with the other worthy.' Richards, pointed out that Lane, having bought in 162 copies, in sheets, as early as 1897, had the better claim; despite his long friendship with Housman, he does not know the reason for this animosity. Perhaps the prickly poet never got over the misplaced amiability of a lunch Lane pressed upon him in 1898.

Though the output of new poetry diminished to a trickle, the firm published a good deal of verse by classic or established poets, sometimes in quite resplendent editions and not always commercially aimed. In 1900 Lane put out a fine edition of the poems of Matthew Arnold, hoping to enhance its public appeal with an introduction by A. C. Benson, eldest and oddest of the four Benson brothers. Benson was also published by Lane and wrote (maybe after receiving a belated royalty cheque from his publisher?) the resounding lines:

> 'Land of Hope and Glory
> Mother of the Free.'

For the most part, though, The Bodley Head turned to assorted anthologies for its verse, and to cheap though attractive editions of selected works by established poets. These were issued in various series, with which The Bodley Head, like other publishers, sought to encourage a book-buying habit, and a taste for literature in an expanding, newly literate, public—an enterprise no less commendable than commercial. Having startled the book world with its then uncharacteristic gardening handbooks, the firm went on with its English Anthologies; those in verse included Epithalamies, Elegies, Satires and two volumes of Nineteenth-century Pastorals. There followed its pretty little Lovers' Library, one booklet to a poet—a long list including Shakespeare, Browning and even Alfred Austin (by now Poet Laureate); and Francis Coutts edited 'Flowers of Parnassus', a series of famous poems sold at 1s. 6d. in leather, 1s. in cloth.

Although these editions were acceptably or even agreeably produced, in terms of stylish production they were, by and large, not the sort of 'exquisite' objects for which The Bodley Head was famous. Still less so were its increasing excursions into new fiction. Early in the new century began the New Pocket Library, offering Borrow, Disraeli, George Eliot and others, clothbound at 1s., and Lane's Indian and Colonial Library in paperback—which apparently gave no thought to the European or worldwide (North America excepted) markets of English fiction soon to be tapped by the Tauchnitz and Albatross editions. The latter, thirty years later, was to provide the practical model for Penguin Books.

Henry Harland, fresh from editing the elegant *Yellow Book*, gave a yelp of anguish at the appearance of *The Cardinal's Snuff Box*. After all, the Keynotes novels and stories had preserved a very respectable standard of style and paper quality. But *The Cardinal's Snuff Box*! In the first place, even after the book, a runaway success, had sold 15,000 copies, he had still received no money for it. And then, he wrote to Chapman:

'I cannot tell you how disgusted, how dismayed I am at the appearance of The Cardinal's Snuff Box—an effect of something written by Jerome K. Jerome and published by Pearson. Only Pearson would never have published anything quite so hideous . . .'

Harland was, as far as books were concerned, living in another world, which had more in common with Wilde and gentlemanly pre-publication subscriptions than with bookstalls and circulating libraries. His remedy had much in common with Mrs Trask of Yaddo, though it was less financially confident:

'. . . the better, the more educated English public will not buy a cut book . . . I see nothing for it but to suppress the whole edition and bring out a new one, *uncut*.'

An optimistic proposal and an over-sensitive complaint. In fact Lane himself delighted in uncut books, and wrote a spirited letter to the *Morning Post* ('I love to cut my own pages') in reply to some disparaging remarks from his own author, A. C. Benson, who in return gave him an inscribed paper-knife; but Lane knew very well that even an educated public, when it came to new novels and whatever the practice in France, would be more likely to buy them in an ordinary commercial form.

In the late 1890s a novelist who less than ten years later was to turn out a living gold-mine had joined the firm's list: W. J. Locke. This remarkable man was born of British parents (his father is described as a banker) in Demerara, in what was then British Guiana, in 1863. Educated at the Queen's Royal College in Trinidad, he became an Exhibitioner of St John's College, Cambridge, gaining mathematical honours in 1884. There followed a period of school-mastering, a profession to which he occasionally refers with some bitterness in his novels, over which he seems to have drawn a veil, and during which he developed tuberculosis. Then, by one of those strange quirks commoner then, perhaps, than now, in 1897 he became Secretary of the Royal Institute of British Architects, and remained so for ten years. He had already begun writing novels, and joined The Bodley Head list with *The Derelicts* in 1897. He did well enough, but it was with his ninth novel, *The Morals of Marcus Ordeyne*, that he sprang to fame in 1905—fame enhanced a year later by *The Beloved Vagabond*, and further by, notably, *The Joyous Adventures of Aristide Pujol* in 1912.

He may be considered the quintessential Bodley Head novelist of the period. He was a first-class story-teller, and the tales he told in concise, selectively alert prose larded with occasional purple patches, were fairy-stories, easily achieving the suspension of disbelief. Reversals of fortune were a favourite theme, or uneasy central figures who already have access to wealth falling in with waifs, ultimately to the general benefit. If initially poverty-stricken, his disadvantaged boys and girls invariably display talent, spirit, and the capacity to take advantage of the luck that comes their way.

His more fortunately born characters, especially his women, are usually seen as enchanting creatures—but enchanting creatures trapped in the numbing complacent triviality of comfortable, indeed luxurious middle and upper class life, revivified by contact with the vitality and zest of the lowly born. His books are, or were when they were considered at all, usually and rightly praised for their charm; but where they touch squalor, they describe it clearly as such, though without wallowing in it. And in almost all his novels his characters develop notably, within the framework of the fairy-story; in his most famous book, *The Beloved Vagabond*, a bombastic, exhibitionist drunkard is gradually seen to be just that, but is portrayed as lovable all the same.

It is little wonder that his stories went straight to the heart of bourgeois readers. Here were all the pleasures of dropping out, without the discomfort. Here was generosity of spirit without need of patience in its exercise. Here were the picturesque joys of poverty without suffering, and the relaxation of riches without the task of earning it. Here was a proper scorn for provincial smugness in others, without the need to abandon its protective cushions oneself.

He, unlike Harland, was not to be treated off-handedly; an instruction sent to the office reveals an eager anxiety:

'Locke: For Heaven's sake pay him his £500 on Wednesday and tell him that it has just come in from the U.S. so that we may get the advantage in the risen £, it makes a great difference—nearly 2s. in the pound.'

This gratifying money-spinner in fact gave Lane a dreadful shock in 1908, when the complacent publisher heard that Locke had gone over to John Murray after eleven years with The Bodley Head. At first he had been published at a loss, 'and never for a moment has my confidence in his eventual success been shaken ... you may imagine my surprise on hearing that the moment of his achieving a great popular success, that moment was chosen by another publisher to lure him away.' Murray did in fact do Locke's next novel (the book of a previously published serial), but then Locke signed an agreement with John Lane to publish with him for the next five years. (Lane put forward a proposal that no publisher should ever write to another publisher's author—a Utopian notion, now as then.)

Indeed this passing infidelity seems uncharacteristic of Locke, even though his notions of honour and decency may not be reflected in the handsome, slightly ravaged face beneath neat, straw-coloured hair, whose portrait gazes out over the heads of the genial topers in the bar of the Garrick Club. Still, after returning to the fold, he re-mained there throughout the war and after; when his health de-manded a better climate, he removed to the South of France, where he lived *en seigneur*, writing relentlessly and entertaining lavishly until his death in 1930.

Whereas in Locke's characters the human was taken for granted, and therefore depicted, if at all, only in its early incendiary stages, a different manifestation of Europe's fascination with the contrast between the upper and the lower classes, but largely motivated by sex, came in the novels of Hermann Sudermann. This German novelist and playwright's methods were naturalistic but melodramatic, moralistic but titillating; they explored with zest the free-living, or even vicious, inter-action between members of the upper and the lower bourgeoisie. The Bodley Head, after publishing *Regina, or the Sins of the Fathers* in 1898, continued to publish his novels regularly until just before the First World War. With *The Song of Songs* in 1910 he set off, or was encouraged by Lane to set off, a hullaballoo of the kind he seemed to welcome.

It is a story of a girl whose good qualities are over-ridden by her muddled opportunism, who delivers herself into the protection of a series of lovers, and altogether goes to the bad in the demi-monde of Berlin, itself described with relish. Lane intended to publish it in an American translation of some vigour; it had sold well in the United States. Before it could appear in Britain, two plain-clothes policemen arrived in Vigo Street, demanding that the book should be handed over. Still anxious to put the firm's reputation for 'off-colour' books behind him (though ever ready to sail near the wind) he withdrew the book; but not to forget it. He commissioned a new translation, described by Lewis May as 'in no sense bowdlerized', but 'a model of good taste'. Which it was, though this was perhaps not quite what Sudermann had in mind. Meanwhile Lane wrote to a number of literary figures—Hardy, Wells and Bennett among them, most of whom declared the book to be a highly moral tale, though some had reservations: Conan Doyle, for instance, 'would not want any woman under 40 to read it.' But George Moore was passionately in the book's favour, and went so far as to offer to join the Society of Authors in order to protect the book's interests on the publisher's behalf. (Not that the Society would have then proved an obvious champion of publishers' rights, given the current antagonism over contracts which divided the two interests.)

The macabre and elegant fable (such as Kenneth Grahame's limpid but anti-feminist *The Headswoman*), the moralistic, or apparently moralistic tale wrapped in a rather titillating naturalism, and the stiff-upper-lip adventurous were increasingly joined in The Bodley Head list by the epigrammatic worldly-witty, which even achieved a Series of its own, the Mayfair Library, though by no means all the books which qualified actually appeared as part of the series.

The most durable of the worldlings appeared in 1904 with *Reginald*: its author, H. H. Munro, writing under the pen-name Saki (nobody quite knows why), had already in his own name produced a splendidly flamboyant *History of the Russian Empire*, but now joined The Bodley Head with a series of books making mock of the upper bourgeoisie, involving them with the supernatural, and, in *When William Came* (1913) pointing a sharp finger at those likely to be collaborators in the event of a German invasion. A saddened homosexual with a gift for a turn of phrase, he was killed while serving as corporal on the Western Front in 1916, though several volumes of short stories were published in his lifetime. By and large, although he too had difficulty in getting money out of the firm, relations remained friendly; only once did a real thundercloud loom, over the jacket for *When William Came*:

'Your letter of the 21st to hand, informing me that you can give no guarantee that the wrapper will not be used.

'It seems a monstrous thing to me that an author should be obliged to beg that his work should not be disfigured by a grotesquely inappropriate wrapper, and I shall make no further appeal on the subject.

'If the wrapper is used with any copies in this country I shall refuse to do anything to extend the sale of the book, and I shall not submit any other to the Bodley Head for publication.'

It all blew over; perhaps this is only the normal small change of relations between author and publisher.

The peripatetic G. K. Chesterton also arrived on The Bodley Head list in 1904, with his first novel, *The Napoleon of Notting Hill*, though he followed it up in Vigo Street with the large-minded but no less spirited consideration of *Heretics* and *Orthodoxy* and his stimulating squib on Shaw 'All windows and no houses'.

In 1907, the offices of The Bodley Head were burgled. Lane wrote a jolly account of the occasion, speculating on those books which were taken and those which were not. He also unearthed a cutting from the *Middlesex Chronicle* for April 6:

'A great disturbance was created on Saturday in Ealing, by a man with a parcel of books under his arm. He paraded the streets shouting at the top of his voice "I AM NAPOLEON".'

Arrested, he continued to answer only 'I AM NAPOLEON'—and the parcel of books was found to contain among, other things, a number of copies of *The Napoleon of Notting Hill.* And the paper sternly added:

'There is a strong and growing feeling that the issue of books of this heady and sensational character should be prohibited. The effect they have on weak intellects (as in this case) is a serious danger to the community.'

Still in his thirties, Chesterton was not widely held to be a menace to society; he was however a source of genial anecdote arising from his absence of mind over the practical details of everyday life, many of which were hardly less hazily managed for him by his brother Cecil. One day in November, 1909, a message arrived from the latter at Vigo Street:

'Mr Chesterton has received a cablegram from Mr. Clifford Smyth, asking if he will send his article by December 20. We are so sorry to trouble you, but we have somehow failed to make a note of what subject it was that Mr. Clifford Smyth wished Mr. Chesterton to write. I remember that you enclosed the letter with an introduction from yourself, and Mr. Smyth's letter was returned to you. I can find no trace of any reference to the matter anywhere.'

Chesterton's appearance one evening, after office hours, at Vigo Street with some corrected proofs rapidly became an office legend. Greeted at the door, after much unbolting, by the sole remaining member of the staff (an accountant, no doubt under stress) Chesterton, still on the steps, produced from his Gladstone bag not only his proofs but a bottle of port and a glass, only to be told that the accountant was a teetotaller. 'Good heavens,' Chesterton is reported to have said in a dismayed falsetto, 'give me back my proofs!'

Chesterton and his wife, too, provide a last and bizarre glimpse of the celebrated and still young Max Beerbohm in a Bodley Head context, when, as Mrs Chesterton reported:

'A delightful dinner party at the Lanes. The talk was mostly about Napoleon. Max took me into dinner and was really nice. He is a good fellow. His costume was extraordinary. Why should an evening waistcoat have four large white buttons and why should he look that peculiar shape? He seems only pleased at the way he has been identified with King Auberon. "All right, all right, my dear Fellow," he said to G., who was trying to apologise. "Mr. Lane and I settled it all at lunch." I think he was a little put out at finding no red carpet put down for his royal feet.'

However agreeable he was to Mrs Chesterton, his links with Lane were already weakening. After *Works* and *The Happy Hypocrite* and *More* parting is signalled in a letter to Reggie Turner: 'No, I don't think Lane for *Zuleika*;' and off he went, first to Chapman & Hall, then to Heinemann.

With Vernon Lee, John Lane's pride and joy, steadily producing, many other women writers made their mark: not least his wife, whose first publication in England was *Kitwyck*, a sequence of short stories set in a remote eighteenth-century Dutch village. They are neatly turned tales. She was liable to be complimented (by, for example, Owen Seaman) on their charm. Charming they are, but as in W. J. Locke, and a good deal of so-called 'light' fiction, the charm does not at all conceal the narrowness, bitterness, cruelty and dumb suffering prevalent in this, or any other, remote rural community.

Admitting that her money removed the spur to greater things, Annie set out to popularise the then almost unknown grapefruit in a pleasing booklet, *The Forbidden Fruit*; she turned to essays and sketches (previously published in a wide variety of magazines) lightly mocking the Bayswater world she lived in, the snobberies and social hazards of what might be called Forsyth country, in a number of books appearing up to the middle of the First World War. In *According to Maria*, *Maria Again* and *War Phases according to Maria* she invented a typically bright, silly, fashion-bound wife whose pretensions offer a crisp (by the standards of the day) analysis of the fads and fancies of the better-off bourgeoisie: among others 'Maria as

Trousered Feminist', insisting that women must stop making themselves attractive for the benefit of men, would be quite at home today.

Mrs Lane was much impressed by Edith Wharton, and on a visit to New York persuaded her husband to snap up that formidable lady's *The Greater Inclination*. But can it have been her appearance on the scene which caused the rapid worsening of relations between Lane and the queenly blonde East Coast widow, originally from San Francisco, Gertrude Atherton? She wrote some forty books, of which The Bodley Head published, *inter alia*, *The Doomswoman*, *The Californians* and *Senator North*, almost as sharp-tongued as the quickly deteriorating tone of her correspondence with Lane. By 1908 the end was near:

'Your ideas of generosity are as amusing as the rest of your performance . . . I more than ever regret that I ever gave you one book, much less half a dozen . . . I will not go to law over trifles. The small sums you deprive me of I can make in an afternoon . . . and if you need those small sums you are welcome to them . . . I have no "malice" toward you, but I have a very natural regret that I ever heard of you.'

Still, she did not share Henry Harland's dismay at declining standards of book production, and nerved herself to say so:

'I will say for you, however, that you get out the best-looking books in England and America, and that your proof-readers are less idiotic than most.'

No wonder that in *The Adventures of a Novelist*, she claimed that 'personally I never liked John Lane. He reminded me of a fat white slug.' This opinion, though later to be shared by a publisher's reader *par excellence*, David Garnett, was not universally held. Maybe Lane was not helped by a weakness of his eyes which often caused him to weep copiously in conversation.

Two Englishwomen luckily did not share this distaste, but provided him and his successors with a steady flow of novels for decades. M. P. Willcocks, a schoolteacher originally from Leamington, but settled in Devon and advertised as 'A Rabelais in Petticoats', offered quite local drama, obviously congenial to Lane.

Rather different was Muriel Hine. Married to a former younger-son knockabout, Sidney Coxon, living in Chelsea, she had already had some success with magazine short stories when Lane persuaded her to attempt a novel. This she did, and produced in *Half in Earnest* a story which failed to pass the propriety test of the [Circulating] Library Association's Committee of Experts, and enabled Lane to attack the would-be censors who proliferated. In most of her nearly thirty novels she ignored conventional proprieties in various walks of life (as indeed did Bodley Head novels of the time); she described with evident relish the onset of sexual desire and the half-eager, half-shocked satisfaction of surrender. She also became an alarming presence around The Bodley Head office, pouring out long and amusing letters in a florid hand, issuing instructions, demanding promotional material, telling Lane to get W. J. Locke to alter a passage, provoking him at one point to advertise her less—no doubt, he added, she had charmed the whole office—which she clearly had, and terrified it too.

One author who joined the Bodley Head list in the rather unlikely guise of a Nature writer was H. G. Wells. As well as being not a little proud to have had a story accepted for *The Yellow Book*, he had got Lane to accept for publication in 1895 a series of articles reprinted from the *Pall Mall Gazette* as *Select Conversations with an Uncle since Extinct*. Was it all Lane's fault if they quarrelled? As usual, Wells spelt trouble, not without reason:

'I hope you are not going to call my "Select Conversation with an Uncle since Defunct", as I see it advertised. My original title, "Select Conversations with an Uncle, now Extinct" refers to the Uncle's extinction by marriage, and *not* in the grave.'

And soon: 'What irresponsible men of genius you publishers are!

Thank Heaven your authors are men of business! . . . Here's your account giving me 10% royalty when I'm entitled to 15%.' In retrospect he might have considered himself lucky to get an account at all, for soon he was to send a lively drawing of a long-haired, furtive fellow sneaking into a shop showing the familiar sign of another kind of uncle, the pawnbroker, accompanied by the capitalised legend: 'Because John Lane NEVER sends accounts, NEVER!'

By that time Wells had already left for another publisher, but in 1911 he returned, temporarily, to The Bodley Head in rather humiliating circumstances, with *The New Machiavelli*. Macmillan had shied away from this work in terror at its probable libels and certain charges of immorality, not to say indecency by the standards of the day; but Frederic Macmillan did not wish to lose Wells, and undertook to find him a surrogate publisher. This proved a problem. Several, including Heinemann and Chapman & Hall, nervously declined, after embarrassed exchanges, much to Wells's mortified dismay—which was compounded when he finished up with John Lane, who had retained from *The Yellow Book* and increased by his consistently anti-Grundy stance, a reputation for outfacing prudishness (or a fondness for publishing 'risqué' books). *The New Machiavelli* was a great and rapid success, despite what Lane called 'rebuffs': a leading Edinburgh bookseller wrote to ask if they could return the work, 'as it is not a book we care to stock or sell;' the Chairman of Birmingham's City Council spoke harshly of both book and author; the *Spectator* refused any advertising from The Bodley Head with Wells's name in it.

This came as no surprise to Wells, who had already written to Lane about the launching campaign:

'One thing I must say at once—that is that I object very strongly to your sending any copy for review to the Spectator, as I am convinced that there is no prospect of a fair or reasonable review in that quarter.'

Otherwise they collaborated well enough. But when Lane wished to charge the editor of a small local paper for a short extract from the

(152)

IX. This Robert Gibbings engraved device was used on title-pages
and letter-paper until 1957.

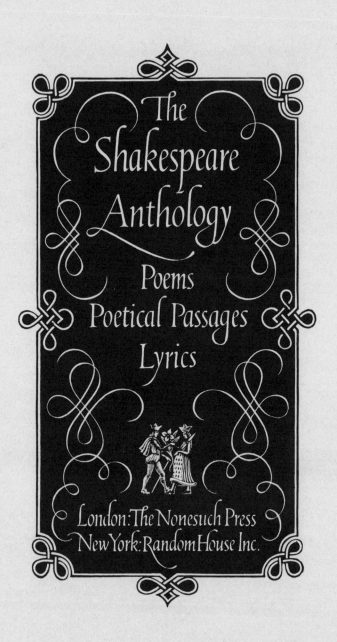

The Shakespeare
Anthology

Poems
Poetical Passages
Lyrics

London: The Nonesuch Press
New York: Random House Inc.

x. Reynolds Stone engraved many pages for The Nonesuch Press
and also Max Reinhardt's publishing device. Meynell and Reinhardt
were together involved in major publications such as the Coronation
Shakespeare (1953) and the Authorised Version of the Bible (1963).
These ventures were co-published in New York by Random House,
as was *The Shakespeare Anthology* (title-page by R. S., *above*).

book, he received a brisk dressing-down from the author—the book's sales having already attained 15,000 copies:

'Dear Lane: Please refrain from that demand of one guinea.

A)   It's mean. You get an admirable advertisement for the New M. for nothing and you want the generous advertiser to pay for it.

B)   He won't pay for it, so that you will only lose your advertisement by being greedy.

C)   It isn't done.

D)   I've written to Mr. W. to give my permission *gratis.*'

And that was that. When, during the war, Lane wrote undaunted to Wells about the rumour of a new book in the writing, he received short shrift, with a side-swipe at Macmillan thrown in:

'Dear Lane: Rumour is a fancy Jade. There is no book available. Macmillan do not advertise well enough for me and they think that authors should suffer for their publishers in wartime. That's the whole story—Yours ever H.G.W.'

An altogether more genial, or tolerant, relationship was built up after Chapman, in 1908, happened to read in that same accursed *Spectator* a humorous article entitled *My Financial Career*. Its author, Stephen Leacock, turned out to be the English-born but Canadian-bred Professor of Political Economy at McGill University, and Lane at once cabled an offer to publish the article, and any others like them, in book form. Thus began an association which lasted long after Lane's death—Leacock lived until 1944. On his visits to London he was a frequent visitor to Vigo Street, tall, tweed-clad and tousled, friendly to all, trenchant, indeed mischievously perverse in his opinions, but demure or pawky in his ever-present humour, though quite often sharply satirical, as in *Sunshine Sketches of a Little Town* and *Arcadian Adventures with the Idle Rich*, in which emerged a comical mockery of plutocrats which must have upset the

(153)

equilibrium of his work as a teacher of Economics. His books were justly summed up by J. B. Priestley in his introduction to *The Bodley Head Leacock* (1957), as, at its best, 'balanced between cutting satire and sheer absurdity'.

The Bodley Head's crowning achievement in fiction, however, was and for some twenty years remained the ambitious and in the end wholly successful translation of the complete works of Anatole France. One of his stories had appeared in *The Yellow Book*, with an appreciative article by Maurice Baring. Ten years later Frederic Chapman persuaded Lane to embark on the edition—under Chapman's general supervision until his long and total decline into illness overtook him. Both Lane and Mrs Lane, the latter herself translating two of the books, threw themselves wholeheartedly into the project. It was to be carried out on a handsome scale, maintaining to the full The Bodley Head's celebrated standards of book production, which Henry Harland had so sorely missed. Great pains were taken over the prospectus, celebrating this 'pagan, haunted by the preoccupation of Christ'; at once 'saintly and Rabelaisian', the pre-emptive (and stimulating) announcement went on: 'His writings are not for babes —but for men and the mothers of men.' As for the Library Edition, it had Beardsley endpapers. Printed in Caslon Old-Face, bound in red cloth with gilt lettering with gilt tops to its uncut edges in demy octavo, it was offered for six shillings—the ordinary price for a new novel. It was reasonably successful, and a luxury edition, lavishly illustrated, bound in a somewhat brooding black and gold, went particularly well in the United States.

It was with the production of a 2s. 6d. cheap edition, using the original plates in a more modestly margined crown octavo size, that France's popularity spread over the land and indeed over the whole English-speaking world and sold well for decades. Its eye-catching binding was said by one observer to have 'turned London orange'. The Lanes went across the Channel to meet the Master. Annie Lane, shaking with apprehension, acted as interpreter. All too eager, she seems to have bewildered the lavishly dressing-gowned author by asking him questions about English writers of whom he had never heard. Meanwhile Lane, monoglot like his host, exercised his delight in works of art and antiques with what one unkind French observer described as 'the air of an auctioneer's valuer'. Annie Lane, though suitably awed by the occasion, recovered enough to write an amusing account of the visit, revealing the fact that she had piously kept the glove which the Master's hand had shaken—but inadvertently sent it to the cleaners.

In return, France visited London in 1913. The occasion had been in the air for months; it assumed almost the character of a state visit, complete with an organising committee. It fell a little short of its aims. A grand reception at 10 Downing Street dwindled into a tea-party presided over by the Prime Minister's wife, at which Mr Asquith was unable to be present. Another reception, at Dorchester House, the American ambassador's residence, fell through because Mr Whitelaw Reid was out of England. But extra rooms at the National Gallery, closed because of fears of suffragette violence, were ceremoniously opened for the magisterial Frenchman, in which he especially admired Goya's 'Dona Isabel Cobos de Porcel'.

In his eagerness to do his best for France, Lane had conceived the idea of having a distinguished British writer contribute an Intro-duction to each book. The scheme produced a characteristic reply from Shaw:

'Dear John Lane: This notion of yours about a preface by me or Walkley or Gosse or by any other Englishman is a mistake. Such a practice can be nothing but an impertinence. A solemn impertinence would be insufferable, and a vivacious impertinence would be like flat ginger ale compared to Anatole's champagne.'

An odd simile, coming from a teetotaller; but France was able to signal his gratitude, or get his revenge, at a reception given for him by the Fabian Society during the visit. Amiably hailing Shaw as 'the Molière of England' he kissed him: and Shaw, we are told, 'wavered for a moment, and returned the compliment'.

While all this was going on Lane was in a transport of delight. The offices of The Bodley Head were thrown into turmoil by the Master's visit, a path cleared through the cluttered outer office, the staff lined up like a guard of honour. If France expressed dismay at his own portrait (by Guth) claiming that it made him look like a ripe camembert, that was only modesty. When shown a charming and enigmatic picture by Gertrude Hammond, entitled 'The Yellow Book', showing a moustachio'd man pointing out a page to a blushing girl, he enquired, as if on cue, 'Why is she blushing?; which enabled Lane to reply coyly, 'He is evidently reading your story to her.' And when France visited the Lanes at 8 Lancaster Gate Terrace, the publisher's cup was full to overflowing, and he recorded 'the *joy* of offering him some hospitality in my own home, where his manifest interest in some of my pictures and *objets d'art* enhanced their value even for me.'

The public climax of the visit came with a banquet at the Savoy, for which admirers were invited to purchase tickets—which they hastened to do, in great numbers. It was presided over by Lord Redesdale, orientalist, sponsor of Houston Stewart Chamberlain's Teutonic fantasies, and grandfather of the Mitford ladies. France made a very long speech, in French, reiterating 'travaillons de concert à la paix du monde,' to an audience which, even if it understood the words, hardly knew what he meant. Eight months later the 1914 war burst upon them.

It is strange that France's real success in English began during that appalling conflict, continued for another twenty years, and died as the next catastrophe advanced inexorably towards us throughout the 1930s. It is hard to see why these tales—ironical, satirical, sceptical and lucid—should in such times have communicated so much to so many, regardless of intellectual fashions. Perhaps, though no man is on oath when writing an 'apology for absence' from the banquet, Thomas Hardy diagnosed at least part of the reason:

'In these days, when the literature of narrative and verse seems to be losing its qualities as art, and to be assuming a structureless, conglomerate character, it is a privilege that we should have, come into our midst, a writer who is faithful to the principles that make for permanence, who never forgets the value of organic form and symmetry, and the emphasis of under-statement, even in his lighter works.'

13

New Recruits

'Take care what you eat and drink. You are not a god and you cannot do things with impunity.' Thus Annie Lane wrote to her gadabout husband from Torquay, where she was prospecting for a comfortable boarding house for yet another recuperative holiday. As he advanced into his sixties John Lane continued to fill his exuberant and neurasthenic life. With bronchitis a regular attendant, arthritis in his hands, his eyes weeping ever more copiously and growing ever weaker, he bustled in and out of the office in Vigo Street, continued avid collecting in many spheres, ate and drank at lunches and dinners without number. Quite early on he received a storm warning—needless to say unheeded—from Frederick Rolfe:

'What your body needs is sun, strenuous physical exercise, and salt water, with a diet of oatmeal and oranges exclusively for three months. You yourself alone can know what will heal your mind.'

Physician, heal thyself, Lane may well have murmured, as he filled his busy days with publishing, travelling (never without visits to bookshops), and endless correspondence on any topic from armorial bearings on bookplates, to post-Impressionist seascapes—a question discussed in the letter columns of *The Times*. (On this he finally observed: 'But for myself, I must confess that I love the sea only in painting and poetry.')

Forever in a welter of controversy, Lane chose to cross swords with that relatively new breed, the literary agent. A charitable explanation, offered by Lewis May, is that he felt that the agent weakened the publisher's personal relationship with the author. He was pained when the very success of M. P. Willcocks's *The Wingless Victory* caused her to put her affairs into the hands of Curtis Brown, and was perhaps at a loss to counter the agent's lofty and rational letter:

'I leave my office very rarely but will be glad to call upon you on your return from Scotland . . . If my appearance in the matter caused her to ask, and get, for herself better terms than she otherwise would have obtained, I am glad to have been of service to her. If, as I understand from you, your arrangements with her are exactly what they would have been anyway, then the fact that a friend of hers advised her to come to me . . . did you no harm. My experience has been that the author who has just made his ~~first~~ [sic] success is rather more likely to ascribe that success entirely to his own merits than is the agent, who realises how large a part the publisher often has in such successes.'

'Say a word for The Bodley Head,' Lane wrote to Willett, 'and d—n literary agents, especially Curtis Brown.'

If nothing else, as the correspondence with the firm shows, agents could, and did, take over the task of getting money due from the firm rather more quickly than was customary. Once at least Lane or his cashiers lapsed in the opposite direction. One author wrote: 'Many thanks for the cheque, which I am returning, as I have already received one.'

Plainly, for all his hyperactivity, Lane—or even Lane and Chapman—could not possibly have handled the necessary business of the firm on their own, especially since in 1900 Le Gallienne went off once again to the United States, and this time never returned except as a visitor. For some years he lived in penury in New York, though continuing to send back both verse and prose. He left his second, Danish, wife in England along with her step-daughter, who became Eva Le Gallienne, a justly successful actress.

Just before, perhaps foreseeing Le Gallienne's departure, the firm was joined by the first of two professionals, Herbert Jenkins. He was a Londoner, though his father had come from Norwich, and learnt his trade as a publisher with Kegan Paul before joining The Bodley

Head. He brought with him an air of masterful professionalism which proved not really congenial to the place. He soon displaced Chapman as manager, though it may well be that the latter was not unwilling to let this happen. Chapman's real preoccupations were all literary, and he was already preparing to oversee his own idea of publishing all Anatole France in English. This immensely successful project virtually killed him or much accelerated his death, through the appalling labour of editing, in some cases practically rewriting, those translators foisted on him too often, according to Lewis May, by his employer's wife. May was a spiteful witness where Mrs Lane was concerned, and where Jenkins was concerned, too, though granting that, even if he did strike an uncongenial note, the firm did well during his time as manager:

'He was extremely able [wrote May] and as energetic as Lane himself. But, with Jenkins, work was very decidedly work, and play, play . . . He had a strong will of his own, and a marked dislike to being treated as a mere employee . . . the atmosphere soon began to grow strained.'

Jenkins also wrote a good deal, in two markedly different styles. On the one hand was a good deal of 'light' fiction, including the Bindle books, concerning the misadventures of a cockney furniture remover and broker's man, as well as detective stories and romances; earlier on the other hand, were a Life of George Borrow published by Murray, and, appearing posthumously, in 1925, though written much earlier in his career, *William Blake: Studies of His Life and Personality*. This seems to have contained the first mention of Blake's trial for high treason after an altercation with a soldier. At least one aspect of Jenkins's own personality may be glimpsed from a passage in an address he gave to the Blake Society in August, 1912:

'It was with a feeling of positive joy that I read in the newspaper a few days back that one man had thrown a knife and another a brick at a parliamentary candidate whose views were anathema to him. *He* had not lost the power of moral indignation.'

Not until 1911 did the next publishing professional join the firm. Basil Willett came down from Wadham College, Oxford and was briefly a printer's pupil before joining Kegan Paul, Trench, and Trubner, of which he quite rapidly rose to be managing director. There being no direction, he came to The Bodley Head as Manager, becoming Vice-Chairman to John Lane in 1921, and—as things turned out much to his regret, no doubt—Chairman on the latter's death in 1925. He knew more about the technicalities of book production than anyone else. Only half facetiously, Lane suggested that he and the rest of them should sit at his feet while he lectured them on the subject. His responsibilities, however, extended far beyond the certainties of technique; they included getting his employer out of trouble when affability had triumphed over sense—as when a W. H. Chesson sent, clearly by request, some less than promising verses:

'Dear Mr. Lane: I enclose the collection entitled "Bogland Blooms and Birds" by the late Moses Taggart . . . a vividness unsurpassed by Wordsworth and Tennyson . . . I would supply a glossary of unfamiliar words.'

In John Lane's time Willett became, perhaps not without satisfaction, the very image of the White Rabbit, a small man bustling about in glasses, gratifyingly overworked. Since Lane spent more and more time away from Vigo Street, roaming the country, or at any rate the South, or recuperating in the house the Lanes had bought at the Kemp Town end of Brighton, Chairman and Vice-Chairman communicated in a series of literally thousands of notes, sometimes several a day, and mostly containing many numbered points. The tone, on Lane's side, is one of great amiability tinged with testiness, and indicates the hard-headed farmer's son leaping on to points of detail, while indicating much relaxed pleasure, with occasional interjections bearing on his health:

I am feeling better today but I shall not hurry back.

Mrs Lane's birthday. This is being celebrated today, and of course the B.H. has to give her something.

The Bodleian. Mrs. Lane feels she wants some more War Work. So she proposes to relieve you of editorship of the *Bodleian*!!

Will you procure me a box of cigars at about 8d. or 9d. each . . . as Mrs. Lane wants them for Captain Norton-Taylor. Charge it to Mrs Lane, please.

I am not keen on theatrical books. There is no money in them, to start with.

Lady Glenconnor: what a nuisance she is. You must be firm with her.

On and on the notes flow. From Weston-Super-Mare he instructs Willett to buy 50 Channel Tunnel shares ('It is so quiet here . . . I want a bit of fun'), to enquire into copper tea urns, wine-coolers, glass goblets, tobacco jars, prints: tells him to look in Groves dictionary of artists (?) and see whether it lists a portrait painter called Mrs Muck. He fears that they are over-advertising Muriel Hine: 'I suppose this is largely due to her charming influence on the whole office, which now seems to me demoralising. But it makes me shiver when you tell me of the 5 tons you have pulped.'

Already there was the first of two notable amateur apprentices on the publishing side. After all, in its expansion, The Bodley Head not only needed more people, it needed more capital. When possible, it seemed best to combine the two, and seek for young men with families willing to sink a few thousand pounds in the boys' futures. Where better to explore the possibilities than in the Devonshire connection? And sure enough, the trail led straight to Arundel Dene, the surgeon who had joined Lewis Lane on a celebrated deer-hunt, witnessed by the little John Lane, when one of the local landowner's deer was shot. The surgeon's son had moved to Beckenham, a southern suburb of outer London, and seems to have brought up his own son, also called Arundel, with grandiose expectations. In

1904 Lane met the father 'to talk about Devon'—and before long was talking about articling the boy to The Bodley Head in return for five per cent of what was foreseen as rising to £3,000, the boy's salary to rise by each £1000 step of the investment from £3.10s. a week to £5.10s. a week.

The young Arundel Dene early displayed signs of juvenile arrogance. Before joining the firm he wrote apologising for not having been in touch on account of 'a bad bout of shingles'. In any case, the letter goes on 'I should like further information on one or two points.' He offers to take six months to learn German, shorthand and typewriting, although 'personally, I had thought that a thorough appreciation of the literary and artistic side of publishing hardly compatible with efficiency in those branches of education designated as commercial'—a common error, now as then.

When he did join the firm in 1904 he was rapidly if not enthusiastically recognised as charming and intelligent. He rose to become under-manager to Chapman and then to Jenkins. He also set up and for some years edited *The Bodleian*, in its earlier years at least a lively, friendly journal, carrying of course extracts from Bodley Head books, but not at all shy of mentioning and even praising books by writers from other publishing houses; there were, of course, many interviews with Bodley Head authors, often in a tone of light mockery. Although the pseudonym was not used until the mid-1920s, 'Mortimer Middlebrow' might well have signed almost every article in *The Bodleian*, and indeed his name adumbrated the firm's policy, boldly affirming its determination not to be bullied by academic puritanism or by threats of censorship, repeatedly affirming its preference, especially in fiction, for the positive. 'People are a little self-consciously ashamed at their predilection for laughter . . . great comedy is rarer than great tragedy and more artistic.'

The Bodleian liked to mock. Its proprietor was twitted on his Devonshire accent. Valuable writers, too, came in for raised eyebrows. What, enquired one of the firm's readers, did W. J. Locke mean when, rather like Homer, he spoke of the wine-coloured sea— 'There is champagne and hock, burgundy and (alas!) claret.' Setting the record straight, Locke briskly replied without equivocation: 'Chateau Lafite 1876'.

Arundel Dene's generally witty editorship began rather uncharacteristically. Some other hand, surely, determined to keep the spirit of the Nineties alive, must have guided the choice of the poems which led off the first few numbers. In March 1909, Volume I, No. 1 announced the new magazine with a 'Nocturne' by Esmé Wingfield-Stratford.

> 'Here in the bower of Night
>   Oh, let me rest!
> Steeped in the balm and nectar of delight
> Spirit to spirit, body to body white
>   Together pressed.'

Strange that poems like this seemed to have aroused, so to speak, no outcry. Surely not merely because it led to a suitably sombre conclusion:

> 'Dream, love! thou shalt awake from Paradise
>   In Hell tomorrow.'

A. C. Benson, in the next issue, offered a suitably moral reluctance:

> 'I would not dwell with Passion:
> When passion throbs and quivers, Love is still.'

And in the third issue Le Gallienne, by no means abandoning his particular imagery, wrote regretfully about 'a bruised daffodil of last night's sin.'

After that, 'Somebody must have said something,' for such sensual images more or less disappeared.

Arundel Dene's initial editorship ended when in 1911 he went with Lane to look into the affairs of the New York office. Since its establishment sixteen years before, the John Lane Company of New

York had certainly provided Lane with an excellent excuse for trans-Atlantic trips, but at considerable cost in trouble and, ultimately, in money. When Lane set it up in 1896 he was ready as always to entrust affairs to a bright young man: in this case a Staffordshire boy, Mitchell Kennerley, born in 1878, at school with Arnold Bennett's brothers—Bennett in fact becoming his brother-in-law—and brought to London when eleven. A self-assured youth, he impressed a bookseller and talked himself into a job. There he met Chapman, and through him Lane; he soon became an 'office assistant' in Vigo Street. Here, 'rather thin and pale and willowy,' as Edward Hutton described him, and 'perhaps rather more interesting than distinguished', what with his long, dark hair, or his Liberty silk tie in green or terracotta. He collected—he was in a good position to do so—modern first editions. He was intelligent and friendly—just the man, said Hutton, for Lane's office.

Even so, it was a bold stroke of Lane's to open his New York office at 140 Fifth Avenue, with an eighteen-year-old in charge. True, the boy picked up a bit of paper on his way through the docks, and was about to throw it away when Lane pointed out that it was a $10 bill. A good omen? Not really, for Lane. Kennerley, left in charge, caused a sensation in book-trading circles by paying Stone & Kimball $1000—an unheard of price—for the plates and publishing rights of Kenneth Grahame's *The Golden Age*, which was and continued to be a spanking seller. He also arranged to have *The Studio* not merely distributed by The Bodley Head but published in America, edited and printed by Americans. This was a disastrous mistake, as it turned out, and was one factor in a fairly rapid rift between him and Lane. This came to a head in 1900, when Lane learnt that apart from everything else, Kennerley was very seldom in the office and gave little of his time to the business but quite a lot to the middle-aged novelist Gertrude Atherton, with whom Lane himself was on increasingly bad terms. So Kennerley went.

He was succeeded by Temple Scott (b. Israel Isaacs) who after various book trade jobs joined Grant Richards's publishing venture (and as a result figured as a viciously anti-semitic caricature in

Frederick Rolfe's *Nicholas Crabbe*). He lasted an even shorter time than Kennerley. Taking over in 1900, he was dismissed in September, 1901, and brought a lawsuit against Lane for breach of contract and slander. He started a publishing house of his own, but was soon arrested on a complaint of Lane's on charges of grand larceny and forgery. Nothing much came of all this, and in turn he went off to a varied book-world career in Boston, in the course of which he was a literary agent, a book-dealer and adviser (forming, *inter alia*, a library for Jerome Kern). He also wrote and edited bibliographies of Swift, the Brontës and St Augustine.

There followed a series of American directors and managers, and a disastrous episode in which a wretched woman cashier was sent to prison at Auburn. There Lane and Arundel Dene visited her, after talking with American members of the firm, as Dene recounts in a brilliant letter from the Murray Hill Hotel in New York. After a dismal train journey they were helpfully received by the prison governor:

'Then we walked along outside the long wall to the women's quarters. Mr. Lane, who was feeling a sort of seasickness at what he considered a nauseous business, managed to blend an intense sympathy for the unfortunate woman with an envy for her enjoyment of the beautiful soft air.

'The Matron received us politely, if without enthusiasm, and after a few minutes that seemed like as many hours, Susan Macomber was transferred to a sort of *Foyer*, where the matron soon introduced us ... She impressed me as a woman of about thirty-nine, with the typically honest face of a dishonest woman. Her eyes were straight and piercing, her features regular and her hands strong and capable, but white and very well shaped. She spoke for about two hours and a half, and in spite of our constant interruptions it seemed like a running narrative ... Though no doubt her womanly malice heightened some of her accusations unduly, yet she gave us much information that we have been able to use since.

'We were particularly anxious to obtain an account of the various facilities enjoyed by Mr. Jewett and Mr. Maupin through what is facetiously termed "exchange advertising". From pianos to lunches there seems to have been a perfect merry-go-round of delight. Even the portraits of Mrs. Maupin and Mr. Maupin's mother-in-law were obtained through "exchange". We came away with the impression that she was greatly to be sympathised with; her salary was undoubtedly very small for the vast volume of work which earned it. And though this does not excuse her dishonesty, it fills one with an uneasy sense, difficult to analyse, of poetic injustice . . .

'Susan Macomber actually confessed to the frauds, which were not detected at all. She wrote a letter, on Lincoln's Birthday, stating what she had done. Maupin laughed, and said "Why didn't you skip?" . . . She considered Mr. Jewett and Mr. Maupin held positions more ornamental than useful. Mr. Jewett's interest in society and Mr. Maupin's in Socialism had so largely increased that a combination of the two conspired nearly to wreck the business.'

Dene goes on to justify this charge with fluent lucidity, before moving on to an account of their social relaxation in New York and Boston. He met and was charmed by Richard Le Gallienne: 'His hair has turned grey but his personality is very youthful and very charming. Women would probably call him, not unjustifiably, "a dear".' He reported a graphic (and of course favourable) account of Eichberg *père*; and having praised a piece by Annie in *The Bodleian*, gently twits her apparent acceptance of the standards of Bayswater:

'. . . does the average author really desire a frock coat: that last stigma of the stockbroker? Now, a morning coat of graceful curves and lines is surely a very different matter. However, I don't suppose the editor of the *Tailor and Cutter* reads *The Bodleian* every month.'

This clear-headed, elegant and lucid letter, slightly tinged, towards both Lane and Mrs Lane, with affectionate impertinence, shows an apparently much-matured version of the Beckenham schoolboy. It comes as a shock to find from future correspondence that the whole time saw Dene under considerable stress—stress which however in no way impairs his wit and much enhances his effrontery.

A letter from Dene, in reply to one from his employer, still in New York, written in June, 1911, soon after their return from the United States, runs as follows:

'You asked me to read your letter with great care. I have certainly done so. I do not think you can have realised the precise purport of its contents, and the fact that you have sent it to me unrevised seems to emphasise my point of view. You ask me, too, to take it that this "plain-spoken" epistle of yours is "kindly meant". And evidently you expect me to take everything you have said in a friendly spirit: to overcome any feeling of annoyance that might possibly seize me at a letter so uncompromising in tone. Accordingly, that is the light in which I regard your attitude; not unnaturally I ask you to extend me a similar courtesy.

'I take your points one by one, so to avoid a long and tedious series of letters concerning unprofitable affairs:

'(1) "The services you rendered me during the three weeks we were together here I was not slow to recognise."

'I have yet to learn that you recognised my services at all, and the rest of the letter is an absolute contradiction to the opening sentence. What were my services? Apart from the general routine of things two facts stand out pre-eminently.

'(a) That through our financial arrangements you were able to set out and fight Jewett with a feeling of independence in your soul, and a sense of victory in your hand.

'(b) Johnson and Canner, in the absence of Jewett, Maupin and Lloyd, were temporarily at least indispensable to the firm. Now both these gentlemen informed me that, had I not been in America to smooth things down, they would not have stayed on. The consequences of such a circumstance you can imagine. It is not in accordance with my custom or inclination to brag about my achievements but, deliberately accused, I have no alternative but to throw them into bold relief.

'(2) "Perhaps you hardly realise that you spent two nights away from the hotel, including your last night (Friday)."

'I do realise it. But the first of these two nights I spent at a Turkish Bath, so as not to encroach on the daytime. I think I told you this the following morning. Now either you have forgotten this, or you do not accept my word. I shall be glad to know what is in your mind respecting this episode. I presume that the spending of a night at a Turkish Bath (an English habit of men beyond reproach) is not in itself a grievous sin, or the mark of a dissolute man.

'(3) "I had to send you $15 so that you might be liberated from a brothel."

'This is absolutely and entirely untrue. I am indignant that this statement should have been made, justifiably indignant, for this is not in accordance with the true facts of the case. Canner returned with me to the Murray Hill Hotel and had no money to go home with. So in spite of my earnest protestations (I advised him to take a room in the hotel and go quietly to bed) he ran upstairs to you while I was still in the hall—a circumstance I greatly regretted then and now. You must be under a grave misapprehension.

'(4) "When I left you at 8.30 that morning on my way to Yaddo you were in a dead drunk condition."

'Very weary and headachy certainly. "Dead drunk", no. Dead drunk, as I understand the phrase, means a person in a state of alcoholic stupor rendering him immobile; a state from which, for the time being, he cannot be translated.

'(5) "The state of your health, as well as your inability to get up in the morning . . ."

'The state of my health, generally speaking, has improved during the last two or three years. So your inference is wrong in this case. And my inability to get up in the morning has dated from the time when I was six years old.

'(6) "You never seem to have a pencil, a fountain pen, or a watch available."

'True, but brains are more than pencils, and watches, and more to be considered even from a secretary.

'(7) "Your bedroom was like a pig-stye".

This must be a humorous remark. I am unable to see any logical connection between my bedroom and a pig-stye.

'(8) "When I gently reproved you for leaving your dressing gown in the bathroom to be trodden on, whilst your linen and clothes were carpeting the room you replied by saying 'That you never did anything which you could get someone else to do for you', which would seem to imply that you were accustomed to a valet, or a millionaire; but all this in its working out meant that you did not pack your trunk, nor did you tip the 'daily' for doing it. No, that was left for me to do on my return from Saratoga."

'I think I will regard this paragraph (less important as it is than some of the others) from "all this working out meant . . ." which summarises it. Well, I have not been brought up to pack bags or trunks and my efforts in that direction would be disastrous to my belongings. The tip, which seems to rankle, since you emphasise it so strongly, might be settled without much difficulty. I think you must realise this sin of omission was purely inadvertent, and the result of hurrying off consequent upon a late night. No-one ever accused me of a meanness. Of course, I might, if I chose to do so, [hide] behind your undertaking to pay "my steamship and hotel expense"—your precise words.

'(9) "You know that I am not a prude or a stern moralist, but your conduct during most of the three weeks disgusted me unspeakably."

'(a) The fact that one person is disgusted with another's conduct does not prove that the feeling of disgust is justifiable.

'(b) "Unspeakably", considering the torrent of words which confront me, is hardly the *mot juste*.

'(c) And how can I regard this sentence in conjunction with your opening remarks concerning the services I rendered you which you "were not slow to recognise".

'(10) ". . . confronted with the question as to whether you were sober on that occasion" (the occasion of the great meeting).

'Witnesses Johnson, Kirby, Jewett, Nichols and yourself can prove the absurdity of this charge. Indeed you, yourself, wrote to

(170)

Mrs. Lane and the office saying that I behaved splendidly.

'(11) ". . . as Mrs. Trask [of Yaddo] assumed you were the dissipated young Englishman I brought over and made a director."

'Why "dissipated"? On what ground? Whence this rumour?

'(12) "You took too much to drink all the time, hence the more or less confused state of your papers."

'I can hardly have taken "too much drink all the time", for my brain has seldom worked as well for your advantage, Johnson particularly complimented me, not in the way of flattery, but in sheer sudden surprise, on my quickness, my grasp of things, and my clearness of expression. As for the state of my papers—my letters and documents are always multitudinous, and being multitudinous, do not suggest order.

'(13) "You possess captivating manners, with what is a rare gift, shrewdness, in connection with your other characteristics."

'Surely it is only a genius who can combine excessive quantities of alcohol with captivating manners and the gift of shrewdness. It was not—correct me if I am wrong—the "captivating manners" and the "shrewdness" that "disgusted you unspeakably during most of the time!"

'(14) "You also have the greatest of possessions—youth."

'Surely youth is a suitable excuse for occasionally indiscreet conduct, where such conduct is noticeable.

'I do not think you will take anything I have said amiss. I have endeavoured to give a plain unvarnished reply to some plain unvarnished accusations. You need no reassurance of my loyalty to you; and you can well imagine the bitter regret that I feel at having behaved more than injudicially on occasions. But, as in the matter of that Friday evening, you will perceive you have overstated the case. Certainly, I did not at all times oppose with sufficient stoutness the dangers that lie in wait for an English constitution under American conditions. But you remember Shakespeare's remark that "Men are merriest when they are from home", and "It is not meet that every nice offence should bear its comment". Again, you must admit that I chose my companions for frivolity with considerable care. For

(171)

instance, Mr. Shuman, Mr. & Mrs. Dreyfus, the Osgoods, Mr. Philip Hale, etc., would hardly think me the dissolute ruffian whom you now stigmatise. The warmly personal note I managed to infuse into my relations with Johnson and Canner was of the utmost service to you. I do not see what material advantage is to result to me from it, although I like them immensely.

'It does not seem to me likely that I should behave injudiciously again. I am sincerely sorry for the annoyance of last Friday, but apart from my (vicious?) enjoyment of a Turkish Bath I had not the opportunity for a single night out in New York, and like a tightly stretched piece of elastic I relaxed when released.

Yours sincerely,

Arundel Dene'

Because, perhaps, of Lane's awareness, and young Dene's reminder of it, of the large amount of money Dene's father had put into the firm, Lane did not in fact take anything in the letter amiss, recognising no doubt the rather touching mixture of juvenile pomp and desperate bravado behind this remarkable letter from a junior employee. Nor perhaps was he surprised that within the year Dene retreated to what was evidently a drying-out establishment. When he emerged in February 1912, Lane became the heavy father:

'Dear Arundel: I learn that you are leaving West Bolton Gardens on Wednesday and I earnestly hope that you have benefitted by the treatment, but I must implore you to remember that the doctors and your friends have done all that is possible for you and all hope for your future must now rest with yourself.

'You will of course have the assistance of your family, Mr. James [the family solicitor] and myself, but by force of circumstances I shall doubtless see more of you than your other friends. To prevent any further misunderstanding I now stipulate the conditions of your return to me.

'i. I shall require you to be at the office at 9.30 each morning punctually.

'ii. You will go to your lunch at 1.30 for which you can take an hour.

'iii. You must not leave the office at any other time without my consent or that of my manager.

'iv. I feel now obliged to change the nature of your work so that you will not be required to be away from the office on any business whatever.

'v. Your salary will be £4 a week until you have refunded the £[. . .] you owe me on account of money given to you the day you left New York and the sum you drew from my cashier on your return together with the amount of £[. . .] for debts your parents are paying for you.

'vi. I have arranged with your parents and Mr. James that you shall take rooms in my neighbourhood sufficiently near to enable you to keep the stipulated office hours and so that I can exercise some control over you . . . Some of your friends are under the impression that I have given you too much liberty and that I have not exercised enough restraint over your conduct, especially as to office hours.

'P.S. This letter has been written in consultation with Mr. James and your mother as it was felt that I ought to have a clear understanding with you before your return.'

Alas! Dene's battered pride and Lane's paternal patience could not arrive at a point of balance. Dene left in 1912, and soon followed Lord Lundy's example and set out for Australia; not to govern New South Wales but, after returning to Europe with the Australian Army in the First World War, to enter the employment of the Melbourne Electric Supply Company, from which on hearing of John Lane's death in 1925, he wrote warmly to Allen Lane. He recalled how John Lane had written to him 'early in the present year, apparently in capital health, full of projects for the future . . . even now I can see him in my mind's eye, proposing my health on my twenty-first birthday at the Cecil.'

And that was the last, it seems, that The Bodley Head heard of its witty, charming, unruly apprentice, save for one more rather shaky letter to Allen Lane, written from an accommodation address in an Adelaide bookshop, complaining, perhaps for want of any other means of renewing contact, of the price of English books in Australia.

14

Fresh Initiatives

On the run-up to the 1914 war The Bodley Head exploded in all directions. The gardening handbooks were succeeded not only by such volumes as *Leaves from a Madeira Garden* but by such unaesthetic companions as the Canvas Back Library, the Sacred Treasury, the Library of Golden Thoughts, the Country Handbooks and even Stars of the Stage, to say nothing of the Spanish Series (sixteen volumes by the same author, A. F. Calvert).

In 1910 R. P. Hearne's *Airships in Peace and War* was boosted by an introduction by Sir Hiram Maxim, but also by a speech in Hanley in which Mr Balfour warned the nation of the dangers of a threatened German invasion. An even more immediate threat was faced by *The Tyranny of Speed*, but *Wheel Magic* and *The Woman and the Car* took a more optimistic view. *Food and Flavour: a Gastronomique Guide to Health and Good Living*, by Henry T. Finck, supplemented Mrs Lane's little book on the grapefruit. To guard against mishap the well-known medical populariser Dr Harry T. Roberts wrote for the firm another series of Practitioners' Handbooks, while another, Dr Zachary Cope, narrowed the field with a book on *Minor Gynaecology*.

John Lane made a contribution to Anglo-German relations with his publication of a book actually banned in Germany, its author being sent to prison: *Life in a Garrison Town* (1909) by one Lieutenant Bilse, signalled by the *Tatler* with a pleasing caricature of John Lane being marched off to prison by a goose-stepping guard. This lively little contribution, along with Saki's bitter romantic satire, *When William Came*, harshly contrasting an idyllic England with the likely collaborationist behaviour of too many of its upper classes in the event of a German invasion, was curiously offset by a two-volume

(175)

History of English Patriotism by Esmé Wingfield-Stratford, and two substantial titles from the pro-German Houston Stewart Chamberlain: *Immanuel Kant* and *The Foundation of the Nineteenth Century*. The latter was at first enthusiastically received, until it was belatedly recognised as paean of praise for Teutonic superiority. Its author was decorated by the Kaiser.

A more congenial, if less commercially viable, nationalism found a voice in Vigo Street with the Rev. Vyrnwy Morgan's *The Philosophy of Welsh History*; but so did another book from E. A. Vizetelly, *The Anarchists: their faith and their record*, not to mention Loraine Petre's *Life of Simon Bolivar*, or Jessie Wallace Hughan's *American Socialism of the Present Day*, balanced by Adrian Dasent's *The Speakers of the House of Commons from the Earliest Times to the Present Day*. And the firm, with its own unconquerable optimism, approached the 1914 war with H. de Vere Stacpoole's *The New Optimism*. Already famous as the author of *The Blue Lagoon*, this former ship's doctor propounded his views of the role of women, pro-feminine but anti-Feminist, and of Anarchy as the best philosophical basis for social organisation, based on the hopeful assumption that 'progression toward the benign is the core of all morality,' as opposed to Socialism 'which wants to destroy society, and build it again on an anti-human-natural ground.'

Religion got its chance on various levels, ranging from the simplest —*Golden Thoughts from the Gospels*—by way of Chesterton's *Heretics* and *Orthodoxy* and Annie Besant's *Esoteric Christianity* to Valdesso's *Divine Considerations*. But there was nothing, it seems, of a specifically Quaker origin, despite Lane's lifelong insistence that he was one.

The firm's old stamping-ground, poetry and belles-lettres, though by no means ignored, faded somewhat into the background, though Vizetelly, undeterred by his spell in prison for actually publishing an all too outspoken Frenchman, wrote an enthusiastic book about him: *Emile Zola—Novelist and Reformer*.

Drama made a very modest showing, though it did of course appear to some current purpose in the continued publication of the works of Stephen Phillips.

Although Lane was not averse to meeting composers, if he thought they had a book in them, it is reasonable to assume that the influence of Mrs Lane goes far to explain the rapid increase of musical books, or at least of books about music and composers, not least those who were at the time quite modern composers. Two popularising series took off, under the indefatigable eyes of Rosa Newmarch and Wakeling Dry: Living Masters of Music, and Music of the Masters. Ernest Newman's *Elgar* went along with *Massenet* and *Debussy*, *César Franck* and *Vincent d'Indy*; while among conductors Henry J. Wood had already won a book to himself. On an altogether larger scale came *The Life and Works of P. I. Tchaikowsky*; and the centenary history of *The Royal Philharmonic Society of London*, proved to have been one of Beethoven's benefactors, bore with some magnificence on its cover, embossed in gold, the Society's handsome medal. But perhaps, in view of his passion for English historical curiosities, John Lane himself may be credited with the patronage of *The Oldest Music Room in Europe: A Record of Eighteenth-Century Enterprise in Oxford*.

After books, painting was John Lane's delight, and after painting, old English glass and almost any other *objet d'art*. One of the firm's intermittent excursions into the East came with *Legend in Japanese Art*, by Henri H. Joly, with hundreds of illustrations, sixteen of them in full colour. Robert Ross expounded the art of Aubrey Beardsley. Charles Conder was memorialised in 1913, soon after his death, in a book with more than a hundred illustrations, a dozen of them in colour. A. E. Gallatin compiled 'an iconography' of *Portraits and Caricatures of James McNeill Whistler*, and Thomas Way, the London engraver Whistler much admired, set down some lively anecdotal memories. George Leland Hunter's *Tapestries: their Design, History and Renaissance* was matched in splendour by Charles Turrell's *Miniatures: a Series of Reproductions in Photogravure of 85 Miniatures of Distinguished Persons, including the Queen Mother and the three Princesses of the House*, to say nothing of *Mosaics in Italy, Palestine, Syria, Turkey and Greece*.

Not that he had given up living artists altogether, though here he began the century with an American bias—influenced, perhaps, not so much by his wife as by the depressed (and surely mistaken) view of that fine Victorian painter and teacher Hubert von Herkomer, that all the best illustrators were American, citing 'Abbey, Gibson (a giant in his way) and Parrish'. So Lane launched upon the British scene first not Edwin Austin Abbey, but A. B. Wenzel's lively social commentaries, and even more effectively, Charles Dana Gibson and his Gibson Girls in several folios of twelve by eighteen inches.

Lane had not, of course, abandoned the Nineties altogether: he was always in search of a new Beardsley. He thought he had one in 1909 with Austin Spare's *A Book of Satyrs*. In 1912 he thought he had two more. Vernon Hill in turn was hailed as 'the most striking, etc., etc.' since Beardsley. And then came the most remarkable of all, the mysterious Alastair. He was mysterious because that is what he set out to be. His name in fact was Von Voigt, born in Trier in 1887 to a well-placed family of soldiers. So different was he from the rest of the military world that he claimed to be a changeling, originally of royal birth. Well educated, he grew up to speak excellent German, French and English of a markedly upper-class kind. He also played the piano, and was accepted as a mime-dancer, his own appearance having something suitably decadent and wraithlike about it. Then, as an artist, he had followed Beardsley indeed, though in a recognisably individual style. He drifted about Europe, one of those people who amuse the upper-classes by their undoubted talent but also by their oddity, and who have a singular capacity for attachment. He was introduced to the London of upper-class Bohemia by Maurice Magnus, a kind of artistic contact man who took him to see John Lane. Here, thought Lane, having met him in 1911, is the man I've been waiting for; and early in 1914 The Bodley Head published, quite in the old style, his first volume *Forty-three Drawings by Alastair*, with 'A Note of Exclamation' by, needless to say, Robert Ross; the edition, bound in cream buckram with Alastair drawings on the endpapers and another, blocked in gold, on the cover. The edition, of 500 copies, appeared from the London and New York offices; the contents included portraits, posters and illustrations to poems, short stories,

Carmen and Wedekind's *Erdgeist*. Meanwhile he had become very friendly with both Lanes, even occasionally staying with them in Bayswater. Whether their enthusiasm was shared by the rest of the office seems doubtful, since Alastair writes even in 1913 complaining of 'not very amicable' communications, including pretended difficulties about getting letters translated from the German.

By the end of the war even Lane seems to have given up, though not for chauvinist reasons; Alastair is reduced to writing 'Have you forgotten me altogether? . . . Do write me one word—one friendly word . . . I do miss London so much.' As late as 1927, after Lane's death, he is still trying to get the money due for his pre-war designs for a luxury edition of *The Sphinx*, which Lane eventually published in London in an edition of 1000 copies, even as The Bodley Head was publishing, in an edition of 1050 copies, Walter Pater's *Sebastian von Storck*—to be followed in 1928 with an 1850-copy edition of Prévost's *Manon Lescaut*, with an Introduction by Arthur Symons. Aestheticism lingered on, though feebly in England. In France Alastair found new patrons in Harry Crosby and Caresse his wife, rich, erratic members of the American group so active in Paris during the Twenties and Thirties. Things did not go well for him, but he survived the Second World War, exotic, hypochondriac, paranoid and picturesque as ever, with the help of yet more bewitched patrons, German this time, and a great deal of translation, until 1969.

Much of Lane's concern with finely produced books was early in the century transferred to the field of biography, memoirs and history, many volumes of which, published normally, rather than in limited editions, bore the marks of great enthusiasm in their workmanship and copious illustration. Three volumes devoted to Memoirs of the Dukes of Urbino and to the Duke of Reichstadt, a later Pepys correspondence, two volumes dealing with the late eighteenth century Sir William Pepys, even the *Memoirs of Mlle des Echerolles*, or a French General's *Life of the Duchess du Maine* could hardly have been expected to produce runaway sales. On the other hand, the *Memoirs of Lady Fanshawe*, *The Diary of a Lady in Waiting*, lives of *The Beautiful Lady Craven* and of *An Irish Beauty of the Regency*, and

Memoirs of the Court in England in 1675 by Mme d'Aulnoy, to say nothing of the interesting career of an English fisherman's daughter, *Sophie Dawes, Queen of Chantilly*, may well have offered the hope, or the expectation, of a titillating read.

Another such would no doubt be *Casanova in England*, by Horace Bleackley, a busy, aggressive, clubland gentleman and populariser, or the same author's *Ladies Fair and Frail*; and surely *Giovanni Boccaccio* (1909), the first appearance of that long-serving and influential figure on matters artistic in Italy, Edward Hutton. Another active populariser, A. M. Broadley, offered *Dr. Johnson and Mrs. Thrale*. Two fat volumes of nineteenth-century reminiscences by Sabine Baring-Gould, that indefatigable clerical folk-lorist, are perhaps more interesting now than they were at the beginning of the century; as is, if only as a source, *The Life and Work of John Churton Collins*, who, though a lively and controversial critic himself, perhaps did English literature no service by long and unfortunately successful campaigning for it to be made a recognised subject of academic study at our universities; all the same, he hardly deserved the description of him attributed to Tennyson—'a louse in the locks of literature'. There may have been a sale of sorts for Oscar Browning's *Memories of Sixty Years*, for he was a well-known Cambridge figure, the butt of many anecdotes deriding his pompousness. The quality of the man is revealed in a letter to Lane describing how he stood as a parliamentary candidate in the Liberal interest; he noted that the average length of his speeches had been an hour and a half, that he was defeated by a wide margin, but remained content with his moral victory.

Another active populariser, Lewis Melville, did well by the firm and the public in 1912, with *The Life and Letters of William Cobbett in England and America*. So did Francis Stuart's editing of *The Last Journals of Horace Walpole*, Mrs A. M. W. Stirling with two books which in fact achieved a considerable success: *Coke of Norfolk and his Friends* and two volumes of *Annals of a Yorkshire House*. Perhaps it was the success of these books, and others such as Albinia Lucy Cust's tales of a great house, *Chronicles of Erthig on the Dyke*, which prompted Lane to put out an advertisement:

(180)

'Those who possess letters, documents, correspondence, Mss., scraps of autobiography and also miniatures and portraits relating to persons and matters historical, political, literary and social, should communicate with Mr. John Lane, The Bodley Head, Vigo St., London W., who will at all times give his advice and assistance either on their preservation or publication.'

No less admirably produced were *The New Letters of Thomas Carlyle* (1904) and *The Love Letters of Thomas Carlyle and Jane Welsh*. So too were some of the steady flow of Napoleonic books which The Bodley Head published early in the century.

An even greater expansion than in the line of biography and memoirs signalled more of Lane's particular interests. Books about places interested him quite as much as those about people and *objets d'art*. Into England north of Boar's Hill, near Oxford, he seldom went. But if he was not in London, he was in Brighton, in Selborne, anywhere in the West Country—and everywhere taking stock, so to speak, of local bookshelves, often making friends of their owners, many of whom remembered him and his persuasive vitality with affection. One result (apart from assorted pictures, glass and the like spotted and picked up on his journeys, along with a sumptuously expressed enthusiasm for *Lady Charlotte Schreiber's Journals: Confidences of a Collector*) was many books of the 'A Detective in . . .' type, along with *Unknown Dorset* and elsewhere, *Hardy's Wessex* and so on.

And although 'abroad' did not beckon him—his trips to North America were strictly for business—books of foreign travel flowed from Vigo Street, mostly reminiscent or adventurously chatty, such as the lively and prolific Agnes Herbert's *Two Dianas in Somaliland*, Cecil Harmsworth's *Pleasure and Problems in South Africa*, Captain F. A. Dickinson's *Big Game Shooting on the Equator*, and indeed a contribution from Muriel Hine's husband, Stanley Coxon, with the characteristic title *And That Reminds Me*.

Many of these books, like the last named (and unlike Vernon Lee in, say, *Genius Loci*), have no literary pretensions but are sprinkled with anecdotes both amusing and bloodcurdling. Some are excellent contemporary studies of their regions, like A. F. Calvert's interminable Spanish series, or indeed Aubrey F. G. Bell's *In Portugal*, which in its preparation landed its author in prison—or Alfred Stead's seemingly unheeded but perennially topical *Great Japan: a Study of National Efficiency* (1905). Baring-Gould deserted the West Country for *The Land of Teck*. An enormous and richly illustrated tome celebrated *Imperial Vienna*. Stephen Graham's speciality was Russia, explored in *A Vagabond in Russia, Undiscovered Russia* and *Changing Russia* (a country, he avowed, in which there was no chance of a revolution, as this was entirely at odds with the national temperament). The genial artist-sailor Donald Maxwell was equally at home in Britain and abroad. Horizons were expanding all over the place. It was a fine time for armchair travellers, and if none of The Bodley Head's peripatetic writers has established him or herself firmly in the English canon, their adventurousness and good humour, and on the whole lack of racial loftiness, deserve a friendly wave.

Lane's interest in publishing magazines did not lapse when he discontinued *The Yellow Book* and its ancillary aesthetic exercises. He was to promote the launching of at least three more periodicals. The first, at the very end of the old century, was the brain-child of Lady Randolph Churchill, and aimed high—too high—in every sense of the phrase. *The Anglo-Saxon* was produced with some magnificence, and bound in leather, and priced at £1 an issue. Lane was to take 12 per cent of the profits—and a job as 'sub-editor' was to be reserved, at £200 a year, for the young Winston Churchill on his return from Army service in India. Rather surprisingly, its contributors included Shaw, Henry James, Stephen Crane, Max Beerbohm, Lord Haldane and since, Lady Randolph wrote to Lane, 'There is no harm in having one French contributor in each issue,' such presumably honorary Anglo-Saxons as Paul Bourget and Maurice Maeterlinck. The latter provoked another of Lane's upper-class ladies to object, in a hand almost as illegibly florid as Lady Randolph's:

'I find the Anglo-Saxon here. It will be paid for— But if such *Vile* literature is contributed as the Maeterlinck paper in this number, I shall cease to subscribe.'

Nevertheless the readership included, we are told, two Kings, three Prime Ministers, three Maharajahs, Cecil Rhodes, Sir Arthur Sullivan, Henry Irving, Ellen Terry and Beerbohm Tree. All were presumably force-fed by the indefatigable Lady Randolph.

Even so the seven numbers lost a substantial amount of money—Lady Randolph's money, needless to say: Lane, initially at least, was to get his percentage of the profits and a hundred guineas an issue for his time and work. But the partnership soon ran into difficulties. The imperious Lady Randolph was ill-equipped to cope with the manoeuvres of the commercially astute if haphazard farmer's son: Lane, however strongly attracted by the social heights involved in the venture, was not so dazzled as to abandon his native cunning. Getting under way only in January 1899, the project was already in trouble by the end of March, when Lady Randolph yelped on discovering Lane's plan for the subscription:

'The order form that you have written out will not do at all . . . It is written out as a cheque to you, and people object to this . . . as to your having the entire control of the funds, *I cannot admit it for an instant.*'

By September, outrage had set in. Lane, having agreed to produce a new order form, had done so without consulting her, and to make matters worse, included her name only in 'microscopic type':

'Considering that I am the proprietor and the editor, and you are merely the publisher, it is rather audacious . . . my patience is nearly exhausted . . . I really cannot see how we are to get on if you are to go back on your word like this.'

Lane's reply failed to mollify Lady Randolph:

'You say you do not know what are my causes of dissatisfaction [she wrote], and you proceed to go into questions I have not raised, and do not mention the only 2 points I pointed out to you in my letter.

'1. The altered order form, which makes the money practically payable to you.

'2. The all but obliteration of my name on the prospectus, which you say has your "entire approval".'

It is no surprise to find her writing stiffly three months later, 'I note that you have decided not to offer any opposition to my withdrawing the Anglo-Saxon from you'. And that was that.

Two more magazine projects came along at the time of the First World War. One quarterly has survived in the cultural history of Britain, short-lived though it was: *BLAST: the Review of the Great English Vortex*, edited by Wyndham Lewis with the usual grumbles at Lane's financial tactics. First published in June 1914, at 2s.6d., it was probably brought to The Bodley Head by Ezra Pound, who was struggling with surprising patience to get the firm to publish his book on Gaudier-Breszka, which it eventually did. It set out to deliver, and in its field certainly did deliver, a smack in the face to long-accepted values. Not least to those for which The Bodley Head itself was still most renowned: book production, stylish typography, elegant illustration. Not that *BLAST* was beyond capitalising on its predecessor in its manifesto:

'The spirit and purpose of the Arts and Literature of today are expressed in *BLAST*. No periodical since the famous *Yellow Book* has so comprehended the artistic movement of its decade. The artistic spirit of the Eighteen-Nineties was *The Yellow Book*. The artistic spirit of today is *BLAST*.'

Jacob Epstein was dragged in as a Vorticist, that movement in the visual arts which included Wyndham Lewis himself, William Roberts and many others in angular, diagrammatic drawings and designs; harsh in colour, mechanistic (even in portraiture), at least it approved lively colours. Its letterpress embraced again Wyndham

XI. From *Drawing for Radio Times*, published by The Bodley Head in 1961, this self-portrait of Edward Ardizzone was commissioned by the BBC for a television talk by the artist.

XII. In the 'sixties, and again in 1985, David Gentleman made
engravings for Bodley Head devices. The one shown here includes a
hart representing Max Reinhardt Ltd, and the tree of knowledge
representing the department of children's books, and of course Sir
Thomas Bodley, founder of The Bodleian Library, Oxford,
representing The Bodley Head.

Lewis, Ford Madox Hueffer (soon to be Ford Madox Ford) Rebecca West—with a story characteristically entitled 'Indissoluble Matrimony' and Ezra Pound, uttering as usual what one establishment figure unkindly characterised as 'barbaric yawps'. And its design was violently in contrast to that of *The Yellow Book*, or any other magazine of the day. Like so many *avant-garde* projects, it pretended that it would be 'popular, essentially'. Deliberately crude and clumsy, it made sure that in appearance it stood in much the same relation to what was (and is) usually considered 'artistic' as a primary schoolchild's work to a Leonardo drawing. Though its memory has lingered on, especially in commercial art and posters (because of its inbuilt aggressiveness) it was effectively bypassed in the post-war years, when the spirit of Beardsley influenced Art Deco much more than this typographical anticipation of the New Brutalism which was to terrorise the architectural landscape half a century later, after the Second World War. The magazine, though not all it stood for, was in two ways defeated by the 1914 war; in the first place the mood was wrong, in the second its splenetic inspiration and editor went off to become (rather appropriately) Bombardier Wyndham Lewis.

Two years later Lane tried again, this time putting the clock back, with *Form*, 'a quarterly of the Arts', edited by Francis Marsden and Austin Spare, yet another artist who had a few years earlier been saluted, at least by The Bodley Head, when it published his *Book of Satyrs* as the best thing since Beardsley. But here again 1916–17 was hardly a time when Decadent ideas could look for much support. Despite contributions from such notable non-Decadents as Frank Brangwyn, W. B. and J. B. Yeats, Edward Thomas, Walter de la Mare, Laurence Binyon and Gordon Craig, in W. H. Davies, J. C. Squire, Ivor Brown and A. L. (Aldous) Huxley, *Form* did become something of an Austin Spare promotion exercise, until he too disappeared into the Army, there to redesign, not too decadently, one must hope, the magazine of the Royal Dental Corps.

The establishment of its house magazine, *The Bodleian*, in 1909, may be said to mark the Firm's maturity. From the day of, perhaps before, his break-up with Elkin Mathews in 1894, Lane had clearly intended to broaden his firm's scope. The remarkable success of his elegant minor poets, coupled with the sensational impact of *The Yellow Book*, had for a few years deflected him. Financial constraints also inhibited the firm's expansion from a very modest capital base; his own way of life, on which much of his firm's success depended, evidently absorbed much of whatever cash was available.

With the personal security offered by his marriage to Annie Eichberg King (as well as her counsel as a trusted adviser) he rapidly increased the firm's output of fiction, history, biography, memoirs and travel books, as well as assorted series. He no longer wished to depend upon the moment's fashion, even if he contributed to it. Proud as he certainly was of his achievement as a fashionable publisher—and of most of the poets he had brought into the light—his own interests were too wide to keep him happy within the range of verse and belles-lettres. By the outbreak of war in 1914 he had established The Bodley Head as a responsible general publisher, though maintaining, in his everyday dealings and through the columns of the monthly *Bodleian* (price 1d.), an increasingly old-fashioned, almost family, atmosphere, with authors and readers alike. As in most large families, its members were often at loggerheads. Some, and among those ultimately the most famous, left home, usually more in sorrow than in anger. His staff were not well paid, and noted glumly his predilection for handsome loss-making art-books—which continued until his death. His authors sometimes, indeed often, had to scream for their money and watch their contracts. If he had a streak of meanness, this resulted from a countryman's natural caution, and was often parried by fits of generosity to those he saw as deserving cases. The firm was run on very narrow margins (and continued so to run, despite his wife's money). Moreover Lane did enjoy 'the rigour of the game', for he was still in it, as Lewis May put it, for 'the fun of the thing'; the driving of a hard bargain was fun in itself, just as it might have been in, say, Barnstaple cattle-market, with the bonus that, at least for the moment, he passionately believed in what he was selling, and usually what he was buying. But *Caveat Emptor* was as deeply graven on his heart as 'Calais' upon Queen Mary's.

15

A Patriotic War

'I never lost my first feeling of almost incredulous jubilation at being at The Bodley Head.' Thus, in 1978, wrote an old man who, within a few days of his 25th birthday, had joined the firm in 1911. Ben Travers had in some ways an unpromising start in life. Small of stature for one thing, he was little inclined, for another, to join the old-established family firm of dried fruit and provision merchants, taking round currant samples to prospective purchasers. His addiction to the theatre suffered a rude blow when he was sent away from the City office to the company's far-eastern outpost in Singapore; his only consolation seems to have been a spell in Malacca, where he found a complete set of the works of Arthur Wing Pinero in the public library. Life did not improve greatly on his recall home; he was unable from his comfortable suburban background to see any way into the sort of world he longed for. Rescue, however, was at hand through the workings of chance and the casual kindness of a stranger.

Thus he found himself one fine day being interviewed by John Lane for a job in his publishing house. Understandably enough Ben Travers knew absolutely nothing about publishing, but Lane evidently detected possibilities in the youth, not to mention the likelihood of his father raising some cash to see his eldest son settled at something. In the event the relatively small sum of £300 saw Travers established as a sort of apprentice, at a wage of £1 a week. Working at first in the firm's trade department in Brewer Street, during the next three years he found himself doing every conceivable job, sticking press cuttings in albums, proof-reading, arranging the tricky *places à table* for Anatole France's banquet, rising even to the position of stand-in manager—and all the time he was in the seventh heaven of delight, not least when taking over from Arundel Dene as editor of *The Bodleian*.

Soon moving to Vigo Street, he found himself in what he optimistically called 'an intellectual beehive'. The staff had, he says, doubled and re-doubled since the early days, 'but it never occurred to John Lane to consider any modifications, except by way of partitions into office rooms of incredibly impracticable shape, size and proportion.' The outer office had to provide desk-space for four assistants, a lady typist and an office boy, not to mention tables piled with books, manuscripts and proofs, all framed by floor-to-ceiling bookshelves. The manager had an office of sorts in a converted corridor. Lane himself had 'a dim, bottle-glass windowed little room tucked in beside the main office', almost buried in books and manuscripts—and eighteenth- and nineteenth-century paintings on the chairs and propped against the other furniture. His secretary, a guarded, virginal lady of middle age, and the cashier lurked in the old servants' quarters at the top of the building.

In that outer office Ben Travers bustled about, gaped at, and occasionally managed to speak to, assorted celebrities. These would have included W. J. Locke, profits from whose books were commonly said to pay all the firm's running expenses, and who was, said Travers, the most courteous man he had ever met; William Watson, 'a Titan of a poet in size and aspect', especially when smashing up the furniture; Stephen Phillips, then just past the height of his brief fame as poet and dramatist, who with a pallid sturdiness, 'seemed to drift from one portion of a dream to another'; Stephen Leacock, rugged, bear-like and abounding in jolly sociability; and of course Anatole France, who gave Travers the impression of having steeled himself to endure an ordeal of utter boredom.

As for Lane himself, Travers over the next twenty years or so became well aware at first hand of his odder characteristics, but remained unalterably fond of him. Short (a common bond with Travers) and jaunty (another) his neat grey beard 'looked as though it should have been worn above a ruff.' His soft voice and slow smile gave little hint of a spirit of wild enthusiasm and impulse, or the fact that 'taking risks gave him a certain glee.' As for his apparently less amiable qualities, 'one could', says Travers, 'and always wanted to find a respectable and even worthy motive for his actions,' while even in the case of those authors, such as Wells and Bennett, who speedily went elsewhere, 'There was something in Lane's nature which inhibited feud or rancour.' This emollient estimate seems on the evidence to be largely true.

Travers's earthly paradise was, like everyone else's, thrown out of joint in August 1914, by the outbreak of the First World War. At its outset Lane departed for the United States, asking Travers to remain at least until his return; but after three months Travers could stand it no longer. His brothers and almost all his friends were already in the Army. 'Why wasn't I? Simply out of conscientious allegiance to Lane.' That allegiance cracked before the greater one, and Travers went off and, with an off-hand insouciance which would have startled his successors in 1939, joined the Royal Navy Air Service, though having previously known or thought as little about flying as he had known about publishing when he joined The Bodley Head.

When Lane did return from America what Travers called his Quaker and pacifist tendencies simply led him to carry on much as before. He could not, of course, ignore the war, though probably he would gladly have done so. In due course his Bayswater house was bombed, which gave him the opportunity of removing to Bath and deluging poor Willett with instructions, sometimes varied with apologies, as when he gave laborious reasons for sending, this time from his Brighton (Kemp Town) house, insufficiently stamped letters. He also urged the staff to do more war work, and promised, rather obscurely, that the firm would pay half of the other half deducted from their pay.

He wrote a congratulatory but enquiring letter to Arthur Waugh and received a brisk reply:

'Dear Lane: I have to thank you for what I am sure is intended to be a very kind letter, but I am sorry to say that on this occasion your goodwill is stronger than your recollection. Some while ago I wrote and offered you this very book, under the same title. On receipt of my letter you invited me to lunch and told me (what I was not in the least surprised to hear) that a book of essays by myself would be of no sort of use to any publisher . . .'

As far as actual publishing was concerned, Lane, the chief publisher of Decadent poems and drawings twenty years before, now told a Toronto newspaper that 'war means death to Decadent Art', which would be succeeded by 'a more virile and wholesome Literature', a prophecy he can hardly have thought fulfilled in the first half of the 1920s. He himself did not care to publish many war books, though The Bodley Head put out many books about Central Europe and Russia before the Revolution. In 1915 he did publish another book by the Swedish Sven Hedin, this time a crisp glimpse of the enemy in *With the German Armies in the West*, of which *The Morning Post* observed with confused hysteria that the book:

'. . . stinks aloud of bribery and corruption; it is the slimiest saurian, shedding crocodile's tears, of a libellous panegyric which ever trailed its many-jointed length out of the cesspools of the Reptile Press . . . It is impossible to condone the publisher's offence in inflicting an English version of this book on us.'

Luckily majority opinion thought otherwise, in a no doubt gratifying number of cases mentioning John Lane by name, as in *The Times*, or, perhaps most gratifying of all, as Holbrook Jackson wrote in *T.P.'s Weekly*: 'Glad that Mr. John Lane, in spite of some opposition, has had the courage to publish Sven Hedin's book.'

By way of pacification, however, the firm also published a parody, *In Gentlest Germany* by Hun Svedend, 'translated from the Svengalese by E. V. Lucas'. But it had also published in 1914 *The Iron Year*, by Walter Bloem, advertising it under the heading WHAT WILLIAM READS, accurately but impassively, as 'the famous novel

(190)

of the Franco-Prussian War which the Kaiser read aloud to the Imperial Family Circle of Potsdam'.

Meanwhile *The Bodleian*, turning smartly on its erstwhile author Houston Stewart Chamberlain, noted that he:

'. . . has been decorated with the Iron Cross for a volume of violently pro-German essays. Surely no Englishman has ever sunk so low.

'Even Judas had the decency to commit suicide after his treachery. He would certainly have refused the Iron Cross.'

Lane became involved with the cause of the refugee Belgians in Britain, and published both in book form and in its house magazine, many bi-lingual poems and some only in French by, for example, Verhaeren and Cammaerts, as well as the embarrassingly titled *Book of Belgian Gratitude*. As a result of all this he found himself, although not until 1920, announced by Albert, King of the Belgians as entitled to bear 'Les Palmes en Or of the Order of the Crown'. He had also busied himself with the American Officers' Club in London and received an almost effusive invitation from Sir Harry Brittain, a noted Anglo-American publicist and Chairman of the Club, to mark, as among 'some of those who gave such splendid help during the Club's existence' the occasion of its closure in 1919 with a dinner.

Patriotism was acceptable to Lane provided that it wasn't too strident. He, personally, rejected a collection of Australian war ballads on those grounds, while Reginald Arnell, much later immensely popular on both side of the Atlantic as a dispenser of rustic charm in the voice of a quaint old Cotswold gardener, was dismissed with his pencil comment: 'Too much like music-hall patriotism. The vaunting is objectionable.'

His powers of persuasion, on the other hand, may be seen at work in a congenial cause when he organised an appeal in support of Theodore Dreiser, whose novel *The Genius* was in America the subject of a complaint from the ambitiously named Society for the Prevention of Vice. Lane's New York office became a headquarters of the ultimately successful protest. What is remarkable is Lane's success in corralling authors many of whom, if only in terror for their sales, might have been expected to hold aloof. Wells and Bennett might have been expected to sign up; and even Hugh Walpole, but W. J. Locke, for example, and E. Temple Thurston might not have been expected to put their heads on the block (though in fairness Locke was a keen and active supporter of Zola). Dreiser was grateful for this transatlantic support; but he soon became discontented with the British sales of *The Genius* and *The Titan*; with the intention of becoming his own publisher, he set out to buy back the British rights of the latter, though he balked at the asking price of $250. Still, as time went by, Lane did better out of the ironical American humour of Harry Leon Wilson, especially *Ruggles of Red Gap* (later a notable film with Charles Laughton and the non-eponymous Charlie Ruggles), and *Merton of the Movies*.

It may be that in the long run the most 'aesthetically' distinguished work to come from the firm during the war years was the first volume of the variously prolific Ford Madox Ford's *The Good Soldier: a Tale of Passion* (1915). An earlier fragment had appeared in *BLAST*. In a manner not wholly unlike early E. M. Forster, it unfolds in a quiet way an Edwardian tale of cross-referred liaisons, madness and a steady succession of suicides. Down the years repeated efforts have been, and still are, made to relaunch this melodrama as a significant novel of the twentieth century. They have so far not succeeded, save perhaps in some academic backwaters.

Another survivor of *BLAST*, Ezra Pound, spent a good deal of time on trying to interest The Bodley Head, and other publishers, in his monograph on the young sculptor Gaudier-Brzeska. With The Bodley Head he was eventually successful. Lane noted in one of his letters to Willett that 'I would not give any advance to Pound on his book, nor indeed would I commission it, but when he has it ready I would read it.' Initially Pound proposed a study of Vorticism in general, pointing out that 'I suppose I need hardly say that there is no other writer so well fitted to do this book as I am.' In 1919, several years later, the book having shrunk in its subject, he was striking a note familiar to the staff in Vigo Street:

'Gentlemen: Yearly account on my "Gaudier-Bresza" was due three weeks ago. The matter is a trifling one, but all other publishers with whom I have ever had dealings, send in their accounts on time and without special requests.'

Pound emerged only once more, in 1925, writing to Willett from Rapallo to urge publication of a mentally unstable poet, R. C. Dunning, whom The Bodley Head had indeed published before the war. Pound seems to have pursued the cause of this unhappy man with what his fellows regarded as unaccountable enthusiasm: Richard Aldington had pointed out that 'Dunning's friends have hawked his work about London for years'. The fact is of some interest that Pound, the cheer-leader of the modern, exercised himself regardless of fashion:

'Let me admit at once that Dunning writes in the manner of Swinburne, the Rubaiyat, Ernest Dowson, etc. . . . but as England has steadily and determinedly refused to have anything to do [with] any more modern style, and as Binyon has just reissued The Golden Treasury, I can't see that this ought to be a drawback in London. If Dunning on the contrary showed any consciousness of the main stream of European literature I should send the book to America, or anywhere else rather than England. I have tried it on various people who liked it, but they couldn't see why I did . . . If you do get the mss., and give it to a reader, for xf's sake don't tell him *I* admired it.'

Perhaps Pound did in fact send it to America, for in the same year, 1925, Dunning was awarded the annual Chicago Poetry Award.

In general The Bodley Head pursued Lane's usual path: minor poetry, some of it not at all bad; 'smart' fiction, a sprinkling of away-from-it-all rusticity; a few war novels, with old favourites like Locke weighing in gallantly as their world was passing away, many new and quickly forgotten first novelists, a quite strong representation of the Frenchman Pierre Mille, self-confessed admirer and follower of

Kipling, and of course the apparently unflagging Anatole France; in non-fiction, a quite deliberate extension of the firm's fancy for anecdotal travel books, on the whole lively first-hand accounts of the military in many parts of the world; a handful of aeronautical books; one or two theatrical books—later to be dismissed by Lane, à propos a suggested reissue of Beerbohm's drama criticism, on the grounds that they never made any money. But then, nor could many of his most enthusiastically championed books have done so—for example, a handsomely produced study by one of his Sette of Odd Volumes cronies, Dr G. C. Williamson, of Ozias Humphry, the late eighteenth-century portrait painter, friend and neighbour of the more famous George Romney. One work, also handsomely produced, with imitation period title-pages, which did achieve a quick success, was F. Sedgwick's at first anonymous pastiche of Samuel Pepys in a diary ostensibly kept during the war, originally published in *The Spectator*, which—perhaps taking its publishers by surprise—soon ran to a fourth edition, and which did neatly and wittily capture the Pepysian tone of 'self-congratulation, self-consciousness and pleased-as-Punchness'.

Nevertheless, although Lane's enjoyment of publishing was still in 'the fun of it', he was tiring by the end of the war. At 64 his manic life had begun to tell on him, and on his staff, no doubt. He was less and less in the office, but increased the flow of his brisk communications and impeded decision-making, since he did not much care for what he regarded as important decisions being taken by anyone else. This was especially the case since the wretched death in 1917 of his long-standing prop and stay, Frederic Chapman; a lifelong devotee of both books and literature, family worries and congenital disease had brought him to collapse, pitifully tearing up and throwing from his windows all the joys of his life, volume after volume of his long-nurtured library.

The firm certainly needed some injection of capital. When Ben Travers, having narrowly survived his naval air service, after what he called 'only eight crashes', came to see Lane, the publisher said to his ex-apprentice, 'I am giving up. I am turning The Bodley Head into a private limited company. Now—I will make you an offer.' This was that if Travers's father would (in 1918) stump up £10,000, he could work for the firm for £500 a year. Father said no.

When Lane, on one of his frequent visits to his North Devon childhood home, tried his hand at tickling trout, he found that he had lost the knack. In the course of turning The Bodley Head into a private limited company he found the task no easier. A Canadian called Miller had been reading for Lane for some months, and expressed great enthusiasm for entering the firm. Alas, his wife's family, bankers, persuaded him to go into banking.

Then there was Mr Kitchin, a young Oxford man, and a great friend of the Coutts family. Alas, again, his family, indeed his late father, had strong legal connections, and wished him away at any rate before thinking of publishing. Worse, the family had already put money into the publishing house of Swann, Sonnenstein, which despite its encouraging name had lost the lot for them. Next was the possibility of Captain Herbert Asquith, who was himself a writer who belonged to the 'Youth Movement' and 'knows intimately all the new writers'. An accountant came on his behalf to examine the books, which Lane felt at that moment were in excellent shape. The trouble there was that these Asquiths were themselves not rich, and consent of the trustees of a marriage settlement—his wife being 'the daughter of a wealthy peer, Lord Wemyss'—was necessary before he could put money into the firm. Evidently it was not forthcoming.

Then one day Willett happened to see an advertisement in *The Times* from 'an ex-officer and an M.C.' who wanted to join a publishing house as a partner. He turned out to be the 32-year-old only son of Sir Benjamin Brodie, Bt., and a nephew of Sir Herbert Warier, President of Magdalen College, Oxford, but nothing came of that.

Another young man, Guy Eglington, proved, at first, to be altogether more promising. Like most trainees, he was first put into the trade premises in Brewer Street. These he found in what he considered a deplorable state of muddle, to remedy which he proposed some radical reorganisation. This Lane much approved of; but then he approved of everything to do with young Eglington, including his literary taste, or at any rate his eye for a winner: not without reason, since it was he who had pressed the firm to take *The Road to En-Dor*, a sensationally successful escape story by E. H. Jones. (Coincidentally, another Jones was to write an equally successful escape narrative for The Bodley Head a generation later.)

He also saw in Eglington yet another bright young Englishman to go and revitalise the New York firm, which continued to give trouble, and in fact never recovered from those 'defalcations' which had caused him some seven years before to take that trip to Albany prison which so upset him that he came almost to commiserate with the wretched woman tempted into theft.

This time, in 1920, it was still the direction but not the staff which was causing his dismay. In fact, Lane had a high opinion of the manager, Jefferson Jones, and had no intention that Eglington should supplant him. In fact, when this energetic and able young man got there, he must have wondered why. True the *Studio International* art journal was in trouble, collaboration with its London end being lamentable; but Lane kept making it clear that he did not wish Eglington to spend too much of his time on it. On the other hand, the John Lane office, though entirely friendly, regarded—or at any rate treated—him as a purely literary adviser, a role which the young man was not at all inclined to accept. Nor, it seems, from Lane's extremely detailed explanations to his protégé of the firm's commercial structure, did Lane wish him to do so.

He, himself, Lane explained, held most of the common stock and some of the preferred, keeping control of the company. The total capital was $100,000, and while the preferred shares had borne their cumulative interest of $19,000, since 1911 no interest had been paid on the stock. The manager had a salary of $100 a week, and he himself had $50 a week, which he had not drawn except to buy all stock which came on the market.

'I want', he wrote across the Atlantic to Eglington with alarming, and unusual candour, 'to freeze some of the preference share-holders out of the concern, because they neglected their duties under the old regime; *firstly*, by not attending the monthly meetings; *secondly*, by upholding the then managing director, who neglected to inform me of the defalcations until three months after the cashier had been imprisoned, and at the same time demanding his salary to be raised from $5200 per annum to $8000. Moreover, the directors, without my consent, awarded the managing director $10 000 of unsubscribed stock.'

'Moreover', he added gloomily, 'not one of the J.L. Co. managers has found and published a really successful author.' Jefferson Jones, the current Manager, was indeed a splendid fellow, but merely a businessman.

'The Bodley Head unquestionably requires the stimulating influence of a well-stored mind of English literature and modern tendencies. Jones of course has too much to do. It is most gratifying, however, to feel that you and he are working so well together . . . Leave lecturing and collaboration until you have acquired a thorough knowledge of your business and the general trend of publishing in the U.S. It will be of the greatest importance to both houses.'

New York, it seems, had been consistently failing to order enough copies from London, while New York riposted by complaining that too many of those they did order were not available. London replied that it had been impossible to reprint during the war, though many had now been reprinted during the 1919–20 financial year, 'which makes my balance sheet look somewhat ugly . . . much money has been tied up in them, and it will take some time to liquidate that sum . . . Nearly all the profits for the past two years have gone into reprints and unpublished books.'

Still, things are humming in London, and Lane even seems somewhat bemused by the growth, quantitively at least, of his own firm:

'I am hoping to have before me on Thursday the figures of my liabilities, the amounts owed to me, the value of the stock, copy-rights, goodwill, etc., which will form the basis of the company. It is now really rather a vast concern.'

A vast concern it was not, by any standards. There was, as luckily there still is, scope for publishing as a small-scale personal enterprise, but as in the farming world in which the foundations of Lane's character were laid, the scale of operations was changing steadily.

Not so, however, John Lane himself. Tiring he might be, but control vested in himself remained his guiding principle as he set about forming his London limited company and re-forming that in New York. However, what he called 'the many inevitable worries of reconstruction' did not deter him. In August, 1920, he noted with satisfaction, trade seemed to be keeping up. '*The Road to En-Dor*, *Humours of a Parish* and *Poets in the Nursery* have sold well throughout the summer, and we have never before had such a strong Autumn List.' Not one of its titles, however, would mean anything today, sixty-five years later, even if a book on the Russian Ballet was 'not only topical but topping'.

All this optimism was in line with Lane's temperament, but also aimed at encouraging Eglington, and even more his uncle, who had expressed his willingness to put £3,000 into the American and £2,000 into the English house. In fact he himself would put in as extra capital the interest-bearing loan of $5,000 he had made to the firm—provided that the Manager, Jones, and Jefferson's uncle would put up the rest!

Occasionally Lane moves into personal reminiscence, and his comments on Mitchell Kennerley, in response to signs of enthusiasm from Eglington, well illustrate his absence of rancour (a trait not always shared by his own enemies), as well as sounding a warning note to Eglington:

'Unfortunately I took him to America too soon. He got a swelled head, which many of my importations seem to have suffered from at that time. He grossly neglected the business ... so I arrived one morning without any notice, and he could not be found. Of course I had to get rid of him there and then, and I found he had been lending money to Le Gallienne and taking money himself, all of which has not even now been repaid [after 20 years].

'You can come to no harm in knowing him, and I quite admit that he is a most interesting personality, but he lacks character, and that in business is fatal; but he is one of the most interesting men known to me. I have no doubt he will be of great assistance to you, but I feel it is my duty to put you on your guard.'

In New York, however, Eglington is showing increasing signs of frustration, not without reason. Despite being told not to spend too much time on *Studio International* he becomes Editor of it on the departure of William H. de B. Nelson—who, as is usually the case, is accused of leaving things in a fearful muddle. He sets about reviving it—'We are the only Art publishers in America and publish the only Art magazine of any standing'—and he wishes to turn it into the champion of American art.

When he hears that Lane has quarrelled with the London end of *The Studio*, which intends to leave The Bodley Head, he thinks they are well out of it. 'The English *Studio* has been getting duller and duller for years'.

As far as the main publishing business is concerned, Eglington is even less happy on both personal and professional grounds. He hears rumours of reconstruction but has some difficulty in getting an explanation out of Lane. Worse, he is in an embarrassing position when asked about it, and cannot persuade Lane himself to come over and sort matters out. As far as the running of the company as it stands, heavily influenced by London, it is a mass of elementary psychological miscalculation. Even if large print orders get a cheaper rate, it is absurd that they should so often be left with so many copies, especially of English novels, imported 'indiscriminately'—in one case no fewer than 10,000 unsold. He does not think buying out shareholders is a good idea, since at $2 they are likely to 'regard them as a dead loss, and hold on to their paper in the hope of improved conditions.' He is exercised as to how to put the American firm on its feet financially. It has been carrying a list much too large to allow any part of its property to be properly developed. On the other hand:

'I am devoted to the John Lane ideal in publishing and I will do all I can to further it . . . The other American publishers are content to succeed. In fact they are more salesmen than publishers.'

Meanwhile, he sends back a stream of suggestions about American books and artists who might go well in London, some of which, after many repetitions—an edition of Van Gogh's letters, for example, or James Branch Cabell's *Jurgen*—are ultimately taken up; in the case of *Jurgen* very profitably, though whether the same can be said for its half-dozen successors is doubtful. Cabell's whimsical improprieties brought about a *succès de scandale*, but seem not to have stood the test of time.

Although he continues to sign his letters 'Yours very affectionately' Eglington is, with reason, increasingly concerned that Lane's ideas for him seem to differ sharply from those explained to him when he joined the firm. The new suggestion that he should spend four or five years in New York horrified him: 'I wish to live in London because I believe it to be my place. It is a town worth living in, which New York is not . . . If my uncle invests the money, it will mean that I am preparing to give my life to The Bodley Head and I must see my way clear.'

Which he could not do, for one thing, if Lane really intended to cut the already inadequate management salaries. Besides, 'You are taking into the London house four partners of whom you propose I should be one . . . You say you would be inclined to prefer one to the other proposed partners of whose compatability you know nothing, and yet you propose to banish me for five years.' And, he added confidently, he certainly would not advise his uncle to invest money in a business with whose management he would have no share.

And that was that. Lane was, as far as London was concerned, in touch with bigger fish than Eglington's uncle. New York became an increasing burden, in management terms as well as financially. The John Lane Company of New York was suddenly sold to Dodd, Mead, who continued to do very nicely at any rate with Anatole France, in the same year as Lane formed his own company, John Lane The Bodley Head Limited, in London, and Guy Eglington went out with the tide.

16

Enter Allen, Exit John

When John Lane felt inclined, at the end of the 1914–18 war, to turn
The Bodley Head into a limited company, he was indeed thinking in
terms of £10,000 investments, in line with his conception of the firm
as 'a vast concern'. When Ben Travers's father shied away, as did all
the others mentioned in the previous chapter, he was perhaps driven
to lower his sights to the more modest £5,000 proposed by Eglington's uncle. But his immense enthusiasm for this young man, his
copious explanations of his financial plans and what almost seems
like excuses for muddles and mismanagement, evidently withered on
the stem with the appearance of two people whose families were
prepared to risk their hopes at £10,000 apiece.

The first of these was Hubert Carr-Gomme, who had been a
Liberal MP for Rotherhithe, for some years private secretary to the
former Prime Minister, Sir Henry Campbell-Bannerman, active in
social matters, especially in London south of the Thames. Quite why
he wanted to come into publishing is not altogether clear. He was
generally thought of as a sleeping partner, though in moments of
crisis he seems to have represented, not always successfully, the
voice of common sense.

The other was certainly to play a much more active part in the
running of the firm day-to-day, though not much to its financial
advantage, and still less to his own. Tall, at least by Lane's standards,
and dark and abrupt in manner, Ronald Boswell came to represent
an earnestness and an overt political awareness not previously notable
in the firm, despite John Lane's liberal, indeed mildly radical, stance.
He came to it, as it were, impersonally; Lane clearly knew nothing
about him when the proposal was first mooted, since he wrote to

Willett from his Brighton house (where he spent more and more time when not, as Ben Travers put it, 'pottering about the West Country') that he had better see the chap: 'Boswell is a gypsy name, which may account for his appearance.' In fact, Ronald Boswell was entirely English for all his Continental antecedents: after Oxford and war service, he had cast around for a congenial and worthwhile line of work, and first joined Werner Laurie (a publishing house much later to be absorbed by The Bodley Head) for a year or two, as 'a stamp-licker, that kind of thing, picking up what I could'. Then, intending to branch out, with his father's money behind him, he was influenced by his father to join Lane's well-established firm in 1919, along with Carr-Gomme, a founding director when the limited company was formed in 1921.

Last, and at the time least, of the new arrivals at Vigo Street, or rather at the trade premises in Brewer Street was a nineteen-year-old cousin of Lane's, Allen Lane. Born Allen Williams, eldest son of an architect in the Bristol City offices, the boy had passed his childhood in what his biographer, J. E. Morpurgo, describes as 'a gloomy house but a cheerful family'. He attended Bristol Grammar School, where he made absolutely no mark, then or apparently later—since even in 1970 his name was omitted from a list of distinguished Old Boys. He did, however, claim later that his headmaster, J. E. Barton, had 'opened his eyes to the significance of design and form.'

Even so, growing up in wartime, the boy formed no very clear notion of what to do with his life. John Lane, however—'Uncle John' to the family—a very familiar and much-loved figure, heedless of Allen's total lack of distinction at school, already saw in this fair-haired, fresh-faced, lively lad a future as his own successor; his flair was at work again. His benevolence in fact extended to the family as a whole; he persuaded them all to change their name to Williams-Lane, its head apparently contemplating without dismay either the modification of the Welsh element in favour of the Devonian, or in the case of the three sons its disappearance altogether when they became simply the Lane brothers.

Allen's first step was soon determined. He came to London and took lodgings with another uncle and aunt in Raynes Park, a modest south-western suburb, and joined the staff of The Bodley Head on Shakespeare's birthday, 23 April, 1919, at a wage of a guinea a week, of which 10s. went to the uncle and aunt. Like John Lane himself— then 65—he retained always a great affection for his parents, especially his mother. His best friends were his brothers and their sister; his Uncle John became, if he was not already, a paragon to be emulated.

Once in the office, he was put to work as, more or less, an office-boy, running messages, meeting trains, taking papers down to Brighton, and performing the usual multitudinous tasks of an office junior. He worked with Guy Eglington, who, once in New York, adopted a rather patronising tone about Allen in letters to John Lane, hoping Allen is getting on all right, although 'he needs someone to keep an eye on him'—and later wonders, it would appear nervously, whether any decision has been made about his junior's future, since he feels that The Bodley Head is perhaps not quite the right place for Allen. If this was intended as a discreet attempt to edge Allen out, it failed, indeed evidently backfired. It was bound to do so, given the latter's admiration for Uncle John, and Uncle John's high hopes for Allen, who 'inherited, learnt, or imitated John Lane's manner of running a publishing house as if it were a great sport in which he wanted all his colleagues to share'—in the sport if not in the material rewards. Allen may indeed have assumed this approach, but, adds Morpurgo: 'Unfortunately for those colleagues, Allen, in this unlike John Lane, changed the rules—and the team—as often as possible, as soon as he was in a position to do so.'

For the time being, however, he was kept busy learning the trade. Soon he went out as a salesman. First with John Lane himself, then with a senior traveller (now known as a 'representative'). He proved popular with booksellers, many of whom were actually interested in the wares they sold. He developed 'some skill in discussing the contents of books which he had never read'. He also, with John Lane's active encouragement, got to know printers and printing, especially the younger printers who became active after the First World War.

Not that these earned Uncle's approbation. In *The Bodleian* John Lane in 1922 declared roundly:

'It can be confidently stated as a fact that there are not more than two firms of printers in the United Kingdom who are capable of producing a book on their own account satisfactorily.'

Not that many people cared; in the case of 'more ordinary books' than limited editions, 'the attitude of both the Press and the public seems to be somewhat apathetic.'

The provincial grammar-school nonentity was busy learning not only the ins and outs of publishing, but as much as he could of metropolitan sophistication. He made his own young friends, among them Ben Travers, with the increasing stage connections; and, professionally more to the point, Raymond Hazell of the printing firm which, as Hazell Watson and Viney, was to play a very important part in Allen's progress.

He was a frequent guest at Lancaster Gate Terrace and there met a wide variety of contemporary notabilities, or at any rate near-notabilities; in fact, he fairly soon abandoned Raynes Park and moved in with the John Lanes, at the same time rapidly advancing in the firm: indeed he became a junior director at the age of twenty-two, joining Uncle John, Carr-Gomme and Boswell, the principal shareholders. B. Willett, by then Managing Director, and T. H. Crockett, Sales Director, also had a few shares, though in fact they had responded feebly to the offer of stock. The group was soon to be joined by Lindsay Drummond, doubly welcomed no doubt because he not only had money—and contributed another £10,000—but also was a cousin of the Marquess of Northampton. He was also, by common consent of surviving employees, 'a perfect gentleman,' easy, affable and thoughtful.

Despite the new money, new blood, new contacts, old John Lane still shaped the firm's character. He wrote many letters to newspapers urging the purchase of manuscripts for the nation (though later by his will, disposing of his original Beardsley drawings to the Brooklyn

Museum, New York) or rashly criticising a fellow publisher (Walter Hutchinson) in *The Daily Herald* in a way which forced him to make a fulsome withdrawal. But there was, in spite of his reputation, some justice in the tribute paid to him in *The British Weekly* by its editor, Sir William Robertson Nicoll:

'He has shown amazing generosity in dealing with the waywardness of genius, and in a perfectly unostentatious way has done many kindnesses of which he has said nothing. He may have had his disappointments in the matter of gratitude, but he has not complained.'

Despite their sometimes stormy relationship, and his office-chair smashing exploits, William Watson was one such beneficiary. His bardic stance had become more and more outmoded; he thought that even the Georgian poets created 'an atmosphere of almost violent reality'. He had acquired a knighthood: on Lane's advice he had delayed publication of the poems in *Retrogression*, and the delay enabled him to add a poem in which he compared Lloyd George, who had just taken over from Asquith, to Merlin, as one Welsh wizard to another, though, as he put it:

> 'Not much beholden to the munificent past
> In mind or spirit, but frankly of this hour;
> No faggot of perfections . . .'

Perhaps it is unfair to both men to suggest that this tribute won him his knighthood. His war poems, unlike his earlier heated observations about the Turks, were at one with public opinion, and with the 'grand style', as he called it, of Rupert Brooke and Julian Grenfell, formed before the long-drawn-out attrition of the Western Front had produced its revulsion.

The firm's taste for the near-the-knuckle continued unabated, though now mostly in the form of illustrated reprints. For some years a leading collaborator in this line of business was a strange Belgian, educationist, artist, poet and quasi-mystic, Jean de Bosschère, who was over in England during and after the war; although he did not make a start with illustrating Bodley Head books he was copious with suggestions of various degrees of impropriety: Defoe's *Moll Flanders*, Apuleius's *Golden Ass*, Laclos' *Les Liaisons Dangereuses*, Ovid's *Amores* and *Metamorphoses*, Flaubert's *Tentation de St. Antoine* and *Salammbô*, Balzac's *Contes Drolatiques* among them.

Several of these were duly commissioned, and duly done, in a curious angular style, part Beardsley, part Cocteau, part even Bauhaus. Of the *Golden Ass* (which sold 3,000 in two months) he thought of the frontispiece, 'You know better than I do. This concerns the sale of the book. It must be the least audicious [*sic*] of the eight.' In the event, in 1923, he was delighted with the result: 'It looks very fine, and does more than fulfil my desires of making, at last, a real illustrated book.' It also got its publishers momentarily in trouble with the law. Undeterred he went on to Petronius's *Satyricon*. The first part, he thought, might seem a little dull and dry, but, 'after that, I will only have to veil the too "realistic" pictures evoked by the text. But if you make it a limited edition, I am rather free.'

Spurred on, perhaps, by part of the firm's reputation, Clifford Bax, the be-caped poetical (and rich) brother of the composer Arnold Bax, who actually lived in Albany between the two sections of Lane's office, wished him to publish his translation of Angelo Poliziano (1454–94), though:

'I must warn you, that neither of us may waste our time, that Poliziano's [version] of the Orpheus story is typical of the Renaissance and might offend modern readers. In fact, he informs us that when Orpheus had lost Eurydice he was so much upset that he decided thenceforth to transfer his affections to the other sex and no longer love any woman.'

Not, clearly, a suggestion likely to appeal to a man with echoes of the Wilde trial still ringing in his ears—although perhaps . . . But Bax stiffly replied 'I never pay for the production of my own work.'

As for James Branch Cabell, Guy Eglington's enthusiasm for

Jurgen carried the day, and indeed proved a considerable success in its mock-Rabelaisian way. The sexual preoccupations of this fifty-year-old Virginian fantasist led to attempts in 1921 to ban the book, the Society for the Suppression of Vice helpfully compiling a list of offensive passages. Encouraged by this absurdity, sales soared; readers evidently wanted the whole book, rather than the selected passages offered in the cause of suppressing vice Lane, even more encouraged, produced a special edition, 'limited' to 3,000 copies, with an Introduction by Hugh Walpole and illustrations by a Huguenot-Scottish artist, Frank Papé. The author sent Lane a note of thanks into which it is possible to read an amiable ambiguity:

'It seems a duty, it is most certainly a pleasure, to express my appreciation of the beautiful dress you have given *Jurgen*. Mr. Papé, hitherto unknown to me, has performed so many small miracles in the way of embellishment, and has added so many purely Papean Flights of Fancy, that even to me the tale comes as a quite new and—heaven knows—a far more opulent chronicle.'

The mutual admiration did not last: Lane had intended only to do *Jurgen*, but somehow (possibly through Eglington) the firm let itself in for twenty more titles, each of which achieved a more disappointing sale.

It would be unfair to saddle John Lane with all the less than magnetic titles which peppered The Bodley Head list during his last years—*One Year at the Russian Court, 1904–5*, for example, or *The British in Corfu, 1806–8*—but it is difficult not to suppose that his tastes prompted many lavishly illustrated books which, however carefully costed, seem unlikely to have solidified the firm's finances: *Astbury, Whieldon and Ralph Wood Figures and Toby Jugs*, for example, *The Churches of the City of London, Mural Painting in English Churches during the Middle Ages, Modern Etchings and their Collectors*, or *The Modern Woodcut*. Even W. Shaw Sparrow's *British Sporting Artists*, with 27 colour and 76 half-tone illustrations at £2. 2s. would have done well to break even—though a special edition of 95 copies at £5. 5s. was sold out before publication. Publication of R. M. Freeman's *The New Boswell*, an ingenious, indeed witty, echo of his three-volume wartime diary in the manner of Pepys, seems more a friendly, if expensively well-produced, gesture than a publishing adventure, especially as, like its predecessor it had already appeared periodically. Three volumes of *Mazzini's Letters to an English Family, 1855–1860*, were surely an affectionate nod to the exiled Italian leader's rooms in Bloomsbury which Lane himself occupied when he first came to London, or a publication within the scope only of a well-funded university press.

Lane's long-standing crony from the Sette of Odd Volumes, Dr G. C. Williamson, was exceedingly active. Handsome studies, in collaboration with Lady Victoria Manners, of *Zoffany: his Life and Times* and of *Angelica Kaufmann* were no doubt valuable in their day, and as much might be said of Williamson's own monograph on *Daniel Gardner: Painter in Pastel and Gouache*, whose work so often, like that of Williamson's previous subject, Ozias Humphreys, was attributed to Romney, and even to Gainsborough and Reynolds. John Thomas Smith's *Nollekens and his Times* edited by Wilfred Whittew, better-known at the time as 'John O'London' was the first complete edition of this celebrated work since 1809.

Contemporary arts were not ignored: in this category may be included *The Russian Ballet in Western Europe*, a six-guinea book of which the most important element consisted of facsimile reproductions 'in full colour and gold', of scenery and costumes by Larionoff, Picasso, Goncharova, Mizia Sert, Bakst, Benois, Matisse, Derain and others. Frank Brangwyn was a good name to have on one's list in those days: the indefatigable Walter Shaw Sparrow introduced *Prints and Drawings of Frank Brangwyn* and *A Book of Bridges*, while one Hayter Preston took over *Windmills*. Finding a writer to introduce *The Pageant of Venice* proved more of a problem. Norman Douglas turned it down but suggested D. H. Lawrence who said no, then said he might, then didn't: the invaluable Edward Hutton stepped into the breach.

The titles mentioned above are a mere selection of the books on visual art and artists published during the last five years of Lane's life. His partners, or fellow directors as they became, were understandably restive. In the field of music Houston Stewart Chamberlain was re-admitted to the fold with *The Wagnerian Drama*. Peter Warlock, under his real name, Philip Heseltine, pondered the art of *Frederick Delius*. A lady called Zoë Kendrick Pyne addressed herself, adventurously for the time, to *Palestrina : His Life and Times*. Dr Agnes Savill produced an extremely perceptive study discouragingly called *Music, Health and Character*. Having dealt so handsomely with the ballet, the firm, harking back to John Lane's youthful enthusiasm (and Allen Lane's, though in his case perhaps less for the dance itself than for its incidental opportunities), offered a *Handbook of Ballroom Dancing*, by, a little incongruously, Paymaster-Commander A. M. Cree, R N.

Though Lane had declared against theatre books in general, and against Beerbohm's reprinted reviews in particular, he did let some through, and those not merely in the genially reminiscent kind of which he was fond. The Bodley Head was early, if not first, in the field with a biography of Chaplin (1922) by a Frenchman, Louis Delluc—as though staking a claim to the comic genius's autobiography which they were to publish forty-two years later. From New York George Jean Nathan, a celebrated critic, surveyed the stage in two volumes, *The World in False Face* and *The Critic and the Drama*. A handful of plays made little mark at the time and none for the future. More to Lane's taste were the Bodley Head Quartos, engaging little volumes of Elizabethan and Jacobean drama edited by G. B. Harrison, and including plays and pamphlets by Henry Chettle, William Kemp, Samuel Daniel, Thomas Campion, Thomas Dekker, Robert Greene, Ben Jonson, Thomas Nashe and others: an admirably planned and executed series of which any publisher might be proud today.

Publication of contemporary literature continued in full vigour though poets were more scantily represented. In 1921 Vita Sackville-West's *Orchard and Vineyard* briefly brought her to the house to join Margaret L. Woods, a good poet in her kind. But for John Lane the death of Alice Meynell in 1923 loomed largest. The Bodley Head had in the heyday of the 1890s published four of her prose works and two of her volumes of verse, and, said *The Bodleian*'s mourning page, 'since the death of Elizabeth Barrett Browning, no woman has soared to the Heights of Parnassus as has Mrs Meynell.' Otherwise, though Lascelles Abercrombie may be remembered again some day, there is little to record save some silly and some pleasant numbers. There might have been, had Lane accepted, even subject to modification, a curious mish-mash of verse and prose by a mid-Western writer sent to him by John Quinn, the American bibliophile whose acquaintance Lane had sedulously courted. But Lane replied, 'Mr. Eliot's work is no doubt brilliant but it is not exactly the kind of material we can add to our list.' Much the same had already been felt by Boni & Liveright in New York. Not until Alfred Knopf accepted the poems on their own in 1919 did T. S. Eliot make any headway, by which time 'that strange young man', as Virginia Woolf called him, had added several of his now more famous poems, too late for inclusion by the Woolfs' Hogarth Press in *Poems 1919*.

Belles lettres, that faded, or at any rate fading, category, was still welcome chez John Lane. It was now that its most celebrated exponent joined the list, and also Lane's consultative staff, in 1923. J. C. Squire, editor of *The London Mercury*, rackety literateur and fine writer of light verse, introduced J. B. Priestley to Lane, and the still youngish Yorkshireman, having survived the Western Front during the war and Cambridge University after it, rapidly became a power in Vigo Street. He claimed to have recommended—unavailingly, in the first case—the first novels of Graham Greene and C. S. Forester.

Introduced as 'a young writer who is becoming well known as both an authority on literary matters and also as the possessor of a graceful and witty style', Priestley wrote and signed a number of agreeable essays in *The Bodleian*, concurring with Lane's general principle of 'accentuating the positive' and deploring the mechanics of reputation-forming: by which, for example, a young writer who demonstrates a sense of humour is all too apt to be tempted, if not by the publisher then by the Press, to write a regular article and thus become a mechanical fun-maker. In that first year he published *I for One*, in 1924 *Figures in Modern Literature*, a varied collection, most of them remembered hazily now if at all: Arnold Bennett indeed, Walter de la Mare surely, A. E. Housman certainly and W. W. Jacobs—but George Saintsbury, George Santayana, Robert Lynd, Maurice Hewlett? In 1925 *Fools and Philosophers: a Gallery of Comic Figures from English Literature* prepared the way for his still admirable *The English Comic Characters*. In the same year he also presented and edited *The Diary of Thomas Turner*, a pleasing picture of the day-to-day life of a small Sussex shopkeeper with a candid, not too remorseful, addiction to the village pub. After John Lane's death, however, Priestley drifted away, to form a lifelong, lucrative and quite demanding association with Heinemann—as an author, at any rate, for he was many years later to be tempted back to The Bodley Head as a director. But of John Lane himself he seems to have retained an agreeable if clear-sighted impression:

'When I first met him John Lane must have been only a year older than I am now [in 1962]. He seemed to me ancient: small and bearded, puckered and peering—his sight was so bad that he could no longer read. His talk and manner contrived to suggest a retired diplomat, a connoisseur who had run through a fortune, and not at all a hard bargainer in the book trade ... he must have felt his particular world had vanished—that small but influential world in which the clever ladies, coping with luncheon parties, cooed and trilled over the latest Bodley Head volume and the current number of *The Yellow Book* ... Nothing had changed in his publisher's technique. After a superb meal at the Café Royal, preferably when a second liqueur brandy had been accepted, there would be a slight shift in his manner, urbane but seigneurial. Out of his pocket would come a contract, originally designed to keep poets in garrets—thirteen copies to count as twelve, a possible rise from 10% to 12½% after 10,000 had been sold, first refusal of the next four books, and an advance of £50—hm., well—even £75. But he was a good host and had many fascinating anecdotes.'

For some writers, Lane worked hard in what he felt to be the right quarters. After André Maurois had scored a great success with humorous evocation of Anglo-French co-operation on the Western Front, *The Silence of Colonel Bramble*, Lane took him up seriously, for example, lobbying both Asquith and Ramsay MacDonald on Maurois's behalf, and evidently treating Maurois himself without the assorted delays and muddles of which so many of his authors complained. Perhaps Lane saw in Maurois a successor to Anatole France. Nor was his judgment confounded by the success of *Ariel* (translated by that *Yellow Book* survivor, Ella d'Arcy) in 1924—which indeed became the first Penguin to be issued by The Bodley Head—sealing an amiable relationship which was to endure until Maurois' death in 1967.

Altogether less amiable was the relatively brief association of Agatha Christie with The Bodley Head, which has become a sort of legendary exemplar of how not to handle an author—and certainly not this author, who, although occasionally pleased, was quite a match for The Bodley Head's sharp if haphazard way of treating her. Devonshire-bred like Lane, though with a genteel rather than an agricultural background, Agatha Christie was only seventeen when, challenged by her sister to write a better crime story than the one she was criticising, she came up with *The Mysterious Affair at Styles*. It was rejected by many publishers, including Hodder & Stoughton and Methuen. The Bodley Head had already ventured into the field of detective-story publication, and presumably the young Agatha's (by now Mrs Christie) manuscript arrived at Vigo Street to be added to the pile of possibles for the genre. Or indeed perhaps it was not thought of at all, since nothing was heard of it for two years. In 1919 she received a summons from Lane, and found him, 'a small man with a white beard, behind a desk in a roomful of pictures, looking Elizabethan, as if he should have been a portrait himself, with a ruff around his neck.' He proposed to publish *The Mysterious Affair at Styles* and offered her a ten per cent royalty on sales over 2,000 copies and on United States sales over 1,000, fifty per cent of any serial or dramatic rights and an option for The Bodley Head on her next five books at a slightly increased royalty rate. At the same time he suggested a number of minor alterations, and a major alteration to the ending. Not long after she had accepted the proposal, Mrs Christie began to feel that she had been taken advantage of, a state of mind confirmed, no doubt, when almost two further years passed before *The Mysterious Affair at Styles* was in fact published—first in the USA—most successfully. The serial rights were sold for £50. By that time she had already learnt to protest at delays:

'Dear Mr. Willett: What about my book? I am beginning to wonder if it is ever coming out. I've nearly finished a second one by this time.'

That book, *The Secret Adversary*, was accepted in 1921 and when it was published in 1922 a keen businesswoman emerged in the correspondence:

'I see you have taken the selling price of *The Secret Adversary* in America as 7s. 6d. Actually it was $1.75, and the average rate of exchange over the period was $4.45 which works out at: 1255, at a price of $1.75, $2201.5 or £499. 5s. at 10%.'

In short she claimed she had been underpaid, having received £43 8s. when she should have received £45 10s. 3d.: 'a very small difference but it all helps in these hard times. Last time, you will remember, you agreed that this was the correct way of working out this sum. Also, I do not see in this account anything for the reprint of *The Mysterious Affair at Styles* brought out by the National Book Company of New York.'

Very soon, chafing at the five-book agreement and with growing experience of publisher's wiles, or at least this publishers' wiles, which she seemed to regard as more egregious than in fact they were, she was contemplating a move as soon as she could. With this end in view she tried a wile of her own. As well as *The Murder on the Links* (1923) and the short stories of *Poirot Investigates*, she submitted a new version of a girlhood fantasy *Vision*, telling her mother that she had sent it in only to make a third in the sequence. By this time she and Willett had locked horns. The Bodley Head refused to recognise *Visions* as the sort of book covered by their agreement, and tried also to insist that *Poirot Investigates*, being short stories already published in newspapers and periodicals, was also not to count as one of the five books stipulated in their agreement. They won on *Vision*, luckily, but lost on *Poirot Investigates*. Her self-confidence was great, and as her biographer Janet Morgan puts it, 'more and more sure of herself, she began to put her publisher in his place. She discovered that The Bodley Head was dependent on her and not the other way round.' When The Bodley Head began to raise the subject of her next contract, it was too late. By that time she had delivered *The Man in the Brown Suit*, but still had one book to go—which turned out to be *The Secret of Chimneys*—when she not only published a volume of poems (at her own expense) with Geoffrey Bles, but signed a contract with Collins, and remained with them for the rest of her life, though not without occasional dissatisfaction on both sides.

She still retained one link with The Bodley Head, in the person of Allen Lane. She had met him by chance when calling at Vigo Street to discuss the jacket of *The Murder on the Links*; a warm and affectionate friendship sprang up between them. He frequently stayed with her in South Devon and was urged to borrow her Morris Minor. He failed to notice her growing attachment to Max Mallowan, the archaeologist, at the end of the 1920s, until she announced, in a letter from Edinburgh, that she was about to marry him: you have met him, she said, but as he never speaks you won't remember him. Professionally she agreed to *The Mysterious Affair at Styles* appearing in The Bodley Head's first and abortive shot at cheap paperbacks, and was quick to offer her books to Penguin, which Allen was to recognise by putting money into some of their archaeological expeditions, as well as buying her an annual Stilton cheese.

Meanwhile the working directors, with some help from Priestley, went on trying to widen the firm's horizons. The steady flow of often

highly readable novels continued—humorous, sophisticated, rural—
though most of them could have been written at any time during the
previous thirty years. The favourite old stagers—Stephen Leacock,
W. J. Locke (who died in 1930) and Muriel Hine—paid no attention
to the onset of the 1920s, though Ben Travers's six novels caught a
little of the winds of change in their exuberant sails—certainly more
than their stage versions, such as *Rookery Nook*. The appearance of
Gertrude Stein with *Three Lives* as early as 1920 signalled at least
an effort to embrace the avant-garde, though in 1923 the first of
Winifred Holtby's Bodley Head books, *Anderby Wold*, was a con-
tinuation of one of Lane's favourite genres, the regional social novel,
looking back to the nineteenth as much as forward to the mid-
twentieth centuries.

Elegant topographic books about London and the British regions,
such as Walter G. Bell's copious series, including *The Great Fire* and
The Great Plague, or Jessie Mothersole's *The Saxon Shore* or
Hadrian's Wall and Donald Maxwell's great output, such as
Unknown Sussex, continued placidly, as did those more adventurous
travellers' tales, such as *A Woman's Impressions of German New
Guinea* or the books of that industrious tropical tramp, Harry L.
Foster, or of that adventurous fellow of Wadham College, Oxford,
R. B. Townshend, with his *Tenderfoot* series. It was now that
Captain Monckton joined the list with his now classic *Some Experiences of a New Guinea Resident Magistrate*. These were occasionally
diversified by, for example, the at first anonymous Odette Keun (one
of H. G. Wells's tempestuous ladies) with *My Adventures in Bol-
shevik Russia* (1923). Lord Northcliffe's *My Journey Round the
World*, his last diary, edited by Cecil Harmsworth, proved unexpectedly well-written, and fitted well into John Lane's preferred category
of books 'gossipy, anecdotal and informative', if not particularly
concerned with another of the firm's favoured requirements, 'to
make us laugh'. And A. J. Evans's *The Escaping Club* joined *The
Road to En-Dor* as a best-seller and minor classic of the First World
War. A sturdy defence, too, was put up in *The Bodleian* of popularising biographies.

Poems

from William Blake's
Songs
of Innocence

*

Drawings by
Maurice
Sendak

THE BODLEY HEAD
LONDON

XIII. Title-page for The Bodley Head's booklet for 1967, one of a
series of booklets issued each year from 1961 to 1984. The drawing
was printed in sepia (*see Appendix*).

TWELFTH INTERNATIONAL CHILDREN'S BOOK FAIR

BOLOGNA
April 4 – 8, 1975

CHATTO, BODLEY HEAD, CAPE
LONDON

XIV. One of the two Quentin Blake drawings for the 1975 Bologna
Fair invitation card.

Reprints, alone or in series, abounded, as Lane senior had rather ruefully written to Guy Eglington. *The Sunday Times* was full of praise for The Novel Library, which among its 3s. od. wide-ranging nineteenth-century choices made yet another, still premature, effort to restore Trollope to popularity by including no fewer than thirteen of his works.

With all this going on, John Lane was firmly established as a front-rank general publisher. He was financially operating on a narrow margin, true; but after all he had brought into the firm £10,000 with Ronald Boswell, another £10,000 with Carr-Gomme, and was about to introduce another such sum with the Marquess of Northampton's cousin, Lindsay Drummond—and all this without losing control of the firm at that.

He reached the age of seventy with apparently undiminished vigour, mental and physical, yet some inner premonition prompted him one day to bring out, in his Bayswater house, 'an enormous cardboard box bulging with letters, photographs and relics of the people and places he had known as a boy'; and he also spoke, to Lewis May, grandson of the Devonshire cleric who had married Lane's parents, of his death as 'if not imminent, at all events not very remote'. Still, he was apparently as brisk as ever in manner and fertile in ideas when in January 1925 he went off as usual to the annual dinner of that French hospital of which he had long been a governor on the strength of his Huguenot origins. From the dinner he went to catch a late train to Brighton for the week-end. The weather was damp and foggy, the train late. Back in London after the week-end, he was plainly unwell and was persuaded to stay in bed. There he conducted business as far as possible normally, with bedside conferences and innumerable telephone calls. But pneumonia set in, and within a fortnight of his taking to his bed the Devonshire farmer's boy was dead, and newspaper placards proclaimed DEATH OF A FAMOUS PUBLISHER.

His will left almost everything to Annie; but he directed that all his portraits and engravings relating to Devonshire and Devonshire men should be offered to the Royal Albert Memorial Museum,

Exeter; all his books concerning Devon should be offered to the City Library, Exeter, or should it already have them, to equivalent institutions in Plymouth:

'I have always loved my native county of Devon, and in the glorious history of its sons I have ever found my greatest inspiration and a constant incentive to be worthy of them.'

He had already given one picture to the National Gallery; in his will he offered them two more of its choice. He had already given one portrait to the National Portrait Gallery, now he offered it two more English portraits of its choice. Five of the original Beardsley drawings already in the Brooklyn Museum, were to go to the National Gallery (two), the British Museum (one), the Victoria and Albert (one) and the Brighton Art Gallery (one).

His body was cremated at Golders Green, his spirit remembered at a memorial service in St James's, Piccadilly. His ashes were taken down to Hartland, and installed first by Annie beneath a granite cross bearing, along with his name, the inscription 'Nothing is here for tears', by the north porch of St Nectan's Church, Hartland: beautiful and familiar. Now a severe but fitting monument to the family marks the place. Inside the church, too, his widow placed a memorial tablet, later to be supplemented by the devoted Allen Lane with a tablet to Annie Lane, and now with tablets to the two other brothers. It is a high, windswept yet sheltered memorial.

17

The Whispering Gallery

In appointing Willett and Crockett as Chairman and Vice-Chairman, or rather letting it be known that they would succeed to those posts after his death, old John Lane presumably had the agreement of the other senior directors; if the usual practice of British business at the time had been followed, no doubt they, as the men with the money, would have taken over the official positions, leaving Willett and Crockett to do—as they did—most of the work. They themselves— Carr-Gomme, Boswell and Drummond—assumed the dignity, however modest, of becoming the heads of the firm.

They had, though, more to worry about than titular distinctions. It very soon became clear that the youngest director, and the founder's surrogate son, Allen Lane, was at twenty-four, already a man to be reckoned with. True, he had sedulously worked on his image as a playboy—which indeed he was, and remained so for over ten years, at home in white tie and tails in the London of the 1920s and 1930s. He cut a dash to some purpose. Ethel Mannin, a fairly 'advanced' novelist of the day, saw an extremely handsome man with fair curly hair across the crowded room at a PEN party, and asked her companion who it was. 'Why, that's Allen Lane,' she was told. She met him and formed a rapid friendship embracing uninhibited gin-swilling parties in the Thames Valley playground—so outwardly different from the relatively decorous and high-thinking Hindhead heights where so many of John Lane's authors mingled sex and seriousness a mere thirty-five years or so before.

But for all his social vitality, the boy from Bristol was determined to make his mark as a publisher. He revered his Uncle John, and intended to emulate him. They had much in common, including a perilous disregard for detail, but in his combination of inspirational leaps and caution he even outdid his exemplar, and certainly did so in that combination of cowardice and ruthlessness which so often marks dynamic personalities. He was no prude, but surely the old progressive Bodley Head was paid a back-handed compliment by that old enemy, Curtis Brown, when he submitted an extremely erotic manuscript with the comment that 'we think it will suit your list.'

Moreover, since memoirs, especially what were then thought indiscreet memoirs, were rapidly finding favour with the British reading public, The Bodley Head in 1926 may just have been the right house to receive the highly readable and exceptionally indiscreet memoirs of a certain retired diplomat. Young Lane, throwing his Uncle's caution to the winds, went with it to his co-directors. They, later professing to wish 'to give the boy every encouragement', approved the book for publication. In so doing they very nearly ruined the firm at a stroke (as opposed to letting it crumble away slowly), and would certainly have ended Allen's days here. If only one of them had checked with their carefully filed readers' reports: there they would have found cautionary words about a previous book submitted by the same author, *Parallel Portraits*:

'Undoubtedly clever and alert, but fundamentally unsatisfying . . . interesting and vigorously written: the manuscript should be examined with exceeding care, however, both for libels and faults of taste.'

The ostensible editor, Hesketh Pearson, had been an actor, and was certainly a spirited fantasist. The new manuscript brought to a credulous Allen Lane was *The Whispering Gallery: Being Leaves from a Diplomat's Diary*, which he claimed to have edited on behalf of the diplomat, whose name he was not at liberty to disclose. It contained recollections rendered verbatim of conversations with the Kaiser, Tsar Nicholas II, King Alfonso XIII of Spain, Lenin, Henry James, H. G. Wells, Hardy and dozens of other contemporary figures, literary and political, most of them portrayed in discreet caricature—but not so obviously as to blunt the excitement of an enterprising young publisher.

The invention had been largely written while Pearson was suffering frightful pain from an old war-wound in the head, which required the removal of a small piece of lead along with quantities of pus. The book had already been offered for serialisation to *The People*, a Sunday newspaper (today it would no doubt go to *The Sunday Times*) and indeed was to be published in the United States by Boni & Liveright, where certainly it sold briskly. John Willis Dunbar of Odhams asked him who was going to publish it in this country. Pearson replied that he hoped Thornton Butterworth, 'but they are very slow, and I am thinking of taking it away from them.' At this point Dunbar pointed him and his manuscript in the direction of Allen Lane. He also asked who was the diarist. 'Rodd,' replied Pearson. 'Who the Dickens is Rodd?' riposted Dunbar, and wrote the name down, having it seems never heard of this well-known Establishment figure, among other things a former British ambassador in Rome. Much later, asked why he had named Sir Rennell Rodd, Pearson said that, regarding the name as a mere formality, on the spur of the moment he couldn't think of any diplomatist less likely to have written such memoirs, and so gave his name as a joke.

To Allen, however, he maintained the air of exciting secrecy, as of course did Allen when reporting his thrilling find to the Board. Indulging the lad, as Boswell later claimed, the Board approved his proposal to publish, on stated terms. These were communicated to Pearson. Allen then suggested that as he was spending the week-end at Bognor, he should call in on Pearson on the way; they accordingly met for dinner at the Dog and Duck Inn, Pulborough. Pearson solemnly assured Allen that the diarist had agreed to the terms offered, and all went ahead. Perhaps Allen was beginning to have doubts; at any rate Dunbar, while giving a warm recommendation to Pearson as one of their contributors, offered the services of Odhams' legal man to check the manuscript—an offer evidently not accepted.

Pearson was then asked to get an indemnity against libel from the diarist. The latter, however, was said to have refused. Allen Lane's response was simply to assure Pearson that 'you can in the first place assure the Diarist that under no circumstances should we call upon him and you to go into the box in the event of a libel action being brought.' To this insane promise Pearson blandly replied that 'Your statement is in every way satisfactory to the Diarist and myself.'

The Bodley Head lawyer, evidently an ingenuous fellow, went through the manuscript, proposing only a little toning-down. Serialisation was again proposed, this time by *The Sunday Chronicle*, but in any case, the other Bodley Head directors were against it, though only on the grounds that it might well harm the sales of the book itself. Pearson, fantasising more extravagantly as time went by, professed to be, perhaps was, extremely angry and demanded that the £250 advance he claimed to be out of pocket as a result of the deal falling through should be refunded by The Bodley Head.

It came to nothing, even though Allen reported to Pearson that after much discussion the other directors had agreed to serialisation *after* publication. Allen then sent a proof of the book to *The Daily Telegraph*, assuring Clement Shorter (rightly, as it turned out) that he knew the author and including a formal statement that he could vouch for the book's authenticity.

Review copies were sent out, booksellers supplied in advance of publication on 19 November, 1926. As that unhappy date dawned, however, the heavens opened:

A SCANDALOUS FAKE EXPOSED

MONSTROUS ATTACKS ON PUBLIC MEN

REPUDIATIONS BY FIVE CABINET MINISTERS

Thus ran the headlines in *The Daily Mail*. A more cynical age, sixty years later, might shrug its shoulders and assume that any cabinet ministers probably would repudiate what they were supposed to have said. In fact, even then, the book was purchased in large quantities and made the firm a profit of more than £1000. Nevertheless, more attacks came from *The Observer* ('a reeking compost of garbage') and *The Times*, couched in the sort of language from which our pussy-footing age would probably recoil; and even, in ponderous solemnity from the Lord Chancellor, F. E. Smith, the Earl of Birkenhead (who might have been expected to enjoy this sort of trick), anxious to counter rumours that in fact he was the mysterious Diarist.

Immediately the attacks began two lists of questions were sent to The Bodley Head, one by *The Daily Mail*, the other by *The Morning Post*. These were given to Allen with instructions to get Pearson's answer. Willett had met Allen at his club that evening, and returned to Vigo Street to await Pearson's arrival. He came at about 11.30 p.m. and produced copies of a typewritten document, saying 'I have had an awful time with the Diarist . . . He is very excited and it is difficult to keep him to the point.' He added that as the Diarist's original (and understandably evasive) statement was in handwriting, he had been home to type out the copies.

Yes, but had he obtained answers to the Press questionnaire? 'I have obtained answers, but they are not for publication.' He then ran through the questions and gave verbally the Diarist's supposed replies. Willett said that he didn't know whether Pearson was in fact reading them or 'relying on memory'. He admitted to having inserted some picturesque details not at all in the diaries and dismissed accusations of mistakes in spelling and in French as 'obvious printers' errors'. As to Lord Balfour calling Lord Robert Cecil 'Robert', the Diarist had replied that he was being facetious, and when Lord Oxford denied ever having called Lloyd George David he was not addressing Lloyd George personally but addressing the company at an informal dinner-party. And when Churchill denied having dined with Asquith in the Spring of 1916, having been at the Western Front at the time, he forgot that he had been back in England half a dozen times on important business. And if they wanted confirmation that Tsar Nicholas II had had a youth flogged in front of his eyes, the Diarist suggested that they should consult Maxim Gorki, who had reported the same incident.

After listening to this considerable imaginative feat, delivered in the small hours after a trying day, poor Willett felt 'for the moment satisfied as to his genuineness and that *The Daily Mail* attack was unjustified.' And so, no doubt, exchanging mutual assurances, they all went home. Alas, worse was to follow, when *The Daily Mail* turned from attacking the book to attacking The Bodley Head, whose directors called a Saturday meeting (a sure sign of panic in a publisher's office) and demanded that both Allen Lane and Pearson should attend, and stopped the cheque for £225 already made out to the latter. First the question of withdrawing the book was discussed. Gentlemanly as ever, they decided that the Diarist must be consulted. Willett himself telephoned Pearson, asking him to make contact. Pearson cheerfully replied that he thought the Diarist would probably be quite glad to have the book withdrawn.

Four minutes later Pearson rang back. He had telephoned the Diarist's house; he was out of town but Pearson would 'get him long distance'. Meanwhile, he asked for the cheque made out to him on the previous night. Having conferred with his co-directors, Willett replied 'That will be all right.' Half an hour later Pearson rang again to say that he had got in touch with the Diarist, who was agreeable to the withdrawal of the book. Arrangements were at once put in hand to make the withdrawal effective after the week-end, and indeed to stop the reprint which had been ordered.

The farce gathered pace. On the following day (Sunday) the directors assembled gloomily in Vigo Street at 10.30 a.m. They then telephoned Pearson and requested his presence; he needed some persuasion but eventually agreed, in the event arriving at about noon. He was then told that they must have *some* evidence of the existence of the Diarist, proposing that he should write a letter to the Diarist in any terms he pleased and give it to Allen Lane for delivery as the only Board member who would know the name.

The game, it might have been thought, was up. But Pearson went on with the masquerade. After prolonged thought (his powers of invention again fully engaged) he said that this could not be done, as any such letter would be opened by a secretary whether marked

'Private' or not. But surely the secretary would not be in the country with the Diarist over the week-end? 'No,' said Pearson. Well then, he should write a letter to the address in the country to be delivered by Lane. 'That is impossible. I have sworn not to communicate with the Diarist by letter. I have never seen him at his own house. I have only met him at his club and at the flat of a friend of his who knows about the Diary. If I communicated with him by telephone the messages had to be cryptic.'

The distraught directors tried another tack, drawing his attention to certain passages in the book, especially the Preface. 'I wrote that Preface myself,' said Pearson—a statement which certainly had the merit of being true. Had the Diarist passed it? 'Yes.' Would he arrange an interview with the Diarist at which Allen could be present? 'No.' Would he telephone the Diarist with Allen listening? 'That could not be done.' Could not a letter be delivered through a third party? 'No.' What about a meeting between the Diarist, Pearson and Allen Lane at a third party's flat? 'No.' Willett then protested that 'If you will not do any of these things our Secretary will have to write to the man concerned, and deliver the letter in person.' 'That, of course,' warned Pearson, 'would be much worse.' The only suggestion Pearson would consider was that he should show Allen a cheque for two-thirds of the money ($£225$) drawn by Pearson in favour of the Diarist, and bearing the latter's endorsement.

At this point S. H. Crockett, the Trade Director, belatedly cast aside gentlemanly niceties and said, 'Well now, not to mince matters, *is* there a diarist?'

Pearson displayed signs of great indignation and cried, 'Of course there is.'

Crockett was not appeased. 'Did you write the book yourself?' 'Certainly not,' said Pearson, who then asked to speak privately to Allen Lane, and they went off to the Chairman's room.

When this pair came back, Pearson said that his position was that he would have The Bodley Head force the Diarist to start proceedings against The Bodley Head: in which case he Pearson would have to give evidence and the name of 'the author' would have to be disclosed. But in that case, added Pearson, 'I should deny that I ever gave you the name.'

The other directors being apparently struck dumb—even Carr-Gomme, who, not surprisingly, as a politician had opposed publication from the start—Crockett reacted sharply to this threat and asked, 'Would you throw us over?' And Pearson replied, barefaced: 'Yes, I should be forced to do so.'

The meeting adjourned for a lunch, for which few can have had much appetite, Crockett demanding that when they re-assembled Pearson should bring any correspondence between him and the Diarist.

When they did resume, with The Bodley Head's solicitor present, Pearson said that after giving Crockett's demand some thought, he could not comply with it. 'What?' said Crockett. 'Do you mean that you are not able to find *any* document connecting you with the Diarist?' 'No,' replied Pearson, 'I knew I had nothing—everything has been destroyed.'

Crockett said that they must make a statement to the Press. Pearson suggested a joint statement, but after some private discussion, the Board said No, and also demanded that Allen should disclose the Diarist's name. He said he couldn't, but after taking his solicitor's advice, agreed to do so. It was Sir Rennell Rodd, he said, adding that he had been to see Rodd, who had denied all connection with the book—a fact evidently known to Allen throughout the meeting.

After that Black Sunday had passed, Willett immediately stopped the cheque already given to Pearson, and wrote abject letters to *The Daily Mail* and elsewhere, shovelling all the blame on 'our junior director' and expressing horror that Allen should himself, without consultation, have written letters giving his personal guarantee of the book's probity. Then the Board lost its head altogether. In a desperate measure to retrieve the firm's reputation (and not to exact revenge) they had Pearson arrested on a charge of obtaining (or attempting to obtain, since he received none) money on false pretences.

He was duly, and by arrangement, arrested at his solicitor's office by Detective-Inspector John Howell, and came up before the magistrate at Marlborough Street Police Court on 26 November, 1926, before appearing before a judge and jury at the London Sessions on 26 January, 1927. His family rallied round; his wife, as Pearson flippantly put it, 'did the Roman-wife touch;' his brother put up money for a £1,000 bail and obtained the services of Sir Patrick Hastings, a most spectacular Counsel, for the defence. Everybody, including his Counsel, urged him to plead guilty, and thus almost certainly to be bound over. Pearson refused to do so.

Hastings, therefore, decided to besmirch the publishers, naming especially *Jurgen* and the series of classical translations illustrated by Jean de Bosschère: Ovid, Balzac's *Contes Drolatiques* and, worst of all, *The Golden Ass* of Apuleius. All in all, Allen Lane did not cut a very convincing figure in the witness-box. He laid himself open to some scathing comment on the inattention with which he seemed to have read Sir Rennell Rodd's entry in *Who's Who*, and by his statement that until trouble came neither he nor, he thought, any other director save Crockett, had read it all. Pearson, however, when asked by Sir Henry Curtis Bennett why he had persisted in lying, simply replied, 'Because I was mad.'

Disapproving of The Bodley Head's erotica, and disarmed by Pearson's belated candour, the jury took very little time to arrive at their verdict: Not guilty. It was a bad moment for The Bodley Head, and a worse one for Lane. (No wonder that more than forty years later, when he invited prosecution over *Lady Chatterley's Lover*, he preferred not to go into the witness-box, or into court at all.)

Nor was the matter ended, for Pearson hastened to bring an action against The Bodley Head. In a last flicker of defiance, the firm's solicitor replied to Pearson's legal adviser:

'If your client or yourselves on his behalf are of the opinion that he has any claim for damages in respect of his recent prosecution at the London Sessions, you will, of course, take such action as you may consider proper. We wish, however, on behalf of our clients to make it perfectly clear that in no circumstances will they admit that such a prosecution was unjustified, nor will they consent to pay a farthing to your client in respect of his pain or suffering or expense, all of which he brought entirely upon himself. Indeed our clients and ourselves are considerably surprised that your client should have the hardihood to put forward such a claim.'

Brave words. But within a few weeks they did pay him £416. 8s. 1d., being the total profits (heavily net, one suspects) made on sales of the book before it was withdrawn. And, the firm defiantly quacked, if that wouldn't satisfy him, they would go to arbitration. Apparently it did satisfy him.

The truth about who knew what in this comical case we shall never know. But as late as 1968 Allen Lane wrote to a retired army officer who had suggested that the Diarist, however edited, must have been a real man:

'I think there is no question that Hesketh Pearson did write the book himself. He was a very well-informed man and I must say that despite the fact that the book got us into a great deal of hot water, I always had a high regard for him.'

Which is more than he had for his fellow-directors.

18

The Lean Thirties

When John Lane died, the firm had re-assembled itself—but still along the old lines. Basil Willett, bristling behind pince-nez glasses, who had been appointed Vice-Chairman by Lane, presided as Chairman over the editorial scene in Vigo Street.

Many books in the John Lane tradition were yet to be published: two elaborate volumes, for example, of Giambattista Basile, *Pentamerone*, translated from a modern Italian version by the eminent philosopher Benedetto Croce, five lavish volumes on the island of Chios by Philip Argenti, no fewer than ten handsome tomes offering the *Collected Works* of Lieutenant-Colonel Sir Reginald Rankin, Bart., were all likely to have been subsidised from outside. But in the tradition of *Topee and Turban* books continued to be published with titles like *Ten Weeks with Chinese Bandits*, or *Thirty Years in the Jungle*, or *Ju-Ju and Justice in Nigeria*.

A young American writer, Milton Waldman, who worked for J. C. Squire on *The London Mercury*, and who had been engaged as a reader, was invited to edit a series of biographies of great British seamen; the first volume in The Golden Hind series, E. F. Benson's *Sir Francis Drake*, appeared in 1927. Milton Waldman himself contributed a biography of *Sir Walter Raleigh*. (Thirty years later the link was re-established when his son went to work for The Bodley Head's new owner, Max Reinhardt, and proved to be one of the firm's longest-serving editors.)

Other series of new titles, too, seemed to keep alive the spirit of John Lane: such were for instance The Quill Library—the letters of, among others, Steele, Sterne, and Burns—or The Bluestocking Letters of George Eliot, Hannah More, Mary Russell Mitford and

Mrs Thrale. Montagu Slater's Barnstormer series began with *Maria Marten*, *Sweeney Todd* and *The Drunkard*—and ended in 1946 with Slater's libretto for Benjamin Britten's *Peter Grimes*. The English Literature Library was an anthologised illustrated survey under the categories of Romance, Essayists, Realism and Allegory, the first English novels under the title 'The Comedy of Life', domestic novels (*Balls and Assemblies*, *Romance in History*, *Rogues and Vagabonds*). The Bodley Head Library admirably reprinted at 3s. 6d. (in parallel with Cape's Travellers Library and Chatto & Windus's Phoenix Library) some of their best books. The Masters of Modern Art series seemed to be looking backward, with among its subjects Blake, Constable, Corot, Gauguin and Manet. The Bodley Head Mysteries tried to impart some cohesion to a miscellaneous crew, and the Week-end Library was a rather up-market catch-all.

An eleven-volume uniform edition of Disraeli's works kept the flag of the nineteenth century flying, as The Bodley Head had repeatedly done for Trollope; *The Bodleian* doggedly proclaimed, some fifty years ahead of its time, that 'the nineteenth century is at last coming into its own,' just as the spirit of the 1920s was reaching its peak. And the death of Flora Annie Steel (1847–1929) prompted the firm gallantly to reissue four of her Anglo-Indian, mildly feminist novels, one a year for four years, beginning with *The Builder* in 1928.

Who will recall the thirteen titles by Mrs Fred Reynolds published during the 1920s and 1930s, or the ten titles of Neville Brand? It is probably due to the generous memory of Graham Greene that the adventurous fare of Marjorie Bowen's fifteen titles have kept a tenuous grasp on the public attention. (It was, the more famous novelist claims, a reading of her romance *The Viper of Milan* which largely determined his own ambition to become a writer.) The five volumes of T. O. Beachcroft's admirable short stories (e.g. *A Young Man in a Hurry*) have vanished, along with volumes by many other excellent writers of the time, not necessarily published by The Bodley Head, such as Stacy Aumonier or A. E. Coppard.

A French novelist strongly recommended for publication by André Maurois—whose perceptive biography of *Disraeli* in 1927 enhanced his reputation as interpreter of English history, was Georges Bernanos. His novels, including *The Star of Satan* (1927) and *The Diary of a Country Priest* (1937) were rooted in French Catholicism; their publication bore witness to The Bodley Head's eclectic tastes.

On the home front, Phyllis Bottome produced *The Advances of Harriet* in 1933 and a best-seller, *Private Worlds*, the next year. Sixteen of C. S. Forester's books came from The Bodley Head, all before his famous stories of Captain Horatio Hornblower, RN, but including his spectacular start with *Payment Deferred* in 1926, *Brown on Resolution* in 1929 and *The Gun* in 1933, as well as a travel book reflecting Forester's pleasure in inland waterways, *The Voyage of The Annie Marble*. Forester read for the firm too, but not to much effect. Over something called *Tranquil God* he pursed his lips: it concerned itself with the sexual adventures of schoolboys, and was 'distinctly low in matter and manner, and the work of a very young author'. The work does not appear to have been acquired.

With the appearance of *Brown on Resolution* in 1929 The Bodley Head resorted to what was surely, and still is, an unusual approach to trade promotion. A full-page advertisement in *The Bookseller* pointed out that:

'In spite of our best efforts we have to confess that notwithstanding an almost unanimous chorus of praise from the newspapers and large sums spent on advertising we have been unable to put Mr. Forester across. Can the trade help?'

A prize of £5 was offered for the best suggestion sent in by a member of the book trade: a modest bait, since had a good idea emerged (of which of course there is no evidence) it would in due course have been worth thousands of pounds to the publisher and to Forester. Perhaps it is no wonder that Forester went elsewhere with the Hornblower books, both parties having presumably lost heart.

Several publishers had already lost interest in, or patience with, the unstoppable John Cowper Powys before he came to The Bodley Head in the early 1930s, to remain with them with both fiction and

(231)

non-fiction for fifteen years, though Jonathan Cape had taken *Wolf Solent* and *A Philosophy of Solitude* and Victor Gollancz *In Defence of Sensuality*, and others were to join the club. He now has a considerable cult standing, which ranges from serious academics to even more serious, or at any rate earnest, lay readers; but at the time of their publication these magniloquent, mythic, tempestuous and writ-inviting tomes demanded, despite their overall success, a bold and patient publisher. The Bodley Head began with a bang, issuing *A Glastonbury Romance* (1933); this, though a West Country book, aroused exceptional interest in Norfolk, according to a Norwich bookseller.

Powys followed it with a striking autobiography written when he was sixty-one, with another thirty-two voluble years to go. These years included, from Vigo Street, *Jobber Skald*, a toned down version under threat of another libel action, of what was eventually published as *Weymouth Sands* in 1963. He and The Bodley Head had already had to settle out of court with a man who claimed to have been libelled in *A Glastonbury Romance*. Powys thought he had invented a West Country businessman who used a private aeroplane and was commercially interested in the Cheddar Gorge in Somerset, to which he was in the habit of taking girls. Soon—and the scene springs vividly to mind—a letter arrived from a West Country solicitor. It was crisp and to the point. After summarising the situation, the letter went on:

'My client is a West Country businessman, he uses an aeroplane to travel about and he is commercially interested in the Cheddar caves. What about it?'

'Our hair stood on end,' said Boswell, recalling the moment. Powys disclaimed all knowledge of such a man. Boswell could get nothing out of him; generously, and no doubt rightly, he assumed that 'this happens with authors—he has read some article and it is filed away in some corner of his mind, and then fished up out of nothing with the associations gone.' Yet the fact that the businessman threatened legal action (but was happy to settle out of court rather than have his reputation publicly cleared) at least suggests that, whatever Powys's sources, 'the associations' had not gone.

Undeterred, however, by such expensive mishaps, The Bodley Head went on publishing him with *The Art of Happiness*, with his tumultuous historical novel, *Owen Glendower*, and with studies of *Rabelais* and *Dostoevsky*, until 1948.

Among what the old firm would have liked to call *belles lettres*, although the term was rapidly passing out of favour, was a strong manger of fodder to feed the insatiable British appetite for sanitised ruralism, always a favourite with John Lane—though to be fair he had long before published the autobiography of a farm labourer which by no means ignored the sordid.

Among what might almost be called the evangelicals were, over the years, no fewer than sixteen titles from the fervent pen of Llewelyn Powys, most of them essays, nature-imbued, which had already appeared in newspapers and magazines, notably on the back page of what was then *The Manchester Guardian*. His output was almost matched by a dozen volumes from Adrian Bell, again mostly culled, if that is not too brutal a word, from pieces in *The Eastern Daily Press* of Norwich: *Apple Acre* and *Silver Ley*, as titles, set the tone.

At the far end of the spectrum, two volumes of H. L. Mencken's *Americana* sharpened the tone, and Gertrude Stein reappeared with a strange farrago, *Useful Knowledge* and the more durable *Auto-biography of Alice B. Toklas*. American humour, an interest of the firm for forty years, since its championing of Charles Dana Gibson, revived with the introduction to Britain of, among others, Robert Benchley. But a new approach, at least in draftsmanship, had already been launched with the recruiting of a visionary American cartoonist, Peter Arno.

A veteran, if restive, associate of the firm, as odd-job boy, editor of *The Bodleian*, translator, biographer and reader, Lewis May, made a surprising re-entry in the early 1930s. In what one would have thought a markedly unsympathetic climate inside the firm, May not only wrote the celebratory but not totally uncritical *John Lane and the Nineties* but had also produced *God and the Universe: a Christian Symposium*, *An English Treasury of Religious Prose* and *The Oxford Movement: a Layman's Estimate*, all in the early 1930s.

The firm was indeed devoting more attention to the twin pre-occupations of religion and sex. The latter as a vehicle for feminism and changing social circumstances had of course always been of interest to John Lane, and had been the subject of much controversial fiction he acquired in the 1890s; and as early as 1924 the firm began (and continued until 1946) to publish fact, such as the preoccupations of Wilhelm Stekel with such matters as *Impotence in the Male*, *Sadism and Masochism* and *Peculiarities of Behaviour*. In 1934 *Sex in Marriage* was introduced by Ernest & Gladys Groves, and soon the name of Havelock Ellis was appearing—with *My Confessional*, obtained from him by Allen Lane after a strong entreaty for a 'sex book'. Havelock Ellis must have been satisfied with the promotion of his book, for he went on to deliver four volumes of a *Study in the Psychology of Sex*.

Verse, the very foundation of The Bodley Head's original success, had taken a back seat, though in 1935 the decline was at least checked by the admirable translations of Heine done by Humbert Wolfe, if not by many volumes of poems by the American Archibald Mac-Leish. Indeed, in 1934 began a series, *The Year's Poetry*, which represented a brave shot at invading the pitch already occupied by competing hucksters, particularly Faber & Faber (to which, to its great advantage, T. S. Eliot had escaped from the bank in which he worked for so long). Five volumes of *The Year's Poetry* appeared, the last in 1938, and The Bodley Head lost money on every one of them. It was edited throughout by Denys Kilham Roberts, a saturnine and most engaging rogue spirit, who for many years ran The Society of Authors, when not at a race-meeting. His co-editors were, variously, Gerald Gould, John Lehmann and Geoffrey Grigson; the first was also a long-standing novel reviewer in *The Observer*, now perhaps better-known as the father of Michael Ayrton, polymath painter and sculptor. The two latter, both highly respected figures as poets themselves, remained as austere judges for many years to come.

Still, some poets, however narrow their talent or wide their pretensions, had their appeal: for example, Ruby Boardman, a French-based portrait painter and poet, originally from San Francisco for whom The Bodley Head published two volumes of verse. Evidently (like Muriel Hine) she was a bewitching if demanding lady. She wrote a series of exuberant letters to Boswell, sometimes complaining—as when her book failed to arrive either in Paris or in San Francisco in time for Christmas, 'and all our efforts (going about the shops personally, etc.) were of not much use'—but more often asking assistance in matters of little concern to her publishers. When she had an exhibition of her paintings—she appears to have moved mostly in the Amazonian circle of Paris-based *femmes du monde*—coming up at a London gallery:

'I would be so very grateful to you, if you would come to make up and send me a list of 40 London authors (playwrights preferred) and poets, with addresses complete, to whom I may send a very attractive announcement of my W. Gallery show. I have the social and painter folk all down on my list, and I haven't the writers round-up. And as there are some lovely pictures of lively exotic ladies—looking mostly as though fished out of the Seine—I would like writer-folk of exotic quality to have a look at them—being sure, by the grace of God, that they would each feel a tingle of ecstasy in looking upon these faces, and would go home and write the better for feeding the lust of the eyes.

'Today I am posting you a photograph of one of the portraits in question. I thought that if you propped it up on your desk, one day, for a few minutes, and took a look at it by the light of the leaded windows at your immediate left hand, and strengthened by the good company of Japanese prints behind you, you would discover in your mind, directly, the men or women of letters I should so like to come and see my show . . .

'And are we, this summer, to have another modest bottle of champagne en tete a tete? I am bringing my sailor to London to cook for me in a little flat, this summer, on account of my health.'

But of course there was a price to pay—the list, duly sent, was the least of it. The lady also got Boswell to organise London-printed invitations to her show and despatch them to, among others, Lady Diana Cooper, Gertrude Lawrence, Somerset Maugham, Beverley Nichols, Margaretta Scott, Noel Coward, Gwen ffrangcon-Davies, Peter Godfrey, Komisarjevsky and Daphne du Maurier. He was also to send twenty invitations with a copy of her poems and photographs (a different photograph for each recipient) including one of herself with Kiki de Montparnasse, 'who is, as you can see, the fat girl of the party, but as handsome as can be, none the less—quite like an archaic Cretan lady.' No wonder she wrote that the invitation 'means more to me than the exhibition itself.' She was painting the British actress Lydia Sherwood, and wanted copies of her book also sent to Tallulah Bankhead and Madge Garland.

She was also a little concerned about the order of her verses in the book: the 'half-weary regret of "Margaret" and "From Sappho" to come last'. She had evidently already exhausted Willett, having asked him to buy for her (taking the cost off her royalties!) 'a small jewel-box so that she can pretend to her mother that she bought it for her in London'. When she wrote apprising him of a further book, he passed her on to Lindsay Drummond, who passed her on to Boswell, to whom the poetess wrote from St Tropez:

'We have had a most awful storm here. The country is streaked with cascades of fresh water running from the river to the sea. The sea itself is giving up hourly corpses of pigs, cows and cats, tables, picture-frames and lumber. I am sitting up in bed in my large, white-washed bedroom, an olive-wood fire burning, bitch and pups steaming before it, and my Greek cook (pederaste) reports from time to time on the latest corpse or art object washed ashore. At the present moment he is sitting on the floor between my bed and the fire, delightedly adjusting a very handsome mahogany shelf-clock which came ashore, glass face, works, chimes, all intact but very wet. "This is my gift to Mademoiselle," says he. "It will be very useful for the studio. Behold the *motif* of bronze. Hark! a musical chime it is not. I shall spend 25 francs of my own to have it set going by the jewellers . . ." Thank you so very much for all your patience, kindness and courtesy. I think I must have been very trying, having always *trop d'idées*. No-one has ever borne with me more gently and to my delight than have you.'

Irresistible, no doubt, and far removed from a cramped office in Vigo Street. But was it worth it? Not in publishing terms.

Hardly had the firm tried to reorganise itself after John Lane's death before a series of national disasters broke over it, like a frightful wave playing with a frail craft before capsizing it. The Coal Strike, the General Strike, world depression, national financial collapse and unemployment—and, especially for Boswell (with his continuing German connections), the rapid increase of anti-semitism in Germany, as the Nazis crept up on power.

By the beginning of the 1930s The Bodley Head was already in a pickle. Life was by no means all happy moments sipping champagne *en tête-à-tête* with a fascinating woman. Boswell was pleased to report progress in getting hold of Walt Disney pop-up books— *Three Little Pigs*, *The Big Bad Wolf*, *Lullaby Land*, *The Pied Piper*— boldy advertised as the Silly Symphonies, with 12 pages in colour and 45 in black and white, 10 inches by 8 inches, at 2s. 6d. each. They did indeed sell well, but were not at all the sort of thing that the idealist (as he described himself) Boswell had in mind when he came into publishing, choosing The Bodley Head because he felt, not unreasonably, that John Lane had been a force for good in British life. Allen Lane's mild radicalism pleased him too.

Now his idealism had tougher meat to feed on. Since the Revolution he had always been interested in Soviet Russia, though he was never a Communist. Then there was India, the new India, so different from those amiable paternalistic travellers' tales. It so happened that Boswell's wife was friendly with that ultimately ill-starred successor to Shaw as a St Pancras vestry man, Krishna Menon, and he was friendly with Pandit Nehru; thus (in 1936) at its last gasp, The Bodley Head published the first volume of his *Autobiography*. They were lucky to get the first book; whether Nehru was is another matter. It had been originally offered to Allen & Unwin, but that firm, fearing that it would be banned in India, offered only a modest advance of £50. The Bodley Head offered £250. In the event it sold immensely well, in India as well as in Britain and America. But The Bodley Head was so hard pressed financially that royalties on the first year's sales went unpaid. With additional chapters from time to time, it went on selling merrily.

Interest in the Soviet Union in fact first brought in Hubert Griffith's *Seeing Soviet Russia* in 1932, more personal than the discouragingly titled *Soviet Trade and World Depression*, by H. R. Knickerbocker, in the previous year. But the successful connection with this celebrated roving reporter of the New York *Evening Post* next year brought his *Germany: Fascist or Soviet?* and *Can Europe Recover?*, 1934, *Will War Come to Europe?*, and Edgar Mowrer's *Germany Puts the Clock Back*, famous in its day.

Fascism had already made its mark in Italy—and if to its German version Britain was slow to react, this was not true of Ronald Boswell, and therefore not true of The Bodley Head. By 1934, in fact, it must have seemed to some that The Bodley Head was publishing little else but anti-Nazi books, and indeed several members of the firm, some of them quite lowly, were put on a black list by the *Völkischer Beobachter* of Munich. In 1934 the firm published 'a pictorial and biographical study of the leaders of Nazi Germany', *Heil!* Among much else of a disparaging nature it contained a rather brave German joke:

'Q: What is an Aryan?
A: Tall like Goebbels, slim like Goering, blond like Hitler, masculine like Roehm.'

(The last-named shortly to vanish spectacularly because of his flagrant homosexuality). Then came Alfred Apfel's *Behind the Scenes of German Justice*, the compilation of documents testifying to *The Reichstag Fire Trial* (1934), and Leopold Schwarzschild's *End to Illusion*.

Probably, in an indirect way, another of Boswell's authors, whom he met by way of his German connections, was the storm-tossed dramatist Ernst Toller. The most notable of the German Expressionists, along with Georg Kaiser and the aptly named Unruh, Toller began writing his plays during the First World War while imprisoned as a pacifist. Ten years later, with many plays behind him, which favoured the group over the individual but approved of non-violent revolution, he was in prison again, having taken part in yet another failed *Putsch*. On release, he came to England, became a British citizen and wrote *I Was a German*. Later The Bodley Head published some of his plays—Boswell obtained the services of the young Edward Crankshaw as translator. Toller, an excitable man and a rabble-rousing speaker, then went on to the United States and there committed suicide in 1939. *Post hoc* but not *propter hoc*, one hopes.

By way of keeping some sort of balance were Louis Corey's *The Decline of American Capitalism* and two books on the alarming figure of Stalin, one by Essad Bey, the other by the French author of a notably bitter First World War book, *Le Feu*, Henri Barbusse.

It also tried to interest readers in the real world with yet another series, The Twentieth Century Library: Eric Gill on Art, Norman Bentwich on the Jews, Naomi Mitchison on the Home, Winifred Holtby on Women, Komisarjevsky on the Theatre among many others, who included an active Communist, Ralph Fox, on Communism. (The Bodley Head also published, appropriately for a man enthralled by Stalin's world, his biography of Genghiz Khan.)

It would be agreeable to report that these well-intentioned books awoke the British to the several perils and problems of the time. In fact, all they brought about was the impending collapse of the firm. Even Albert Einstein's *The World As I See It* sold miserably; *Hitler Re-Arms* achieved in 1934 a sale of fifteen (15) copies. Struggling out of the Great Depression, Britain in the early 1930s recognised the truth of these anxious warnings—and there were plenty more in other publications—but preferred to think of something else, or better still not think at all.

The firm's financial position weakened steadily. Boswell, whose worthwhile books had contributed so handsomely to the firm's losses, sold his (or rather his father's) shares, originally worth £10,000, for a derisory 5s. a share. Still an idealist, he eventually went to work on the administrative side of the BBC, which he rightly regarded as a worthwhile form of public service, and remained there happily until his retirement in 1960.

His shares were bought by Lindsay Drummond, who—connections with Drummond's bank notwithstanding—thus surely confirmed the friendly judgment of what may be called the lower deck of the firm: that he was too good-natured a man, too much of a decent English gentleman, ever to succeed in the cut-throat world of publishing. Drummond was not really a success, either, as Advertising Director, apt to spend the firm's money on small advertisements in what a colleague unkindly called 'all sorts of useless provincial papers and half-baked literary journals'. Very tall, and straight-backed, with a greying, rather military, moustache, and amiability personified, he eventually left to set up his own publishing house; but that failed too.

The other investing director, Carr-Gomme, was widely regarded as a sleepy sleeping-partner. He did in fact appear to edit, or at any rate sling together, *The Bodleian*, by now a half-hearted quarterly in a much smaller format. When this change was brought about, in 1932, The Bodley Head indulged in another of its whimsical fits of self-deprecation, as it had when asking the bookselling trade to provide ideas for selling the novels of C. S. Forester. This time it announced that though it was usual for its promoters to claim that the first issue of a new, or newly-styled, publication had been an immense success, welcomed everywhere with open arms, they candidly admitted that with the new *Bodleian* this had not been the case, and asked its readers to suggest means of making it better. Three years later it ceased publication, and with it went the old-style

Bodley Head as John Lane had established it—a firm at first specialising in belles lettres, then capturing the general reader, but always designed for a leisured and essentially leisurely world.

19

The Brothers Lane

Despite his setback over *The Whispering Gallery*, Allen Lane's resilience had remained unimpaired, though a good deal of his energy was directed towards the life of a man about town—he needed some distraction from the suspicion of his colleagues.

Nor did he forget that he had two younger brothers, who could certainly be called in as allies, even though neither was as committed as Allen to publishing, or to the memory of old John Lane. The senior directors looked on apprehensively from their quaint and crowded refuges in Vigo Street and Brewer Street (a few minutes walk away, on the other side of Regent Street). Their misgivings were not allayed when first Allen, then Richard, moved in with old Mrs Lane at Lancaster Gate Terrace. And hardly had the furore over the Hesketh Pearson affair begun to abate than she died, leaving to Allen all the shareholding in the firm which had been left to her by John Lane. Though he did not yet control the company, he was clearly becoming even more of a force to be reckoned with.

While Mrs Lane's estate was being wound up, on both sides of the Atlantic, the brothers went on living at Lancaster Gate Terrace in stuccoed, Forsythian splendour, and gave lavish parties, entertaining such new luminaries as Beverley Nichols (also from Bristol) and the glamorously emancipated Ethel Mannin, Mrs Porteous. She became friendly with all the brothers, though her way of life was alarming to these would-be sophisticates:

'Renée tells me Dick [Lane] called on Monday [she wrote]—it is never wise to call unexpectedly—I am so liable to be caught in 'a compromising situation' . . . and that would be an embarrassment all round.'

Not that her sexual freedom was altogether consistent. Allen sent her James Hanley's *Boy*, about a young sailor on a merchant ship, for a professional opinion:

'A terrible book . . . no amount of cutting or editing could possibly make it publishable—the whole book is nothing but buggery and brothels and filth and horror piled upon each other in endless repetition . . . I don't believe in the author, nobody comes alive.'

There perhaps she was wrong, even though the book was prosecuted when it did get published. Allen presumably thought well enough of it to become involved with its author in a plentiful correspondence full of pain (on Hanley's side), mostly about money and his disastrous family.

Appeal follows appeal: 'It was real nice of you to write me like that, I appreciate it. It is very kind of you to offer to help' . . . 'I am moved to write you once more to ask if you can still see your way to help my people.' He is 'hoping to work on a political book with [D.H.] Lawrence,' and 'I think it is very decent of you to help my mother—and if you could let me have that £50 before next Wednesday I would be more than grateful. I hate even reminding you of it once more—but you advised me to.' Three weeks later: 'If I wrote to you concerning the promised help for my mother it was only at your suggestion . . . It is rather disappointing to me (how much to my mother God knows) but thinking the matter over I have decided not to bother any further.' And then, even more painfully, 'I feel like a damned bum standing here in your office, but because I know that things are really bad, I hope you will see me. If of course you feel you can't now, I won't trouble to come in.'

It is more than possible to feel for both sides in this wretched little story, for the desperate beggar and the harassed publisher for whom too 'things are really bad'. As it happens, Ethel Mannin seems to

(243)

have revised her opinion of *Boy*, not least in the light of 'the sex book I'd thought of writing'; and there were other distractions. Ethel Mannin sends a postcard from Jersey where she is with, of all people, her husband, and adds a postscript: 'Did you go to the Spencers' vice-party? How are things. Love to Dick. Love E.M.' Then there was that bizarre lady, Elsa Lanchester, who married that equally bizarre actor, Charles Laughton; she continued to write warm and lively letters to Allen even when she had gone to live in California. And there was Peggy Wood, singing actress, who caused Allen to patronise Noel Coward's *Bitter-Sweet* many times. And of course there was Agatha Christie, bubbling away in her letters about painting the garden furniture green with her then teenage daughter, and what a wonderful year 1930 was (no doubt it was, for her). It seems likely that Allen, like Uncle John, though delighting in female company, was not so much a Don Juan as a ladies' man. He certainly set out, in those relatively earlier days, to be his authors' friend as well as their publisher, whatever their sex—a tricky business, since in the nature of things some were likely to respond better than others. Usually he was successful, for his eye, if beady, was bright and invigorating, and he and his brothers all became welcome presences around the smarter Bohemia.

Dick Lane, on leaving school, worked first at an agricultural research station, then went off to work as a jackaroo in Australia. At one point his mother, or so his father wrote to Allen, entertained the notion that the entire family should emigrate to Australia, an idea that vastly amused his father, but even in his frustrated condition did not appeal to Allen. In fact, Dick returned to England just in time for the General Strike of 1926. Allen first found him a job in a north London bookshop; on a tiny salary he too maintained a high style of life.

When they eventually had to move out of Lancaster Gate Terrace, Dick first went off to live in the house of a friend (who worked for Chapman & Hall) in Hampstead. But soon all three brothers were sharing a series of far from luxurious flats in which they assiduously played up their landlords until they moved to a self-contained flat in

Talbot Square, north of Hyde Park and even nearer to Paddington and their Bristol home than had been Lancaster Gate Terrace. Here Allen, in pursuit of style, painted his room green and the three brothers wove daydreams about how to discomfit the senior directors.

It took some four years to get the younger brothers established in the firm. John, smaller and darker than his brothers, had come to London to work for the London and Lancashire Insurance Company. Dick wanted to be an actor, but had to give up the stage for a more secure job as secretary to A. J. A. Symons, then running the First Edition Club, an establishment the finances of which were even more precarious than those of The Bodley Head.

Needless to say, Dick had no qualification whatever for this bibliophile's delight, but he got on well with Symons (biographer of Frederick Rolfe and picturesque elder brother of Julian Symons, soon to become, with Geoffrey Grigson, a young and severe luminary of the poetic scene). He had helped Allen to dispose of John Lane's extensive library, which brought in more than £2,300. Perhaps Symons would gladly have helped Allen get rid, not only of Uncle John's books, but of his pictures, or what Allen supposed to be his pictures: it seems that publishers, having commissioned artists to illustrate books, bought the resulting pictures outright (perhaps they still do). At any rate Allen, without consulting the senior directors, sent every picture he could lay his hands on, whether from the Lane's household effects or from the cluttered office, to be sold at auction. As soon as the other directors discovered what was afoot, Allen was in trouble again. Solicitors' letters were exchanged, Counsel's opinion was taken; there was a long and irksome process of sorting out which pictures in fact were Allen's by inheritance, and which were the property of the firm.

Gradually the dispute died away. But Allen was in greater disfavour than ever with his co-directors; and for his part, was even more determined than ever to get rid of them. This was not as easy as it might seem; as the firm's turnover and its overdraft increased steadily together, the atmosphere in Vigo Street grew tenser. It was, however, diversified by a number of younger enthusiasts, mostly of Oxbridge descent, and few if any of them paid. Among those who actually were in receipt of a wage, however small, were two who were to play an interesting role: Edward Young, a youthful designer, and H. Arnold, a boy from South London who had been at pains to acquire some simple skills of an administrative kind which at that time, rare in the gentlemanly air of publishing, were to stand Allen in good stead in the early 1930s. There too was Frank Baker, office boy in Ben Travers's time before 1914, and now, as production manager, another of those one-eyed employees who, if not kings in this country of the blind, at least provided some framework of every-day competence.

There was a distinctly upstairs-downstairs relationship between Vigo Street and Brewer Street. For all its hugger-mugger partition-ing, its lost Adam fireplaces, its general clutter, Vigo Street kept its fallen dignity about it amid the discreet grandeur of Albany. In Brewer Street the two converted shopfronts, for all their brave dis-play of new Bodley Head titles, were unashamedly grimy and com-mercial. The ground floor was divided by a waist-high trade counter. The waiting-room was merely the street-side of the counter. Offices, mostly no more than cubby-holes, were patched up out of any avail-able corner. Up a spiral staircase from the middle of the packing-space the accounts were kept. Vast ledgers, some in pen and some in pencil, were pored over at high sloping desks by clerks on high stools in a tiny office. Parcels of books arriving from the binders were shovelled into a basement presided over by a retired sergeant-major.

One director, the persistent Crockett, presided over this Dickens-ian scene. He was a chunky, likeable Scot, who had begun his working life with two Edinburgh booksellers, Foulis's and Grants, then came to London to Stonehams, became The Bodley Head's London representative (or traveller) before old John Lane made him Trade Director. He was credited with a legendary feat: knocking down, during the General Strike of 1926, a picket who tried to stop him loading the firm's van (needless to say, The Bodley Head was totally non-unionised).

Crockett had his more persuasive side. One day the chief cashier offended a director of a large wholesale firm, seizing him by the arm and demanding to know why his firm had not paid its account. Voices were raised in anger. Crockett emerged from his little office, disengaged the visitor, led him back into relative, if cramped, privacy. They eventually emerged in a state of great affability, Crockett having extracted from the wholesaler a large order for 2s. novels, and a guaranteed date for settlement. On some afternoons, to the evident amusement of his junior staff, he left quite early, announcing in a loud voice that he was going over to Vigo Street and would be back at about five o'clock (the weekday office hours were from 9 a.m. to 6 p.m.). He may have visited Vigo Street, but why, the others wondered, did he take his golf clubs? And somehow he never did return at five o'clock. But in 1930, failing to follow doctor's orders, he died. Unusually for the period, and less than triumphantly for the firm, a woman took his place: Winnie Endicott was one of many Bodley Head ladies described by survivors as running their departments with 'a rod of iron', and much respected by Allen, though a chain-smoker given to getting tipsy and telling dirty stories. Perhaps it was not wholly her fault that a rod of iron and a penchant for smutty stories proved no substitute for the actual selling of books, which steadily declined throughout her time.

Though the substance of the accounts department weakened annually, they were at least well-kept, up their spiral staircase, first by the veteran Roland Clarke, who had also accumulated his share of legend; an American who had been brought by John Lane across the Atlantic, he was widely supposed to have been a cowboy in earlier life; the damage to his right eye was said to have been caused by a fall from his horse. Clad in a heavy overcoat in winter, a light overcoat in summer, and sporting an umbrella at all times, Clarke was as regular as could be in his daily progress to the bank with whatever cheques and cash had mercifully come in (no fear of mugging then). When he returned, some time later, it was evident to all that he had made his usual visit to the Bodega bar in Regent Street, so conveniently placed between the two offices. The reins, however, were swiftly and meticulously taken up by his deputy, Ernie Jennison, who was to grow white in the firm's service, having exchanged, so to speak, the cut and thrust of a timber merchant's accounts office for the balancing act of this curious circus. A portly pipe-smoker and beer-drinker who in later years assumed a somewhat prim, Victorian manner, he was a lively fellow and very strong, a fact that he was apt to demonstrate by lifting the heavy turning-spokes off a letter-copying press and holding it shoulder-high for several seconds. Others, challenged, proved unable to lift it at all, much less hold it out at arm's length. He was also a master of instant mental arithmetic.

More than maintaining the old-world atmosphere of the place was Mr Brunger, the accountant. He was in charge of royalty accounts (more often credited than paid). Seated on his high stool in a shiny black suit, in crooked wire-framed spectacles bought from a stall near his home in the East End, he lacked only a quill pen to keep the clock back a hundred years. He had but three topics of conversation, his aching feet, his large but apparently very happy family—and the horses: these last led him every week to catch Jennison and ask for a loan, or advance on wages, 'till Friday'. He was eventually replaced by another Dickensian figure, the white-haired, dignified Ashley, in his high white collar.

As for the ledger clerks, their work would today seem a hell, or perhaps a peaceful haven, to those so employed in an electronic age. Apart from transferring, by pen or pencil respectively, details of pencilled invoiced amounts to pen-and-ink ledgers for booksellers' accounts (and very slow payers they were), they had every morning to extract from the invoice books the number of copies of every title appearing in them on the previous day. Two sets of books were kept alternately. For this extraction of titles a large ruled sheet, some 24 inches by 18 inches, was used with an index from two catalogues pasted up at the edge. This sheet was laid out on a large oak table in the so-called waiting-room (where mostly messengers from bookshops sat with their sacks, to carry books ordered). One clerk called out the title and number of copies, the other entered the number and title on the ruled sheet. These were totalled at the end of each month

BROOKE CRUTCHLEY

To be a printer

THE BODLEY HEAD
LONDON SYDNEY
TORONTO

xv. The letters B H, drawn by Michael Harvey, were used as the Bodley Head device for about ten years. Brooke Crutchley's autobiography appeared in 1980.

xvi. Rex Whistler's design for a double-image of Sir Thomas Bodley
for *Oho!* by Laurence Whistler published by The Bodley Head in
1947.

and sent, entered on the relevant royalty account, up to the accounts department. With luck—and the intermittent appearance of a cash-flow of sorts—they would pass under the scrutiny of Brunger's crooked spectacles, and so be forwarded to a hopeful (sometimes despairing) author.

At this table, when the clerks were not filling in their list of grati-fying sales, sat on many afternoons a faded, stooping figure called R. Brimley Johnson, who was editing the Quill series of letters from such as Sterne, Steele, Fanny Burney and others. Between spurts of reading and writing he would stop and roll thin cigarettes of ex-tremely strong tobacco, and then gently drop off to sleep, regardless of the noise around him.

These years, good-natured enough in the trade department, were increasingly gloomy for the firm, and death, the fell sergeant, con-tributed. In the four years 1928–32, while the directors remained unscathed, six of the practical labour force died after short illnesses —Crockett, Clarke, Brunger, the office manager Hunt, and the London traveller among them. Allen understandably preferred the company in Brewer Street. He had ceased to be Company Secretary at the time of the Hesketh Pearson mishap, his place ultimately pass-ing to Jennison. Allen, now nominally Advertising Director, spent as much time as possible in Brewer Street, where at least the neces-sary work went on with reasonable cheerfulness; at Vigo Street, the results of misjudgment were oppressively plain to see, and he was regarded as a vengeful pariah by his fellow-directors. Besides, at Brewer Street it was easier to get at the petty cash.

Now his brother Richard had joined him, doing quite a bit of very unsuccessful travelling on the firm's behalf. Probably, casting aside his white tie and tails, he preferred what might be called the social, certainly the sporting side of staff activities. Dick was a keen cricketer; perhaps it was Allen's idea to see that a Bodley Head team held its own at least by wearing a smart cap in blue with a white peak and the initials BH emblazoned on it. It was not a club in which the other directors took any interest, still less in the football team. The Bodley Head being a small firm, any team it put together was likely to contain at least a leavening of outsiders. They played mostly other publishers on a pre-booked pitch in Regent's Park, on Thursday or Friday evenings, afterwards adjourning to one of the pubs, The Queen's Head or the Artichoke, in Albany Street (running parallel to the Park, and nothing to do with Piccadilly). Playing against Heinemann down at its comfortable works in the Surrey heathland made a more stirring expedition. The Bodley Head team being on one occasion soundly defeated, Allen Lane bestirred himself to fix the return match, and engaged two Middlesex players. Heinemann could not get these two out, and when the captain (an invoice clerk at Brewer Street ominously named Frank Harris) declared, one of the Middlesex men also proved to be a bowler, and skittled Heinemann's out in no time. Similar sporting tactics prevailed on the soccer field. Playing an export firm, William Dawson, The Bodley Head team went down to the spectacular tune of 0-40. The winning captain unwisely said, 'Bring a better team next time.' So The Bodley Head made up its team with two schoolboy internationals, and won 9-0.

Allen Lane had by this time a well-regulated idea of how far the brotherhood of man should go, despite his professed Socialism and improbable admiration for the works of Bernard Shaw. When, one very hot day, Dick sent out to buy ice-cream for the whole staff in Vigo Street, Allen was far from pleased.

From his office he had an escape route to the upper floors. This he often used, especially when certain women were announced—including, no doubt, the demanding Muriel Hine, and very likely the imperious historical novelist Doris Leslie, who was apt to turn up in riding breeches, carrying, if not brandishing, a stock. The staff were required to exercise prodigies of tact and invention until the ladies went away—just like the old days, some of them must have murmured, remembering John Lane.

Allen also spent a good deal of money converting part of the building into a flat for the use of himself and his brothers, as well as going to 'vice-parties' and cavorting with Ethel Mannin and her bohemian friends in the gin-soaked pleasances of the Thames Valley. But behind the all frivolity his mind was working—or at any rate his instinct, since systematic thought was no more to his taste than it had been to old John Lane's. He had two problems to solve. One was to preserve a future for the firm; the other was to find the best way to get rid of his fellow-directors and take charge of the firm himself. He succeeded in the second, but before they all went they had by their obstruction sealed the fate of the first, at least in the short term.

20

The Penguin Offshoot

It is amazing that any worthwhile books were being published at all, in the current atmosphere of suspicion and dissension. The slide into chaos had accelerated by 1932. A strong recommendation from André Maurois (a recommendation rejected, though the books came back later) brought them Roger Martin du Gard's *Les Thibaults* and *Jean Barois* in the firm's enfeebled years, and in due course the lucrative *Lust for Life*, Irving Stone's Life of Van Gogh, and its successors down to much later days. But even successful books did little to help the firm's financial position—partly on account of erratic costing. Allen was certainly alive with ideas, but the admirably produced Peter Arno cartoons and the American children's books, including the Walt Disney spin-offs, for example, sold extremely well—and lost money on every copy sold.

At this time Dick Lane acted, in the long run not to his own advantage, as Allen's financial minder, in a process of 'collaboration by opposition'. When Allen, once again emulating Uncle John, took to frequenting Sales it was Dick who went round quietly in his brother's wake, cancelling extravagant offers; he also, though to little effect, frequently questioned Allen's costings. Manuscripts were sometimes, especially in the case of established house authors, sent off to the printers without copy-editing but simply with the curt message 'Print as before'. On the other hand a handwritten note from J. R. Ackerley suggests the sort of copy-editing excesses still inflicted in some houses by know-betters:

'Dear Mr. Lane: Thank you for the proofs which I am returning corrected. I agree with you that the writing technique we go in for here should not be adhered to for your publication purposes; but I think perhaps your editors have been a little extreme, and I've restored a paragraph or two which seem to me necessary either for sense or balance. The air of apology inherent in my opening paras doesn't make sense unless the sentence I've re-introduced is put back, and since the personal note can't really be eradicated— and I see no reason why it should be—I would like to have it restored . . .'

To add to his troubles, Allen Lane was confronted meanwhile by a series of menacing letters from his own solicitors. As early as 1932, for example, he was warned in the words of Section 275 (1) of the Companies Act 1929 that:

'If in the course of the winding-up of a company, it appears that any business of the company has been carried out with intent to defraud creditors of the company . . . any of the Directors shall be personally responsible without any limitation of liability for all or any of the debts or other liabilities.'

Perhaps, added Mr Sidney Davis of Bullcraig & Davis, he should draw attention to a recent action in which 'it appeared that a certain company was, to the knowledge of the Directors, insolvent and unable to pay its debts. Nevertheless, they ordered further goods, which were delivered but not paid for,' with disastrous results. Of course, the solicitor consolingly went on, fraud 'does not mean in law the turpitude popularly attributed to the word.'

A few weeks later the accountants Smedley, Rule & Co. wrote to Allen Lane (at Brewer Street):

'Candidly the situation in which the Company finds itself is desperate and demands that you take most drastic steps to deal with the position, otherwise, on the present volume of sales and overhead charges, it is only a matter of time before the business will have to cease trading.'

(253)

The situation was not much helped by The Bodley Head's customers, the Depression-ridden booksellers, who owed the firm £14,000. Economy must be the order of the day, declared Mr Rule, though of course if the company can hold on long enough, it will be helped by any improvement in the general economic climate; and of course a best-seller would help. There would be no point in a reduction in the company's capital, or in writing down the values placed upon copyrights, authors' advances and stocks. These, he said firmly, are only what are now called cosmetic accountancy procedures; and anyway it would be advisable to leave the Bank 'to form their own opinion as to the values placed upon these assets in the Company's Balance Sheet.'

Then there was the question of the Board of Directors and their remuneration. The plan of getting rid of them and their generalised hostility progressed slowly. It was easy enough to show Willett the door (he had hardly any shares) even though he was nominally Chairman, and one morning the staff noticed that this kind, harassed and pince-nez-primed little man was no longer at the Chairman's desk; Allen Lane was. His more than twenty years of faithful service and expert knowledge (at least of fine book production) had left him far behind. He went, it seems, without ceremony, and found in due course another job with a paper-making firm: it was a sorry, indeed a brutal end to his time with The Bodley Head.

With Crockett dead and Willett disposed of, there still remained the three very different men who had each a good deal of money in the firm. Carr-Gomme never forgave Allen for the *Whispering Gallery* debacle; probably ill-pleased by the cavalier treatment of the former chairman, he took himself off at the same time as Willett. Lindsay Drummond, the perfect gentleman, did not matter very much either way, though he was quite useful in the meantime. Ronald Boswell was the difficult one. 'We shall have to watch Mr Boswell very carefully,' opined Allen's solicitor in writing, while Allen manoeuvred for control of the company without himself owning a three-quarters majority of the voting shares.

Again, in this matter too, Counsel's opinion was sought; Mr Cecil

Turner pursed his lips and observed that they could not simply remove a fellow-director. However, the Articles of Association 'are in a very unsatisfactory form, and by no means accurately or consistently formed.' Perhaps this worked to Lane's advantage, for a few months later the solicitor, Sidney Davis, was expressing his amusement that his opponents had 'caved in'. He felt obliged, though, to point out that Allen could not legally prevent payment of Participating Preference Shares. Also, he added, perhaps it would be as well if he and his brothers (they too evidently equipped with some shares) refused to pass the accounts, as part of a move to embarrass the other directors:

'If you did so refuse, it is quite likely that the Bank might feel that there was something wrong with the Company's affairs, and appoint a Receiver.'

He should decline to have the copyrights written up; he should confine himself to a comment that the wise course would be not to pay any dividends at all but to reduce the amount owed to the Bank. And, added Mr Davis in an evident warning against Allen's perfunctoriness in matters of detail: 'Of course, avoid signing the balance sheet and accounts . . . and also avoid signing any cheques in payment of dividends.'

In the end, Allen Lane and his two brothers were left as sole directors. They seem to have made the most of it while the going was good. It was soon decided that John should go on a world tour on behalf of the firm. Armed with assorted letters of introduction as the bearer of an honoured name in British publishing, and encouraged by an exuberant farewell party, he set off eastwards, and by and large did pretty well, though apparently, in the eyes of employees, always in the shadow of brother Allen. On his return he was confirmed as Export Director. In this post he exhibited at least a touch of the family waywardness. At one point he disappeared entirely for a week, only to announce on his return that on the spur of the moment he had gone to Paris with the London manager of Hachette, the French publisher and bookseller.

Dick and Allen also proved to be enterprising travellers abroad on behalf of the firm, cultivating assiduously such promising markets for Bodley Head books as St Moritz in the winter sports season, and the bull-rings of Spain.

These enterprises developed slowly. In the early 1930s the Old Guard Directors still had to be placated as far as possible while being got rid of. Nor were these the only matters occupying Allen's mind, along with keeping the Bank tolerant, if not happy. The fame and fortune of the firm must be restored somehow, if possible without doing violence to Allen Lane's radical feelings. He was widely, perhaps understandably, regarded as a playboy by his fellow-publishers. His professed socialism was not taken very seriously. Yet behind his apparently frivolous vitality lay always his respect for the virtues of books in their many forms. It certainly was not merely the commercial possibilities of paperbacks which attracted him. Had that been so, his idea might well have been stifled at birth by The Bodley Head's first paperback experiment.

There had, of course, been many paperback reprint series already; but, save for a few such as Benn's Ninepennies, they were all aimed as reprints of old books at a level of undemanding entertainment, like Hodder & Stoughton's Yellowbacks. The books, too, were taken from their publisher's own list.

Even so had begun The Bodley Head's paperbacks. It had a long back-list of extremely popular novelists—but, with one obvious exception, they were all novelists of a lost world—W. J. Locke, Muriel Hine, F. E. Mills Young, for example. The obvious exception might well also have been classified with these past successes, but conspicuously escaped from it—Agatha Christie, whose works continued to flourish where the once popular crime stories of say, J. S. Fletcher or John Ferguson had faded into oblivion. But these were the traditional names with which The Bodley Head attacked the paperback market, with bright but tawdrily romantic covers, advertisements for such as Cherry Blossom boot polish on the back, and many of them printed in double-column. They proved a total failure in no time at all and cost the hard-pressed Bodley Head £9,000.

Neither the books themselves nor their style of presentation and production were what Allen had adventurously in mind:

'Reprints of good quality fiction and non-fiction, the books to be produced in attractive paper-covers and sold to the public at the unbelievably low price of sixpence—the price of ten cigarettes.'

Mass production, he said, was the answer, and sales outlets far wider than in conventional terms—Woolworth's for example (whose rallying-cry then was 'Nothing over Sixpence'). There is a legend, or perhaps myth, that the idea came to him when, returning from a visit to Agatha Christie in south Devon, he found himself wanting to change trains at Exeter (or, in another version, Newton Abbot) with nothing to read and nothing but rubbish on the station bookstall; and that, having brooded all the way to Paddington, he expounded his idea to his sceptical brothers in their communal bathroom next morning. If they were sceptical, the reception of his idea at the annual Booksellers' Conference (dominated, as usual, then and now, by publishers), at Ripon Hall, Oxford in October 1934 was venomous. After all, this chap was virtually a failure; his firm was on the rocks; his idea was fortunately impracticable in itself—if it were practicable it would be the ruin of the book trade.

Needless to say, when he had put the notion to the directors of his firm, they didn't like it. Hardly anybody did, but The Bodley Head Old Guard by this time did not care for anything he did. There was, for instance, the matter of *Ulysses*, by this chap James Joyce. Everybody knew it was a filthy book, constantly being confiscated by the Customs in various editions. True, an American publisher, Bennett Cerf of Random House, had issued it, after bringing a test-case on the basis of an imported copy which with the help of a famous defence attorney, Morris Ernst, he had won, but still . . .

The Lane brothers had by this time reached a reluctant arrangement with the Old Guard that Allen and his brothers should, while still working for The Bodley Head, back certain fancies of their own with their own money: thus, much to the firm's profit, came those Peter Arno cartoons. After the successful defence of *Ulysses* in the American courts, it might have been thought that British publishers would have been clamouring for the rights. Joyce himself wanted Faber & Faber to publish it in Britain, but T. S. Eliot, its resident guru, though an admirer of Joyce's earlier work, supposedly backed away. In fact, Allen's was the only offer.

The Old Guard, terrified, insisted, though the Lanes would use their own money to publish and publicise it, on a £20,000 bond as a guarantee against legal costs in the event of the book's prosecution. Eventually the Lanes found this money; but affairs had dragged out until 3 October, 1936 when an edition of 1,000 copies was published, 100 to be signed by the author, under the imprint of The Bodley Head. By then Allen and his brothers had in fact left the firm, which continued to make money out of the book; so much so that Allen had much later to pay a large sum to his successors for the paperback rights.

It has often been noted, and it is true, that almost everybody at the time even remotely connected with Allen Lane or The Bodley Head has put in a claim to have inspired him with the Penguin idea. It hardly matters, since only he, in the prevailing conditions, could have shaped the notion, and with an inspiration at once haphazard and calculating, have carried it out, to the great advantage of Western civilisation. But one of his young employees certainly has as much claim as anybody to having shared the vision when it was still only a vision: H. A. W. Arnold, the clever working-class boy who at fifteen came straight from school, at a wage of 15s. a week, though by 1934 it had risen by 2s. steps (10p) to 32s.

When Allen moved over into Willett's seat in Vigo Street he took Olney, the Trade Manager, and Arnold with him, with two specific jobs as well as the usual odds and ends—doing, for example, letters for travellers, or royalty statements. Arnold sat at a tiny desk in Olney's room, as Assistant Trade Manager, on the ground floor; to look after the mailing list he sat in a tiny room on the top floor. There was by this time a number of the bright young Oxbridge types, probably unpaid but fashionably keen on 'going into publishing'. If nothing else, they provided company of a sort for Allen; in his early thirties he was a good deal nearer their age, and a great deal nearer their mental attitudes, than to those of the remaining Old Guard. But few of them, including Allen, could match the young Arnold, an omnivorous reader only too happy to find himself in such close proximity to books, of which he had previously felt starved. The public libraries then aspired, in general literature, no higher than the popular favourites of the Nineties, or so it seemed to him; a fastidious youth, he saw no point in *buying* second-hand books. There was, he felt sure, among the increasingly educated working-class, a ready and unsatisfied appetite for cheap new books.

A possible way of achieving this dreamed-of feast grew in his mind. Opposite him across the corridor on top of the Albany was the Trinidadian-born Edward Young, another all-purpose young man, mostly drawing and designing advertisements, for Boswell and Drummond. Although by background he had more in common with the Oxbridge folk, he was the only one who shared Arnold's greed for books. One day Arnold confided his passion and his dream to Young, who was doubtful but urged him to see Allen: a dubious project, since Allen was so seldom there. Towards the end of August 1933 Allen did after all send for him. Arnold, naturally shy, awestruck in the presence of this famous man, and excessively conscious of the difference in their backgrounds and their looks, trembled and spoke up for his idea of a really cheap—sixpenny—series of good books to cater for an expanding market, if only of out-of-copyright books. Allen thought for a moment or two: Arnold, he said eventually, must be aware that the firm had recently lost a large sum of money on the 9d. paperbacks, and had no clear idea of how to recoup the money. His co-directors certainly would not agree to spending more money, even if it could be found, on a similar series at an even cheaper price. Still, he thanked Arnold courteously for bringing him the notion, and would bear in mind what Arnold had said about the expanding market of an educated working-class. He certainly did bear it in mind, for the notion was already part of his mental furniture.

Lane's non-committal answer was what Arnold had expected; he was not unduly dismayed. Having told Edward Young what had transpired, he got on with whichever of his various tasks was to hand. It might have been a diversion, such as getting rid of Aleister Crowley and his black arts; or, more seriously, holding a balance between S. H. Olney and Frank Baker—both of whom, though they were often at odds, he found ready teachers and wellsprings of technical information. Olney, the rather resented newcomer, was small, smartly dressed, with smooth brilliantined black hair, and lived in Sidcup. Baker, the old-stager, was a rougher type; though still within the clerkly mode, he was not above chatting up, through the Vigo Street window of his office, the pride of prostitutes who gathered there every afternoon, as they had done every day since the Albany was built.

Such distractions could not long restrain the eager young Arnold from his bookish path, nor from the ideas that seeded themselves along its margins. He was perhaps disappointed when, early in 1933, Olney came back from lunch with Allen and handed him a couple of paperbacks, one Tauchnitz, one Albatross (two paperback series of English fiction on sale on the Continent but not in Britain) and told him to start costing them at 6d. each. For some six months Arnold and Olney worked sporadically on the project.

This had already led to another boardroom unpleasantness. Allen was told that it was one thing to use Bodley Head staff to produce those books he and his brother were underwriting, quite another to take them away from their proper work to plan a whole hare-brained series. Nevertheless Allen managed to retain the use of Olney and Arnold; and as it happened his vitality and excitement had attracted the loyalty of many of the younger members of the staff, as they were soon to demonstrate.

By August 1933 Olney and Arnold had come up with a costing which indicated that not only was it possible to publish paperbacks at 6d., but that provided they could persuade other publishers and authors to accept a royalty of $\frac{1}{4}$d. a copy, they need not restrict themselves to out-of-copyright works. So began the arduous task of persuading authors (beginning with their own) and even other publishers to accept their proposal. The grand design was under way. Perhaps Arnold was disappointed when neither then nor at any other time did Allen, though consistently friendly, say a single word about the interview in which Arnold had expressed his enthusiasm for what, as far as he knew, was at that point a mere dream of his own for a mind-expanding plan for The Bodley Head —in whose time, and with whose resources, eventually including money, or at any rate credit, the whole foundations of a great enterprise were laid.

The first ten titles were chosen, with André Maurois' *Ariel* as flagship, an in-house arrangement. The rebuffs suffered by Allen in trying to persuade other publishers to let him have their books must have made him even more thick-skinned than before. He had already undergone a considerable ordeal when, by the autumn of 1934, he felt ready to unveil his plan at that Booksellers' Conference at Oxford. Not all publishers were as laboriously civil as Harold Raymond, Chairman of Chatto & Windus:

'Dear Lane:—Your suggestion of the sixpenny series has led to long discussions among us here, but I am sorry to tell you that we have decided not to co-operate.'

The booksellers, he went on to suggest in polite language, were horrified at sharing the market with vulgar people like Woolworth's. Moreover:

'The steady cheapening of books [a view once forcefully expressed, as it happens, by old John Lane] is in my opinion a great danger to the trade at present, and I sometimes think that the booksellers have to be saved from themselves in this respect. It is they who have so constantly clamoured for us publishers to "meet depression with depression prices" . . . Possibly these arguments might have been over-ruled in our minds if our hopes of the possible profit accruing from the series were greater. But unless we are considerably under-estimating the sales . . .'

And so to his graceful dismissal:

'I am so sorry to be saying no, but I can assure you that we have given the idea very full consideration and we shall remain very grate-ful to you for giving us the chance of considering it.'

Whether this velvet-glove approach, or withdrawal, was any more acceptable than the much ruder response of some other publishers cannot be known; in any case the replies must have been bitterly disappointing and hurtful. Allen welcomed like a drowning man the adventurous if derisive hand of rescue held out to him by Jonathan Cape. Along with the offer of some of his titles he observed genially that as the venture was bound to fail, he might as well take some of the money while it was going.

By that time the name of the new series had been chosen. The Lane brothers and one or two others, including Edward Young, were gathered in Vigo Street discussing the matter. In Young's account:

'We were all sitting round the table suggesting one bird or animal after another. None of them seemed quite right. In the corner of the room typing away at her desk, was A.L.'s secretary, Joan Coles. Suddenly she turned round and said "What about Penguin?" We all looked at each other. "That's it!" we said. It was a unanimous decision, taken without further discussion . . . Joan Coles it was who actually suggested the name.'

That same afternoon Young went off to the Zoo to fix the Penguin image in his mind and, as it turned out, in the minds of millions. Chatting to young Eric Norris at the Trade Counter, he rashly said,

'I'm off to the Zoo to draw some penguins.' 'Penguins! Whatever for?' 'Oh, . . . a . . . some new idea of Allen's.'

Allen's other problem was to keep the old firm going. To this end, among other things, he himself actually lent The Bodley Head £2,360, while John Lane came up with £200, Dick with £25 and the patient Lindsay Drummond a further £4,000 in a second debenture. Economies proposed included a wholesale clearance of stock, mostly stored in the crypt of Holy Trinity Church, Marylebone, still reeking of rubber from the stored tyres of its previous tenants, Dunlop. Away at knock-down prices went all those finely produced, if cumbersome, illustrated editions—of, for example, Fielding's *Tom Jones* or *Rabelais*—and the less ambitious Black and White Classics such as *Salammbô* and *Daphnis and Chloe*. All surviving poetry, including the strangely shaped square Helicon series, was sold at 4d. a copy. Some of all these books, not yet bound, were put into hardback as quickly as possible. Regardless of the original cost, Allen saw such sales as a splendid way of not only saving but raising money.

Another idea, pressed upon him by his advisers, was to give up the Brewer Street premises. A hasty search for cheaper quarters ensued. The idea of putting everybody into a rather de-populated Vigo Street was set aside. Premises in Lambeth were declined. Eventually what seemed suitable premises were found in Bloomsbury. Galen Place was a cul-de-sac off Bury Street, and hard by the British Museum. The Bodley Head's entrance was approached by threading one's way through, or over, the packing cases of a neighbouring greengrocer. An enormous concrete-floored groundfloor had a trade counter installed on the left of the entrance; offices, in a manner almost as haphazard as at Brewer Street, were fitted up as best could be, the rest of the ground floor serving as the book-store, and packing area, complete with its resident sergeant-major, regarded as a bully by juniors. Also among those transferring was the 'looker-out', whose job it was to find the volumes required: a very old gentleman, he suffered a permanent hernia, and couldn't carry a book or parcel of any weight.

The move to Galen Place more or less coincided with the publication of the first ten Penguins, issued jointly with The Bodley Head, the names being printed on either side of the front cover, as indeed they were on the first eighty titles. Allen had not yet given up the struggle to keep Uncle John's foundation going, with Penguin as a part of it. He did, however, mark the occasion by sacking, or as it would now be called making redundant, no fewer than six junior members of the staff, a procedure jocularly referred to by the victims as 'the slaughter of the Innocents'. One of these was the eager Arnold, who with Allen's help was found a job in the City. This proved so distasteful, and the call of books so strong, that after a week away he persuaded The Bodley Head to take him back. In April 1936, though, he left again, and with Allen's help as before (a silent acknowledgment, perhaps, of Arnold's role in setting up Penguin), joined the staff of the British Museum, where he served for forty years, ending up—a strange fate for the boy from Tooting—as an expert in the lesser-known Oriental languages.

Before he went, however, and even after, he threw himself whole-heartedly into operations in the crypt of Holy Trinity Church. Stripped of its dusty piles of unwanted, excess stock, it had become the powerhouse of the Penguin operation. There, as the fateful day of publication, 30 July, 1935, loomed, enthusiasts worked all hours. Access was difficult. There was a goods lift, once used for the descent of coffins, mostly, for some reason, having contained the corpses of retired civil servants from the West Indian island of St Vincent. Nude pin-ups offset pious memorials and dismayed the godly. There was also a steep sloping ramp from which books were delivered from printers or binders. There humped and sweated all three Lane brothers, Edward Young, Eric Norris, Arnold, Bill Rapley, van driver and notoriously hard-swearing Roman Catholic, and Ron Blass (another van driver who in due course rose in the Penguin hierarchy).

At times, of course, the travellers, including the Lane brothers, went out to sell their pride and joy—with, initially, a marked lack of success. Allen himself made a fruitless circuit; Richard, tallest of the brothers, amiably round-faced, did little better. Woolworth, in the shape of the Manager's wife, came to the rescue: a salvage task nearly wrecked when Marks & Spencer joined in, but discovered that they were being charged 3¾d. a copy as against Woolworth's 3½d., which forced Lane to credit them with a great many copies to make up for the extra farthing.

But Allen was, after all, still Chairman and Managing Director of The Bodley Head, and by 1936, for all his loan, and Lindsay Drummond's and an inexplicable shot in the arm from Martin's Bank, The Bodley Head was sinking fast.

As if launching Penguin were not enough, by 1936 Allen was trying hard to sell it along with The Bodley Head. Various gentlemen advanced and retreated, or were retreated from. The Bristol printers Purnell & Sons considered the matter carefully and eventually offered a floating debenture of £30,000, to carry interest at five per cent per annum, the whole to be 'redeemed out of profits over, say, ten years, all work to be done by Purnells'. Not worth it to you, said Lane's advisers. Nothing for it but to put The Bodley Head into voluntary liquidation (just in time, the staff thought, to avoid creditors, notably the Banks, foreclosing). This he did, early in 1936, having formed with his brothers a £100 company for Penguin Books Ltd.

Set down thus, all appears a fairly straightforward financial juggling act. Yet apart from all the offers, rejections, pessimistic advice ('the company is hopelessly insolvent'), the unsatisfactory offer, the evasive answers ('The chances of finding private money are not great ... I hope the matter will be arranged to your satisfaction')—apart from all this there was, after all, an emotional element: it was Uncle John's publishing house that was at stake, and Vigo Street, where the young Allen had cut his name with a diamond on a window-pane all those years before. Whatever some people might think, he was not a cold fish. It is no wonder that he swore one day to get Vigo Street back. And so he did—in 1967 when he set up there a hardback division, Allen Lane the Penguin Press. This was at best a relatively short-lived venture. Vigo Street was sold again, but at least in 1985 his widow came back from Australia to unveil a plaque which served as a memory of old Uncle John.

Meanwhile, The Bodley Head 'went along quietly', out of Allen's reach, under the Receiver until that gentleman found an interested and interesting buyer.

———◆———

21

Sir Stanley Unwin to
the Rescue

An outsider, viewing the purchase of The Bodley Head by Sir
Stanley Unwin, might have seen it as a transaction carried out between Praise-God Barebones and Toby Belch. Both sides, however,
had more to them. Allen Lane might have become, but obviously was
not, a superannuated Bright Young Thing. Stanley Unwin, for all
his puritanical nonconformist background and quirks of behaviour,
amply displayed in The Bodley Head offices as elsewhere, had several
other sides to his nature—including, surely, a sense of mischief.

This is apparent even in his notorious cheese-paring. As his son
David (Severn) put it in *Fifty Years with Father* (a touching and
illuminating book, worthy to be spoken of in the same breath as
Edmund Gosse's *Father and Son*), he felt it necessary to parade his
parsimony; it is difficult not to believe that he secretly delighted in
the stories going round about him. And a man who heads a chapter
in his autobiographical *The Truth About a Publisher* 'How to Make a
Nuisance of Yourself' cannot be altogether absolved from the charge
of feeling a certain malicious pleasure even when pursuing worthwhile causes, which he frequently did as an official of many bookselling organisations, and even when a member of the British Council
—a splendid body, but ripe for mockery.

Again, it is not hard to imagine the barely concealed glee when, one
Saturday morning, arriving (in an ancient Daimler) at his office, he
was able to telephone another publisher, Hamish Hamilton, leisurely
at home, and report what he had observed while on his way: 'Ah,
Hamilton, good morning, I am at my office . . . and yours is on fire.'

In that same autobiography the man who at his own wedding

commissioned a book from the officiating clergyman in the vestry, strikes off asides which cannot be reconciled with the image of the busybody puritan he was at pains to present to the world:

'The telephone contributes far more to the inefficiency than to the efficiency of a publisher's office.

'I am probably more widely known in non-literary circles for my letters to *The Times* than for anything else I have done; they are thus part of my life, and a most amusing one.'

John Lane was rightly said to have been publishing 'for the fun of it'; the same could well be said about Allen. And surely the same applied to Stanley Unwin, however different his way of showing, or concealing, the fact. When tenders were invited by the Receiver for The Bodley Head, he reflected that:

'the business was insolvent at the time of John Lane's death . . . It is astonishing for how many years a book-publishing house can continue its insolvent way before the showdown comes . . . and it suddenly occurred to me that it would be amusing to run the John Lane business co-operatively with two of my competitors.'

So he approached Wren Howard of Jonathan Cape and W. G. Taylor of J. M. Dent, suggesting that they should come in to the tune of one-sixth of the purchase price each. They too, as he put it, thought it an amusing idea. It is difficult to see why, since they must have known that they would play practically no part in running the officially joint operation. Would they like to check his valuation? No, they said, or so he says; what was good enough for him was good enough for them. He was in Copenhagen when his bid was accepted, and on returning to London 'I was chairman of something new in publishing—a business owned by three competitors.'

It soon became a difficult business. The war (which by 1937 he must obviously have foreseen) did not help The Bodley Head's indigent condition. Profits were ploughed back to finance the growth of the business. Not until 1947 did they pay any dividend, and then a small one, for that year only, and even that was a mere nuisance as he explained in one of those letters to *The Times*:

'A company was formed in 1937 to acquire the assets of a bankrupt concern, and is now doing a substantial export trade. The chief proprietor [himself, needless to say] drew no remuneration, and, to finance the development of the business, no dividend was paid on the ordinary share capital until 1947, when a small one was declared, yielding the proprietor £100 gross. But the income tax, surtax and "special contribution" on this modest remuneration for ten years' daily attendance at the business amounts to £127 10s. plus, it may be added, 2 per cent interest, because the proprietor was in New Zealand on business when the assessment was made. We thereafter refrained from paying dividends.'

What possible reason could there have been for all this save 'the fun of the thing', even if the fun was not wholly shared by his employees?

At least they had the satisfaction of working for what is known as a 'character' who provided plenty of opportunity for indignation or rueful amusement, according to taste. Galen Place was, from Allen & Unwin's office, only a few minutes walk—or in his case run—one hand folded across his middle to hold together the flaps of his unbuttoned double-breasted coat; and the similar building in Little Russell Street to which The Bodley Head moved in a few years was even nearer, all of them in those eighteenth- and early nineteenth-century streets which huddle round the forecourt of the British Museum like cottages round the lodge gates of the Lord of the Manor.

In his letter to *The Times* Unwin hardly exaggerated when he wrote of 'ten years' daily attendance at the business', his own as well as The Bodley Head's. In theory he was supposed to know and approve everything that went on, though in view of what The Bodley Head got away with the theory cannot have been very widely applied in practice. It was his practice to go first from his bleak Hampstead home to his own office in Museum Street to open the post and give any relevant instructions.

The gnome-like, bearded figure would then trot down Little Russell Street to The Bodley Head, into the building, up the stairs, scattering 'Good morning, good morning, good morning' as he went. He was then received by the portly Jennison, who had already slit open the morning's post. He had not, however, removed its contents; that was done by Unwin, who also removed the stamps from the envelope (for sale), and any enclosed for return postage (for use)— 'My only untaxed source of revenue' he was apt to say, as he tore away with deft, surprisingly long-nailed fingers. Meanwhile Jennison was dealing with the envelopes in two ways: either by leaving them simply slit open, so that they could be used again, or opened up so that, smoothed out, they could be used as what was known as 'rough paper' in the office. The proceedings were occasionally punctuated by sharp comments—'Ha! Have to watch them, they don't pay!' Then, after a few minutes with the current manager, off he would go.

On Friday afternoons he would reappear. Once again he would be met by Jennison, and the weekly ceremony of wage distribution began. The pay packet would have been prepared, each in its un-sealed, re-used envelope, all arranged in a cardboard shoe-box, carried by Jennison, in the pre-arranged order of a fixed itinerary round the office. Jennison removed the appropriate envelope, passed it to Unwin; he handed it to his gratified employee, who replied 'Thank you very much, Sir Stanley,' and was shaken hands with. Sometimes, if one of them happened to be out of place, he or she got the wrong envelope; Jennison, at least, must have known who everybody was, yet so established was the system that he simply gave out the top envelope, and the next in line solemnly received it. Only afterwards would those concerned swap envelopes.

For a few years, some oversight on the part of the Treasury enabled, indeed encouraged, the firm to pay, or rather give, a Christmas bonus. This was distributed in the same way, even when, owing to some downturn in the firm's business, the envelope contained nothing but a letter regretfully announcing that this year it was not possible to provide a Christmas bonus.

On one appalling day Unwin arrived in the office to find an unaccustomed air of eager expectancy. What was going on? he enquired. With much, and justifiable, unease, it was explained that the staff had organised a sweepstake, at 1s. a ticket. Sternly against gambling, Unwin was appalled. Never, never, he cried, must anything of the kind happen again; and made the cowering, if sulky, organiser return all the money. There were, however, happier discoveries: one day Unwin discovered that one of his packers was an amateur cobbler, and frequently did repairs for other members of the staff. Now it so happened that for some reason the nimble Unwin bore down more heavily on one heel than on the other. It was the work of a moment for him to work out that it had always been wasteful for him to have both heels repaired at the same time. If he had one renewed half as often as the other (and for half the price, naturally) he would in due course save the cost of a whole heel's repair. Accordingly a junior employee was detailed off to take the single hard-worked shoe to the amateur cobbler when required, and the other one half as often. Unfortunately the Hans Sachs of the packing department was detected in some misdemeanour, and despite his worth in terms of domestic economy had to be dismissed.

Even Stanley Unwin could not run, in addition to his own firm, what was in spite of its financial exigency a quite large publishing house. The existing staff had no-one of sufficient authority or experience to manage the firm; but at the right moment Martin Secker's firm collapsed. One of its directors had been P. P. Howe, long (and still) recognised as biographer and editor of William Hazlitt, and Unwin put him in as manager. He did not last long. He was even more briefly succeeded by Lovat Dickson, born in Australia but bred in Canada. Meanwhile, although Fred Warburg, not Unwin, had acquired the assets of that excellent if uncommercial publisher, Martin Secker, there were several more small publishers of interesting or admirably produced books going to the wall, and Unwin acquired a taste for picking them up. He did not attempt to run them

all as separate entities, but merged them with The Bodley Head—
there was little competition for Cobden Sanderson, Martin Hopkinson, Gerald Howe and Boriswood. The latter, nervously financed by
John Morris, a pianist good at figures, was run by C. J. Greenwood,
whom Unwin brought into The Bodley Head while Lovat Dickson
was still there. An embarrassing few months followed before eventually Lovat Dickson went off to Macmillan, and Greenwood was
appointed Manager. He had already been described in *The Bookseller*
as 'the brightest of the young publishers'.

Presumably Unwin recognised in Greenwood the sort of passion for publishing which he could respect. This must have been
almost the only thing about his new manager that he did respect.
In temperament and character they had nothing in common, and
their relationship was ever edgy. The ageing, though energetic,
commercially-minded nonconformist son of suburbia and the
erratic descendant of a long line of north country spendthrifts,
wealthy enough on wool, made an ill match. Greenwood was born,
to the sound of the 5 a.m. knocker-up and the clatter of clogs, into a
well-off but far from stable family in the small village of Cornholme,
in the hills between Burnley and Halifax, on the very border of
Lancashire and the West Riding. His grandfather had been managing director of the largest firm of bobbin-makers in the world; his
father was an alcoholic who before long left home; because of his
father, Greenwood was despatched to a Lancashire boarding-school,
while his mother devoted herself, or at least gave most of her time, to
looking after her parents, both of whom had had strokes. At school
Greenwood formed the ambition to be a farmer—an out-door occupation, since in childhood tuberculosis had left him with only one
lung.

Accordingly he, like Richard Lane, went to an agricultural college.
After a while, however, he realised that, especially in the middle of
the Great Depression, he would not have enough money to set himself up as a farmer, and would not consider any other way of staying
on the land. On the contrary, in partnership with an Armenian
friend he set up shop in Liverpool—books this side, carpets the other.

This notion was not a success; in due course he came to London with his mother and they set up house in Chelsea, where an uncle already lived. In London Greenwood started the Beauchamp Bookshop by South Kensington Underground station and became interested in printing; he bought a hand press, and in a state of less than blissful ignorance cut the string around the type that came with it so that it all cascaded to the floor. Undaunted, he thought about printing books.

At about this time, he got to know, and much to his mother's dismay invited to live with him, the difficult novelist James Hanley, later to prove such a trial to Allen Lane: afire with enthusiasm he set an early work of Hanley, *Resurrexit Dominus*. This was—no doubt it all seemed explosively daring—about a Roman Catholic priest in Liverpool who fell in love with one of his parishioners, a poor Catholic girl, having seen her embrace the figure of Christ in his church. He then substitutes himself for the Christ-figure and, as she touches him, ejaculates. Greenwood printed 100 copies on hand-made paper, and bound them in white vellum (white for purity, perhaps). These were never sold openly, most of them in due course being ruined by a leaking tank.

Meanwhile, like Allen Lane, Greenwood supposed himself to be a Socialist—if not actually a Communist, be it only of the 1930s kind, with vague ideas gradually subsiding in the ideological quicksand and its practical consequences. He certainly made a number of Communist friends, such as Montagu Slater and Alec Brown, an apparently forgotten novelist, to publish whom was one of the reasons why Greenwood and friends set up Boriswood Ltd, with an office in an old house in Frith Street, Soho, opposite Alfred Marks' Bureau for hiring waiters. Here his political acquaintance broadened to find room not only for poet Edgell Rickword but even for a man of the Right like Roy Campbell. In between, at various points, were Hart Crane and Georges Bernanos, whose books went with him to The Bodley Head; in *The Diary of a Country Priest*, Bernanos gave the renewed company its first real best-seller.

The memory of Boriswood as a firm lingers on, if at all, in the memory of two court cases. The first arose from James Hanley's *Boy*, the book of which Ethel Mannin at first so disapproved when it had been offered to The Bodley Head: all about a ship's boy and, as she put it, buggery and brothels. A complaint was laid in Birmingham and there Greenwood and his partner Morris were hauled into the dock. Morris was so sure that they would both be sent to prison that going up in the train he bought only a one-way ticket. But they escaped with a substantial fine and a Court Order to destroy the books.

Hardly had this panic more or less passed when a book of a very different kind brought them to the London Sessions: *The Sexual Impulse*, by Edward Charles, or possibly 'Edward Chorles'. This was a deadly serious book, and the court was hard put to it to keep a straight face when, this time, the Judge himself read out passages from the book, including a recommendation that sex was best enjoyed in the open air, or, if indoors, gave a detailed description of a type of chair in which to make the most of sex—and how. Another fine.

Their best literary find, however, was Rex Warner. Greenwood's partner John Morris had a daughter at school in Surrey at Frensham Heights, a more or less advanced establishment where Warner taught. Although since Oxford a friend of Spender and Auden (who dedicated one of the sections of *The Orators* to Warner's son), Warner had not had much luck with his poems until Greenwood took them. Then part of his novel *The Wild Goose Chase* was published, and handsomely reviewed by Spender, in an early, hardback volume of John Lehmann's *New Writing* (also first published by The Bodley Head before being taken over in paperback by Penguin). First *The Professor* in 1938, then *The Aerodrome* made his name in the early 1940s. The Kafkaesque nightmare was thus naturalised in Britain. The time for those books was ripe. But Warner was also a classicist, and produced a number of translations from the Greek and Latin, which were soon to adorn the Penguin list.

C.J. (Greenwood disliked his first name, Cecil) looked after all his authors well. He was attentive and indeed gallant towards the ladies who might have a book in them. One day as Inez Holden, the eccentric author of *Night Shift* (who during the war was apt to come to supper in her pyjamas, in case the Blitz compelled her to stay the night), was walking down Jermyn Street with Greenwood's wife, Mrs Greenwood happened to mention, as they passed L'Ecu de France: 'C.J.'s having lunch there with E.M.A.' This was the charming and agreeable E. M. Almedingen, Russian author of *Frossia*, another best-seller (1943, followed by some sixteen more titles). 'How awful for you,' said Inez Holden; 'I don't know how you stand it.' To this Mrs Greenwood replied that publishers must be allowed a bit of their romantic image, and after all C.J. was very good-looking. As E.M.A. was not, she may have posed little threat to Mrs Greenwood.

C.J. had what might otherwise have been (in his widow's words) 'a rather too pretty face', interestingly corrected by a huge scar on his forehead, caused by going through a car windscreen. Tall, slim and graceful, he went to Sadlers Wells one day to call on Bodley Head author Ninette de Valois, only to be told by the stage doorman that Miss de Valois was not taking on any more male dancers today. His innate kindness was reflected in his voice and a quiet way of talking. It came in two timbres: the one, an intensely earnest tone, presaging, says one of his authors, an extremely serious and usually quite non-sensical discourse of an intellectual nature, to which one had to resign oneself; and the other, an eager, though still quiet, expression of glorious prospects opening on all sides for the firm, or the person with him, or even for himself. This was usually the state of play after lunch, which might take place at L'Ecu de France, or, for much gratified members of the staff, at the Black Horse in Rathbone Place, or even, as the sherry to which he was devoted took hold, never stirring from the congenial fug of Long's Wine Bar, just off Tottenham Court Road. Here the hours would pass as C.J. smoked his Craven A cigarettes, between puffs standing them up vertically on their cork tips, and shared dreams of a rosy future. And in the evenings he liked to sit in a Chelsea pub, his concentration on the manuscripts he read enhanced, he claimed, by the noise around him.

Out of all this did emerge some interesting authors, more and more of them left-wing. James Aldridge, who had made a success with *Signed with their Honour*, published by Michael Joseph, was poached by C. J. Howard Fast's *Freedom Road* was very left-wing. Budd Schulberg, too, who joined the list in 1949 with *The Harder They Fall*, and went on to write the bestseller *Waterfront*. There was Jack Lindsay, an extremely agreeable Australian of radical sympathies. And of course that upper-class romantic revolutionary figure, Christopher Caudwell (St John Sprigg), with his poems and two volumes of *Studies in a Dying Culture*.

Another Bodley Head discovery of his was Jocelyn Brooke, a tall, thin, rather scruffy homosexual who lived in Kent and devoted himself to wild flowers (*The Military Orchid*) and fireworks—to celebrate publication of *A Mine of Serpents*, practically the whole Bodley Head staff went down to watch a most spectacular firework display culminating in the *feux d'artifice* which gave the book its title.

Others, though, went their way in search of bigger royalties and bigger sales. C. J. was much chagrined when John Pudney went off—after all, Pudney had been a friend, had in fact carried friendship so far as to lend the Greenwoods his house: this offer turned out to embrace full contents including his Alsatian bitch and her four puppies, but food was short, even dog biscuits were unobtainable, and the creatures grew hungrier and hungrier, and started throwing fits. Perhaps it was to make amends for this, and in recognition of C. J.'s persuading him so profitably to write children's books, that Pudney gave C. J. the original manuscript of his famous poem 'Little Johnny Head-in-Air', one of the poems about the RAF, in which Pudney had served originally as Duty Shepherd, the duty being to keep sheep off aircraft runways.

These losses of good authors occurred for two reasons. One was that in his continual battle with Stanley Unwin, who never had any interest in fiction, C. J. was seldom successful in getting what he regarded as adequate advances, at least for novelists. Some said that, left to his own devices, C. J. would have published nothing but poetry. But the other reason was the curious one that, admirable

(276)

talent-spotter that he was, he admired and courted potential but often backed away from success.

As the Second World War drew to its end, new faces appeared, and old ones reappeared. For all his weaknesses—and all his staff spoke and still speak with nothing but warmth and gratitude of C.J. —they realised that he was no business man. 'He was a lovely man,' said Michael Legat, a young man who has done well as publisher and indeed as author, after starting straight from school at 15s. a week. 'I only wish he had lived long enough for me to realise how much I owed him, and to thank him.' So did several others, partly because he could always spare time to talk and encourage—and to circulate his own letters, and expose his own failures to the younger newcomers.

One significant development, the establishment of a full-fledged children's list, was initially due to the last man to buy himself into the firm, though not on the scale of the old guard back in the 1920s. Martin J. C. Foster, as he seems always to have been referred to, was a conscientious objector and member of the family owning, among other things, the celebrated Black Dyke Mill in Yorkshire, and its even more celebrated band. He simply paid what may be called an apprenticeship fee of £500. Very soon he was grandly called Publicity Manager, working from a large upstairs room in or around which almost the whole office was ranged—C.J. in a room to himself beyond it, and beyond that the invoicing room with its big handwritten ledgers, still every night trundled down to the safe in the basement and trundled up again in the morning. There, too, was a partly partitioned area where the mailing of catalogues and advance announcements was handled, more or less the whole staff turning to when necessary. At such times, said one member of the crew, it was like coaling a ship in the old days, with everybody taking part except the Captain and the ship's doctor. The whole place had what another survivor called a dirty, musty, fusty air. Apart from Martin Foster, one or two juniors and the all-rounder Len Lake and strong-arm Jennison, there was Frank Baker, the Production Manager, who controlled the ordering of paper, print and binding. Behind a partition lurked Skinner, the man with the difficult job of squaring the royalty statements, which he wrote out in beautiful copperplate till his retirement in 1957.

Martin Foster in fact soon began to take a much larger part in editorial matters. It was thus that he began the strengthening, or reconstitution, of the Children's Book Department; when not regaling the rest, during the war, with horrific tales of his experiences during the Blitz with the Heavy Rescue Squad of the Fire Service, he would sit stolidly reading manuscripts in which perhaps he was not very interested; but then it was an area in which nobody else seemed interested either, so he could make it his own. In due course Foster was joined by a 24-year-old ex-RAF officer, Richard Hough, who had emerged from six years' service with a wife and family and no visible means of support save a £2-a-week allowance from his father. Fancying a publisher's life, possibly swayed, but certainly not helped, by the fact that Jonathan Cape was a governor of his school, he eventually arranged to see Wren Howard, Cape's second-in-command. Howard had nothing to offer, but passed him on, not as might have been expected, to the firm of which he was at least nominally a part owner, but to Philip Unwin of Allen & Unwin. Philip Unwin had nothing to offer either, but did at least pass him to the firm of which his Uncle Stanley was the supremo. So young Richard Hough, much later to make his name as biographer and naval historian, was interviewed by C.J. In the course of their talk his eye straying along the bookshelves, he involuntarily exclaimed 'Oh, you've got Rex's books!' 'Yes, we publish him. Do you know him?' Indeed, it turned out that Hough had been a pupil at Frensham Heights, and that Rex Warner had taught him Latin.

The job was his, such as it was, at £4 a week, no bad sum in 1946. The very first thing was what was innocently called a stuffing job— putting catalogues into envelopes. But the horizon expanded. There was soliciting bookshops, for instance, where he found how very well he was received in left-wing bookshops. Then there was the task of cutting out reviews, at which point he felt entitled to take over Martin Foster's title of Advertising Manager. Before long he began to share Foster's concern with children's books. One day in 1950, Hough gave a temporary job to a young friend who had just come back from an *au pair* job in Canada, and a few months later he suggested to C.J. that this young temporary, Judy Taylor, might be invited to stay on permanently. She agreed—a momentous step for her, certainly a momentous step for The Bodley Head, and ultimately a momentous step for Hough himself.

Others came and amiably went, or came and stayed, as did the elegant Barney Blackley. After the Army (the 17/21 Lancers and the Tank Corps) and Oxford, and a brief glimpse of the book distributors Simpkin Marshall, Blackley put an advertisement in *The Bookseller* which produced some strange answers and one which led to C.J. taking him on in 1952—like most people doing something of everything, but in particular, selling foreign rights, at a wage of £4 a week, increased to £5 10s. when he married a year later.

The whole office, not to mention visitors to it, was dominated, if not cowed, by the alarming Mrs Josephine Digby, yet another in that line of authoritative women who appeared from the start of The Bodley Head's history. Tiny, another compulsive smoker ('I like a good fag'), she is said by some—though others were too terrified to observe it—to conceal a kindly heart beneath her prickly manner. Nominally she was Greenwood's secretary, though she would do typing for others, with an apparently poor grace but great speed and efficiency: she also doubled as Crime Story Editor. The office's day was more or less governed by her success or otherwise with the *Times* crossword, to solve which all were pressed into service.

Nor were all the versatile Bodley Head crew under one roof. Down near Moretonhampstead, on the southern fringes of Dartmoor, Norman Denny lived. This stocky, sandy-haired, heavily be-spectacled and beaming labourer in the vineyard was himself a capable writer of children's books under the pseudonym of Norman Dale (and of several unsuccessful novels); but he was also the firm's chief reader, replying to vast parcels of manuscripts with crisp opinions characterised by his spidery signature. He also seems to have done most of the copy-editing; Michael Legat spent hours altering American spelling, but there seems not to have been much work on manuscripts done in the office, and a good deal of the care-free practice (not by any means confined to The Bodley Head) of sending off books to the printers marked 'set as before'. He was also a copious translator. After the war the firm published many French novels and Denny, for example, translated most of the neglected but admirable Marcel Aymé.

Survivors from the former regime soldiered on, notably Len Lake and Frank Baker. It was their practice, usually, to eat sandwiches and chat at their desks at lunchtime, then go for a stroll through Blooms-bury. Baker's always monocular sight deteriorated rapidly, and he frequently, as Lake put it, 'scared the daylights out of us' by his cavalier way of crossing the road with complete disregard for the traffic. Perhaps it is no wonder that Unwin became dissatisfied with him, even though by 1950 his salary amounted to no more than £400 a year, for a highly responsible job.

Although C.J. was amazingly successful in getting marginally better pay for Bodley Head employees than was available to their opposite numbers at Allen & Unwin, it was at this time that staff, especially of course its younger members, tended to leave in search of better-paid jobs. The production managers, i.e. designers, were particularly prone to move on. Edward Young, having gone with Allen Lane to Penguin, was replaced by Wat Tyler, less rebellious than his name suggests. His place had been taken during the war by a witty, sardonic and rather contemptuous man, Denys Kay Robin-son, soon and gladly off after the war and in turn replaced by Michael Legat. When Wat Tyler returned, Legat was demoted. But now Tyler went off in search of more money (later, like poor Willett, becoming a traveller for a paper firm) and—under C.J.'s eye and within his favourite typefaces, Perpetua, Bembo and Centaur—Legat became Production Manager again from 1946 to 1950; along with all this and the copy-editing and being allowed to do some blurb-writing and even translation from the French. But then he too went off in search of a better-paid job.

So, between the upper millstone of Unwin's rigour, and the lower millstone of C.J.'s relaxation, The Bodley Head somehow continued

1. The young Max Beerbohm, a caricature by Sic from *Vanity Fair*, 1897. (*BBC Hulton Picture Library*)

2. André Maurois

3. Kenneth Grahame

4. H. H. Munro (Saki)

5. G. K. Chesterton. (*BBC Hulton Picture Library*)

7. Rex Warner

6. C. S. Lewis

8. Stephen Leacock. (*Karsh, Ottawa. Pictorial Press, London*)

10. Norman Hunter

9. Mitsumasa Anno

11. Shirley Hughes. (*Carole Cutner*)

12. Pat Hutchins

13. Edward Ardizzone

14. Maurice Sendak

15. Charles Chaplin signs the contract for *My Autobiography* in the presence of his wife Oona, and Joan and Max Reinhardt

16. William Trevor

17. Graham Greene with Max and Joan Reinhardt. (*Wilcock Woodward*)

19. Allen Lane in his thirties

18. John Lane

20. Sir Stanley Unwin (left) with Max Reinhardt when
The Bodley Head changed hands. (*Mark Gerson*)

21. Sir Francis Meynell with Kathleen Lines. (*Mark Gerson*)

22. C. J. Greenwood and his wife

23. Judy Taylor (left) with Barbara Ker Wilson. (*Camera Advice Centre*)

24. Margaret Clark flanked by Margaret Meek (left) and Naomi Lewis. (*Mark Gerson*)

25. Jill Black (left) celebrates publication of the first Historical Novel Prize winner, *Gallows Wedding*

27. David Machin. (*Tom Miller*)

26. Two generations of Bodley Head editors: Milton Waldman and his son
Guido at the party to launch *The Sky Falls* by Lorenza Mazzetti (left).
(*Wilcock Woodward*)

Max Reinhardt

AND *The Bodley Head*

BOOKS FOR AUTUMN AND WINTER

1959-60

28. Heather Copley's drawing of The Bodley Head's Earlham Street office (1957 to 1966), the corner building in the centre of the picture.

BODLEY
HEAD

July to January 1966-67

29. The Bow Street office occupied 1966 to 1985, drawn by
Roy Spencer

30. Barney Blackley (right) and Euan Cameron present a copy of Peter
Jennings's *The Pope in Britain* to Pope John Paul II in Rome. His
Holiness subsequently joined the Bodley Head list (*Be Not Afraid!*,
1984). (*Felici, Rome*)

31. John Ryder. (*Penny Abrahams*)

to acquire books. Occasionally it still published a book suggesting the old days of John Lane. In 1939 it had put out, for example, *Lord Chelmsford and the Zulu War*, by Major-General the Hon. Gerald French, DSO, with a Foreword by Sir Bindon Blood, GCB. *Chin P'Ing Mei* or *The Adventurous History of His Men and his Six Wives* had the advantage of an Introduction by Arthur Waley, and indeed achieved a sequel, *Flower Shadows Behind the Curtain*, twenty years later. Three volumes of yet another translation (by J. D. Sinclair) of Dante's *Divine Comedy* achieved a solid backlist presence, unlike *Home Truths*, a book of comic verse by a youthful William Douglas Home. The middle of the war saw the beginning of an annual sequence which lasted for four years: the highly successful *Glory Hill Farm* books by Clifton Reynolds, a businessman in the furniture trade who began by seeing his adventures in agriculture simply as a contribution to the war effort and ended by finding them best-sellers. More enduring has been the association, begun in 1943, with the English scholar, Christian moralist and fantasist C. S. Lewis, whose science-fiction trilogy, starting with *Out of the Silent Planet*, has remained regularly in print to this day.

C.J. also brought off a singular feat in getting into print apparently without Unwin's knowledge a series of arts books: *Ballet Now* (with special reference to Sadlers Wells Ballet, just beginning to ascend to glory), *Opera Now*—hence Slater's libretto of Britten's masterpiece, *Peter Grimes*, and so on. These were written by C.J.'s impoverished friends and acquaintances, who received the striking sum of £250 for a text running to about 10,000 words. Not all to C.J.'s taste as a publisher, though in the event highly profitable, was a succession of books in a tradition established by Allen Lane, or indeed by John Lane. Uncle John had inserted his brand of soft porn into a more (in this respect at least) hypocritical society by presenting it as illustrations to literary classics. Literature with sexual overtones had continued in the list with the publication of *The Body's Rapture* by Jules Romains, not long after *Ulysses* had come out under the Bodley Head imprint.

Nude studies, which had already visited the list as early as 1933 with Alice Bloch's *The Body Beautiful*, now re-emerged too. Rather surprisingly, Unwin, whatever he thought of the classics as an excuse, had no hesitation in pursuing the publication of nude pictures on aesthetic grounds. He kept a close eye on the development, however. Perhaps with the same motives that induced old John Lane to scrutinise Beardsley's drawings with a magnifying glass, Unwin himself brought *Nudes of the World* to C.J., and always insisted on examining the original photographs of plastic ladies, with what seemed to some of his staff an excessive zeal, before the pictures had been air-brushed (that is, in an all too suitable phrase, touched-up—or toned down). John Everard's series of albums, with titles like *Artist's Model* and *Sculptor's Model*, contributed mightily to the firm's financial health in the 1950s.

Books for children had appeared regularly and successfully from the early days of John Lane, notably from the pen of Kenneth Grahame and Evelyn Sharp. But the firm had no name as a publisher of children's books until Unwin first saw possibilities in this direction. A major impulse was provided by David Unwin, Sir Stanley's much-loved son, when he wrote a children's book under the name of David Severn. Cautiously the book was submitted under this name to The Bodley Head. But when it had been accepted—the first of an agreeable and successful series of tales in what might be called the Ransome vein—father went into action unashamedly. He more or less acted as his son's agent, demanding, and not surprisingly getting a twenty per cent royalty for this unknown writer from the start. He also, of course, allocated the paper ration, which in those years virtually determined the sale. David Severn was duly allotted twenty-five per cent of the ration allowed for the whole list; and his sales were reported to him every day. Even M. E. Atkinson, though a relative of Wren Howard, and also receiving preferential treatment, got enough to print only 8,000 copies a year.

As David Unwin [Severn] acknowledged, 'the Manager of The Bodley Head—a man in a most invidious position—had his own friends and protégés to support, and when they sent in their manuscripts their contracts were drawn up on similar lines to my own. This was not at all what my father had intended! He had to gun them down. He had taken the firm over in order to build it up—it was in a poor state when he had acquired it—and he was accepting no fees for his services. He saw my inflated royalties as an overdue reward for the work he was putting in gratis.'

Besides, as Unwin sharply told Greenwood, 'You must get more money coming in;' and forbade him among other things, to publish any more verse. The situation was wretched. Dick Hough was by now running the children's section, with the promising Judy Taylor as his professional prop and stay; he was also himself writing children's stories. The firm had inherited, even from Allen Lane's time, some useful children's authors—not least the gaily surreal Professor Branestawm stories of Norman Hunter. Allen Lane, in fact, improbably claimed to have heard the first of these stories when they were broadcast on the BBC Children's Hour. Their author, now (1987) a genial octogenarian with a home-made working model (complete with lighting, stage machinery and audience) of Drury Lane Theatre more or less filling one room in his house, was a professional illusionist who toured the world with his wife and occasionally (as we shall see) entertained his publisher's children.

After Martin Foster's departure Hough and his group had built up a more than adequate Juvenile list, at the start of the astonishing renaissance of children's books, in which The Bodley Head soon acquired a considerable celebrity, with Methuen and Oxford University Press.

Nevertheless, the firm was running down. Greenwood could act with a wise and gentle paternalism towards his staff; but he stood in mortal dread of Stanley Unwin. No wonder. He was certainly not making money for The Bodley Head despite his good list. Worse, he spent a great deal of his nervous energy in devising means of pulling the wool over Unwin's eyes and desperately hoping not to be found out. A bowl in the office contained bills due for payment. Every day the credits were totted up and put to pay as many bills as they could meet in order of date; a particularly big bill would have to be put back in the bowl, as available cheques could not meet it. Absurdly too, he devised a scheme of different coloured Memo Sheets: white for general circulation, blue for those not to go to the Chairman—a ruse of which Unwin was perfectly aware. In fact, C.J.'s incompetence as a manager must have maddened Unwin, though not as much as Unwin's severity distressed C.J. Undermined by these pressures, his health deteriorated, and ultimately cancer of the throat was diagnosed. By this time he had begun to think of leaving the firm, and even in 1955, in his last weeks, he buoyed himself up with thoughts of a link with an American firm to launch a new paperback imprint.

It was of course too late. Hough took over as manager. He had himself been long distressed by the predicament of C.J., of whom, like everybody else, save perhaps Stanley Unwin, he was extremely fond. And he was hardly less upset by the spectacle of a long-established and still respected publishing house wasting away—not least because of the failings of a man to whom he owed much and towards whom he felt so warmly but who, he felt, should never have been put to run any company. The rumour was soon put about, over sundry professional luncheon-tables, that Unwin was proposing to sell the whole firm lock, stock and barrel.

So in 1955 Richard Hough left, taking up a part-time consultancy and then a directorship with Hamish Hamilton, and nursing extremely unbenevolent thoughts about Stanley Unwin. Now it was the unfortunate Barney Blackley, scarcely out of his twenties, who was left to run the rump of the firm and guard its still far from contemptible list. This he did, until one day Unwin appeared with a tall, sturdily built man of picturesque cosmopolitan appearance, with a broad-brimmed brown hat and an air of calm and affable command. As Bernard Shaw wrote of another Max impinging on another publishing venture, there 'stepped spritely in the incomparable Max.'

III

THE REINHARDT IMAGE

22

Max Reinhardt
Enters Publishing

Max Reinhardt was just under forty when he took on the enjoyable
task of revivifying The Bodley Head. He had already lived a life
crowded with incident. It had brought him from Constantinople to
London by way of Paris, and from, in his own simplification,
'importing nuts and exporting bicycles' to his real ambition, British
citizenship, and his real love, the world of books and the making of
books.

Students of hereditary tendencies would find much to interest, not
to say amaze, them in this cosmopolitan's progress. His paternal
grandfather was what might well have been called a merchant-
venturer, ranging in the late nineteenth century from Vienna as far
afield as Japan. Max's father was born in a village in southern Austria
and studied architecture and architectural engineering in both
Vienna and Prague. Joining an architectural partnership, he was sent
to Turkey, and there remained. A loner, though a friendly one by
temperament, he nursed a passion for the music of Wagner, was an
indefatigable walker, and designed many public buildings for
that architect of modern Turkey, Mustafa Kemal Ataturk.

Meanwhile the young architect—fretting somewhat at the bad
taste of the new Turks—had met and in due course married Frieda
Darr. Though she had been born in Constantinople, her family came
from another part of Austria not far from the Reinhardts. The Darrs
were a close-knit family, at least as far as was compatible with being
spread all over the world. They too prospered in many kinds of
business, with interests in shipping and insurance and agencies for
many foreign firms, British, German, Austrian, Italian and so on.

There was plenty to do when Max's maternal grandfather established the firm's branch in Constantinople, then a free port.

Thus Max was born, on 30 November, 1915, into a thriving international community. He grew up, first in a flat, then in a house, attended by for the most part Greek servants. French was largely spoken in the household, though Max tended to speak German with his father (and Turkish in the street). His education, both in Turkey and in Paris, was paid for by his mother's younger brother, Richard, a potent influence in his life. The uncle did not, however, control its course, Max's father having determined that, despite the family's central European orientation, the boy should have an English education. Despite family teasing about his unpractical notions, Max's father stuck to his guns.

The headmaster of the English High School in Constantinople in these late 1920s and early 1930s supervised his reading—he needed no encouragement—along firmly traditional lines, strongly featuring Scott and Dickens. The Chairman of the School's Governors, too, saw the potential of this pupil. He was Sir Telford Waugh, brother of John Lane's crony and slighting mocking contributor to *The Yellow Book*, Arthur Waugh, and therefore uncle to Evelyn and Alec. He was also British Consul-General to Turkey (and as it turned out, much more).

Max became adept at games, notably at tennis, and the family spent four months of every year, like almost everyone else in the rather privileged international community north of Constantinople, at Therapia, where the climate was cooler, the water more pleasant, boating and tennis the order of the day.

Looking at Max's future, both Telford Waugh and the headmaster wished him to go to an English university, but here the family, that is his mother's family, put its collective foot down: they had not, they said, any strong English connections and it would be far more suitable for young Max to go to Paris. Uncle Richard, who had largely paid for Max's education, was after all installed there and had opened a branch of the family firm, a point dwelt upon by Max's mother.

(288)

In Paris he was duly enrolled in the prestigious Ecole des Hautes Etudes Commerciales, and found many friends from his own part of the world, as well as a number of Frenchmen, including the publisher-to-be Robert Laffont. From Paris he was able to make frequent trips to London, and in 1938, at twenty-two, he persuaded the family firm to let him set up a proper London branch. This was done reluctantly at first, but proved a boon to the family firm later. At first he lived in a boarding house in the Bayswater Road, playing bridge with, mostly, members of the Greek community, which included the father of the historian Peter Calvocoressi, and buying books from Denny's bookshop in the City of London.

His accountants, Spicer & Pegler, found him space in their office premises, and he managed to arrange some excellent agencies for the family firm back in Constantinople (by now renamed Istanbul) and elsewhere—Richard Thomas & Baldwin, for example, in the steel business, and Dewhurst the cotton people, from his eyrie in St Mary Axe. Active and profitable life in the office, active and enjoyable life among bridge- and tennis-playing friends of many nationalities was supplemented by establishing his own home in a block of flats, Kensington Close, then under construction behind Barkers. Here squash courts were readily to hand, and Max took to the game with zest; it was to lead him in an unexpected direction.

Life was opening out, and extremely enjoyable. Gradually, too, he was bringing about a markedly pro-British swing in the family business, by the agencies he got and by sending representatives of the firms they represented to stay with the family in Turkey.

By the late 1930s it became evident that there would soon be war. Agitation seized the family: Max, who was carrying an Italian passport following the territorial adjustments after the First World War, would be an enemy alien. He was summoned home: but he would not go. Sure enough, in September 1939 war came, and Italy joined Germany's side. What to do? At first, Max did his best to ignore the whole thing and the honorary Englishman wished to serve his preferred country. Since they were still in touch, he thought he would consult Sir Telford Waugh, now living in retirement in Wimbledon.

At Sir Telford's suggestion, he wrote to the War Office offering his services. He was soon called for an interview. By this time the French had collapsed and the real war started. Max was briefly interned with many Italians and some Greeks who also had Italian passports but the War Office pulled him out after a short time and a Mr Stewart, of Stewart & Lloyd, one of the companies whose agency he had been working to obtain for the family firm, thought they might have a job for him: 'Go to Turkey. Be Number Two to Number One.'

'What will I have to do? . . . I want a clean job. How would I get there?'

'Four passports—Turkish . . .'

'I only want one, British.'

'. . . Italian, French, British.'

'And how would I go?'

'By plane. It's now Friday. Give me your answer by Monday.'

Back went Max to Kensington Close, and so to the Public Library to borrow books on spying. One of these was by Telford Waugh, who, it turned out, had been head of the British Intelligence mission in the Middle East in the First World War as well as Consul-General in Turkey.

'I've read your book,' Max observed to Sir Telford over tea. 'I know I shouldn't but I must ask you . . .'

'What they want is your connections. Turn it down. If anything happens you would be looked after, but your family and friends . . .'

On Monday Max did go to the War Office and turn its offer down. But he somehow felt cowardly. Wishing to serve as himself and not through his connections, he went to an RAF recruiting office. After they had seen all his papers, and consulted the War Office, and he had passed the medical, he joined the RAF as, more than likely, the only enemy alien in the Royal Air Force. Not, however, to trail clouds of glory. His nationality did make for complications over promotion, though he was—surely rather strangely—posted to the Operations Room of RAF Northern Ireland. This proved dull, professionally speaking, despite an abundant flow of secrets. Reading was one consolation (plenty of time for that) especially of Shaw. Somerset Maugham and Bertrand Russell also shaped his thoughts; but his road to promotion was blocked, despite the efforts of his Commanding Officer who knew of his command of many languages and his knowledge of the Middle East. He went once more to see Stewart at the War Office, but there was nothing for him now, as Turkey was overwhelmed by agents from the Balkans. He was to put his qualifications to better use later on.

But before long he had stumbled into what was to prove yet another stroke of luck. Having kept on his flatlet in Kensington Close as an anchorage, he went while on leave from Northern Ireland down to its squash courts. There was, he was told, a gentleman looking for someone to play with. They were introduced:

'Lieut-Commander Richardson, this is AC2 Reinhardt, who'd be happy to give you a game.'

They played, took to each other, formed a friendship which lasted for the rest of Sir Ralph Richardson's life; in good time this encounter changed the course of Reinhardt's life—in more ways than one.

When he was discharged from active duty, Max determined to resume his long-forsaken studies, interrupted by an interesting trip to the Middle East: he opted for international relations at the London School of Economics, then evacuated to Peterhouse, Cambridge. He was accepted on the strength of his French degree, and given all facilities, including the right to attend post-graduate lectures by the already admired Bertrand Russell. His own teachers in the theory of international relations were a very right-wing South African and, much more to the point, Harold Laski, who ignited in Max the spark, always there but in danger of lying dormant, of the 'Excitement of Learning'. Thus began his turning away from commerce as the principal point of life (though not from its skills).

Back in civilian life, Richardson put him up for membership of the Savile Club. The part played by the Savile in Max Reinhardt's progress can hardly be exaggerated. Both professionally and personally it was to stimulate him and console him. The Savile was rich in literary and broadcasting personalities, among whom Max found new bridge partners. One of these was A. S. Frere, the head of Heinemann, a firm which, established three years after The Bodley Head, had continued to grow. Frere was to be very helpful to Max.

Max found the family firm's business in London more or less moribund, or at any rate dormant; so that when his friend young Richard Pegler of Spicer & Pegler asked the formidable senior partner Mr Ernest Evan Spicer, 'As Reinhardt is so interested in books, why doesn't he buy our little publishing firm?' the idea was appealing.

This was a small business, HFL Ltd, which took its name from one H. Foulkes Lynch, the first accountant to establish a college in his devious craft—it celebrated its centenary in 1985. Spicer & Pegler, foreseeing (and how right they were) a tremendous demand for accountancy, and the training of accountants after the war, set out to produce text-books. Since Spicer & Pegler were themselves immensely busy, a deal was agreed. Max should have the copyright of the books for £5,000 which was the money the company had at the bank, provided only that he would also buy The Stellar Press, the small printing works in Barnet they had acquired to print their text-books, and which was badly managed and losing money. This Max did, and so took his first steps into publishing, or at any rate publishing of a sort. He was totally ignorant of the field, but received some guidance from R. H. Code Holland of Pitman's, expert in the educational field. He told Max, for instance, how to get a larger paper ration through a governmental organisation known as the Moberley Pool. Thus refreshed, the turnover of HFL Ltd increased from £2,000 a year to £15,000 a year in two years (it eventually reached £130,000 a year, and was sold only in 1985 to Butterworth).

On the strength of this rather limited experience Max conceived the idea that publishing of a more general nature might indeed be fun—a notion stimulated by conversations with Richardson and with another actor, Anthony Quayle. Constantly the talk returned to the theatre—as in the meantime Max had married a budding

actress, Margaret Leighton, soon to become famous in her profession
—and to celebrated books now out of print. Excitement flared at the
prospect of a new publishing venture riding on the back of HFL.
Richardson and Quayle agreed to join Reinhardt as directors of Max
Reinhardt Ltd. On 14 May, 1948, Max signed his first contract as a
—more or less—general publisher with Bernard Shaw and very
successful this relationship would prove to be.

Young Pegler was married to the sister of Dwye Evans, another
leading figure at Heinemann and the son of Charles Evans, the chairman before Frere. Pegler also had a brother who was looking round
for a job after the war. If Max would take him into partnership,
Dwye Evans said he would, while remaining with Heinemann, join
the board of the infant company. So he did. The firm got under way
rapidly, and acquired a staff of about ten—including Laura Coates,
daughter of Wells Coates, a leading architect. A dogsbody of sorts,
this busy and efficient lady started by making tea for the staff and
doing more or less all there was to be done on the editorial side; she
suggested authors and books; Stephen Potter's (a good friend of
Max's) very successful anthology, *Sense of Humour*, was one.
Another was one of Portugal's most famous writers, Eça de Queiroz.
Roy Campbell, the distinguished poet, translated many of his books.

In the meantime Max's marriage to Margaret Leighton was breaking up as each had careers to follow which often clashed and neither
was ready to sacrifice theirs. The marriage had lasted a few years and
the parting was sad but civilised. During this time the Savile Club
provided something of a sanctuary.

To tap the American scene, Frere gave Max on his first trip to the
States letters of introduction to leading publishing personalities.
Frere's letter of introduction to Simon & Schuster in New York
resulted in Max being summoned to the office of Richard Simon.
There sat the great man with his feet on the desk, smoking a cigar.
Going straight to the point, Max said, 'I've come to buy some
best-sellers.' They were joined by Peter Schwed (who later became
Chairman of the firm).

'Peter, I want to give a best-seller to Max.'

(293)

'Well, what about S. J. Perelman's *Westward Ha!* with Al Hirschfeld's illustrations? The English publishers say it's too expensive to produce.'

'I'll buy it,' said Max.

In fact, the firm published it and several more Perelmans, thus establishing a line in humour, with books by Paul Jennings from *The Observer* juggling deftly with the Oddlies (and they were many), and other authors of the contemporary scene. Wilfred Taylor's *Scot Free* and *Scot Easy* from, indeed, *The Scotsman*, Michael Ayrton's *Tittivulus* and cartoonists from *Punch* and the *New Yorker*. No less successful were Ivor Brown's word books, in which he explored the curiosities of language, and of English in particular, with a light and graceful touch.

By 1954 the firm had already moved out of its birth-place in Spicer & Pegler's to an unoccupied corner of another large publisher, Dent, in a handsome building in Covent Garden. It was supported by the inconspicuous but highly profitable HFL Ltd and its accountancy text books. By then John Hews, a brilliant accountant, had joined the firm and took HFL under one of his wings. Max Reinhardt himself had long left Kensington Close and was established in the first of a series of increasingly up-market London addresses. Having entered publishing, like John Lane before him—though less frenetically—he was finding publishing fun, and was rapidly learning its difficulties too.

His next adventure came from another member of the Savile Club, Sir Francis Meynell, founder of The Nonesuch Press in the 1920s, and it brought in a touch of publishing distinction. Meynell was a remarkable man. His mother was the poet Alice Meynell, his father Wilfred a man of letters, a copious journalist and managing director of the Catholic publishers Burns, Oates & Washbourne. He was also a dedicated expert in book production, and it was in this field especially that Francis followed him.

Born in 1891, Francis grew up, and remained, a man of strong leftward views and dandyish appearance, in maturity always wearing shirts with exceptionally long points to their soft collars. He was above all a poet and a typographer-designer, with a marked taste for the ornamental in style.

Over a game of snooker Francis offered Max the opportunity of restarting The Nonesuch Press with him. Meynell found in Max an effective and congenial ally with his 'combination of business acumen with unfailing courtesy and good humour'—qualities certainly needed in dealing with Meynell's temperamental and perfectionist approach to typography and book design (he had been known to attempt more than forty examples of a single title-page). But his determination to produce handsome books not only in limited editions but at reasonable prices in unlimited editions was widely appreciated.

The agreement signed on 5 February, 1953—and never again referred to in the twenty-two remaining years of Meynell's life—stipulated that Max Reinhardt Ltd should be responsible for producing Nonesuch books, to be planned and designed by Francis Meynell, advertised and sold at agreed prices, Meynell to have prior approval. Reinhardt joined the board of The Nonesuch Press, Meynell the board of Max Reinhardt Ltd.

This rapidly led to the 'Coronation' Shakespeare, dedicated to the new Queen, illustrated with engravings by Reynolds Stone and introduced by Ivor Brown. Selling at £7 7s., the four volumes had a runaway success—4,500 sets went within five months in Britain, the rest equally fast in the USA through Random House, a pre-war ally of Meynell's. Cautiously, Max had arranged that their chosen printers should be paid over a period of three years; in fact the bill was cleared within six months. Thereafter with a modest annual output of titles, Max kept the imprint financially afloat. Perhaps the most distinguished later offering of this still prestigious imprint was a celebration of the 200th anniversary of the birth of William Blake with an expanded edition of his *Complete Writings* in 1957, edited by Geoffrey Keynes.

Nonesuch in due course under the aegis of The Bodley Head also gave rise to junior editions, Nonesuch Cygnets: between 1963 and 1968 there were eleven of these pleasing volumes, carrying a wood-engraving of a swan by Joan Hassall, in front of Nonesuch Palace, Henry VIII's long-since vanished pleasure dome south of London.

Max's interest in book production and typography had been much stimulated, understandably, by his association with Meynell and before him by that with another distinguished typographer, Will Carter, who designed all the Reinhardt books before Max merged his company with The Bodley Head.

Max was also in association with Sir Gerald Barry, most genial of journalists, man of letters and in 1951 Director of the Festival of Britain, that forgotten post-war tonic. This in turn led to a new edition of *The Week-end Book*, a cheerful conceit, first published by Nonesuch in 1924 and soon becoming a small-scale institution for the upper-middle-class. Max's main contribution was to suggest an essay by Fred Hoyle, who had just delivered the first Reith Lecture on the Universe, instead of one of the poetry sections.

With experience gained in successfully publishing a small and choice list, Max Reinhardt gave rein to an ambition to continue expanding.

23

. . . And
Acquires The Bodley Head

When a new door opened to him in the early summer of 1956, Max was ready. This was when he was introduced by Ralph Richardson to L. A. (Boy) Hart. The two had served together as officers in the Fleet Air Arm, and Hart was now a director of the merchant banking firm of Ansbacher's. Hart had a proposition: would Max be interested in joining them to purchase the publishing house of The Bodley Head?

The suggestion came out of the blue, and naturally required some thought. After all, while The Bodley Head was not a giant among publishers, it was several sizes larger than the pleasing if still modest operations of Max Reinhardt Ltd.

By 20 August matters had advanced to the point where Hart wrote to Stanley Unwin making him a firm offer for the shares. Unwin had already sent to Reinhardt details of stocks of new books for 1955 onwards, and of advances to authors outstanding at that date, sales figures for the previous four and a half years and a salaries list. This, incidentally, disclosed the fact that young Barney Blackley, who, in Unwin's absence on a world cruise, had for a year been left in charge of the day-to-day running of the firm (while Frederick Muller stopped by each day to keep an eye on things), was receiving a magnificent £950 per annum. At this time he thought it reasonable to ask for more. 'Ask the new owner,' replied Sir Stanley. No doubt Blackley did so: with what result may be inferred from the fact that he retired from the firm only in 1987.

Nor did the agile Sir Stanley feel disposed to give the firm away, any more, perhaps, than did his partners in the enterprise, Wren

Howard of Cape and W. G. Taylor of Dent. Moreover he—or probably all three of these experienced publishers—detected in Ansbacher's a certain unfamiliarity with the publishing world. This enabled, or encouraged, them to indulge in a good deal of commercial and tax-conscious backing and filling, a certain amount of veiled implication, and a good deal of doubtless highly enjoyable moral indignation and highmindedness, the wording of this last being mulled over with evident relish—as in a letter from Unwin to Ansbacher's solicitors:

'What I am asked to do is impracticable as well as unreasonable. Surely they must realise that I cannot give guarantees on behalf of two publishing houses [Cape and Dent] of which I am not even a shareholder, let alone a director . . . They don't appear to realise that the two businesses of John Lane [all three partners persistently refer to the firm as John Lane rather than as John Lane The Bodley Head] and Allen & Unwin are *completely* different. If the Lane business had been suitable for incorporation in George Allen & Unwin Ltd. I would gladly pay more than £72,000 to absorb it. But it is not.'

If, he went on sternly, an expert on linguistics wrote a children's book published by John Lane, why should Allen & Unwin be debarred from publishing the linguistics book? Nor, he thundered, did the prospective purchasers seem to understand that:

'I have never cast eyes upon, or personally corresponded with, the vast majority of John Lane authors; juvenile authors have been seen by Miss Wilson and the novelists by Mr. Blackley. I have seen the readers' reports, authorised offers, signed contracts, but that is all.'

Moral indignation was now building up a fine head of steam:

'If what is wanted is an undertaking that I will do nothing to impair the goodwill of the firm I have laboriously built up, I will gladly give it, ridiculous as such a request seems to me . . . If an undertaking is wanted that I will not during the next five years publish any novel by a John Lane author other than Bertrand Russell and my son David (Severn) I will gladly give it, though the request is superfluous because George Allen & Unwin is not interested in fiction. I will gladly include Lane's most profitable authors, such as Helen Dore Boylston and John Everard.'

The latter was, as earlier mentioned, a photographer of feminine charms which Unwin had himself pressed, and most profitably, upon the reluctant manager, C. J. Greenwood 'because they are not up George Allen & Unwin's street.'

At this point Max himself was compelled to intervene in the negotiations, pointing out that Ansbacher's were not prepared to increase their offer of £72,000: 'A banker must, of necessity, only consider bargains.' In the end the three partners in The Bodley Head accepted Ansbacher's offer, having fended off various suitors. They felt able, furthermore, to offer some sharp advice to these ignorant financiers as, presumably, a fair return for having backed down from their asking price of £80,000. Max made characteristically emollient noises:

'. . . If by some happy chance you and Hart come to terms I promise you that The Bodley Head will continue to be well run.'

In return Unwin advises him 'to keep Blackley and Miss Wilson' both being first-rate and 'worth substantial increases as from January 1, which I should have granted . . . The two Miss Taylors do admirable work in their respective spheres.' One of these was Judy Taylor, soon to establish the Children's Book department as a leader in the field; the other was Iris Taylor, who joined the firm straight from school in the middle of the war as secretary and later assistant to the Chief Accountant, and was to be placed in charge of authors' royalties by Max, a charge she still fulfils. Under her aegis the delaying tactics of the old Bodley Head became (admittedly with the help of Max's financial stability) a thing of the past, and all

Bodley Head authors should call down blessings on her name. 'I would be happy,' Max wrote with a touch of grandeur to Stanley Unwin—having sorted out a few disputes about the valuation of stock:

'. . . to receive The Bodley Head into our group, and take good care of all that is inherent in its rich tradition. I have also promised you that the company's staff will be well looked after, and Spicer & Pegler, from whom I bought HFL (Publishers) Ltd and The Stellar Press, will confirm to you that we are in the habit of doing this.'

What called forth these anxious reassurances was a dark suspicion on the side of Unwin, Howard and Taylor that, whatever might be the case with Max, Ansbacher's, these banker fellows, were not only ignorant of the financial aspects of publishing, but moved in a different world, with absolutely no understanding of the human element. Unwin wrote a draft:

'While it is, of course, true that publishers must depend to some extent on keeping the authors whose work they have published as well as by attracting new authors, it is a mistake to look upon authors as a kind of property to be bought and sold at will; for in fact authors will not submit to such treatment, as every publisher knows.'

Wren Howard thought this too mild, and proposed:

'. . . it is a mistake to regard and treat authors as if they were cattle or sheep to be bought or slaughtered at will.'

On the other hand both Unwin and Taylor recoiled from the generous suggestion that the contract of sale should offer some 'post-sale aid' by way of steering books to The Bodley Head if 'thought more suitable to their list than to our own'. All, however, consented to a contractual agreement that there should be no 'detrimental action against The Bodley Head or its authors, at least for a five-year period', and at least 'as long as Max Reinhardt personally manages the business.' Perhaps, though, the vendors wondered, there should be a reciprocal quid pro quo to prevent The Bodley Head from poaching in *their* preserves.

Thus, laboriously, among what Ansbacher's representatives repeatedly claimed to be 'normal business practice', hair-splitting and scarcely veiled innuendo, together with a last-minute frolic when Ansbacher ingeniously but unsuccessfully tried to make The Bodley Head their accomplices in dodging Stamp Duty, agreement was at last reached, and The Bodley Head passed into Max Reinhardt's hands. Or, as Unwin put it in his autobiography, with a perhaps characteristic mixture of factual truth and fanciful mischief, the firm 'was bought by the merchant bankers Ansbacher's, who put Max Reinhardt in to run it.'

Some years later Unwin told Max that his success was a cause for pride. 'But why were you so rude to me?' asked Max, still smarting under Unwin's abrasive negotiating manner. 'Rude?' said Unwin, 'Me? Tactics, my dear chap, tactics.' But he also told his son Rayner (later Chairman of Allen & Unwin) that Max Reinhardt was the only man with whom he had done substantial business for whom he retained real respect.

24

A Little Empire-building

One morning early in 1957, on the actual day of the sale, Iris Taylor was at work in the cheek-by-jowl Bodley Head offices in Little Russell Street. It was about the time when Sir Stanley was due to make his bustling entrance, though for some time rumours (the same rumours that had already persuaded Richard Hough to leave the firm) had been circulating which suggested that Unwin was about to sell them all off. Suddenly, a stranger appeared and startled, she said to herself, 'H'm, it seems we're in for some changes here.'

And so they were. It was at Reinhardt's suggestion that Unwin had brought him along to meet the staff. Barney Blackley, too, managing the firm, such as it was, was startled when, alongside the small, busy, beaming, teetotal, non-smoking figure of Unwin, appeared pipe-smoking Max, diffusing quiet panache, an air of cosmopolitan worldliness, a sense of flourish without ostentation. Nobody could say as much for the Bodley Head offices—or Allen & Unwin's for that matter, grander though they were. The first change arose from the fact that Max was already busy arranging new premises for his own firm. Looking only to the needs of Max Reinhardt Ltd, he had found a block being rebuilt in Earlham Street (conveniently close to the Ivy Restaurant, then at the height of its gossip-columnists' fame), and bought the lease, subject to the building being completed. This now also had to embrace The Bodley Head, and proved to be too small. A floor of office space across the street became available and he took it as an annex.

After their usual Sunday game of squash, he had taken Ralph Richardson to see his principal premises, which had by this time a small roof garden, and was approaching completion. 'What about money?' Richardson had asked. More was needed, replied Max. 'Well,' said Richardson, producing a cheque book as if by magic, 'how about £5,000?' 'Must have a written contract,' said Max. 'Oh well, if you insist.' That, they thought, would finish off the ground floor, give the firm a shop window. So it did, and the roof was pressed into service for a while, complete with sunshades, as a fine-weather entertainment area.

Meanwhile the fifteen members of The Bodley Head staff moved to Earlham Street and were just as cramped as they had been before. Old Bodley Head traditions for distinguished typography and design were encouraged, or revived, by Will Carter, and before long he was replaced by a younger man who remains an important figure in design and book production: John Ryder.

Born in London and born to be a designer, Ryder has to the present time spent all his working life in that city. Perhaps not surprisingly, on leaving school after the middle of the 1930s, jobs were difficult to find. But he did get one in a bookshop. Also he bought a typewriter and set about making a number of typewritten books for himself. These were typed in folded sections and later sewn and bound by a local craftsman. The bookshop was John Baker's Phoenix Book Company which later managed the selection and running of Readers Union. The stylishness of that book club already showed signs of what were to be the typographical hallmarks of Ryder's style.

Three months after the declaration of war in 1939 Ryder was called up, stood before a tribunal and was registered as a conscientious objector. For just over five years, as a private in the Army, he worked on east coast defences, later was engaged in loading supply ships in Cardiff and later still in digging for unexploded bombs in Bedfordshire until the final stage of active non-aggression led to airborne operations in Normandy and over the Rhine at Wesel. Both operations were performed without arms as originally registered, and were carried out by small surgical units dropped by parachute between the front lines. A period of six months to unwind from such intensity was spent in Palestine and, in 1946, he was demobilised and went back to John Baker who had by then transformed the bookshop into a picture gallery and publishing office, Phoenix House, a subsidiary of J. M. Dent.

Then from 1946 onwards the next ten years were spent in designing and producing books for Phoenix House. Both John Baker's and John Ryder's reputations were established in this period. Then in 1957 Ryder moved upwards, on Will Carter's recommendation, to work at The Bodley Head. But before that happy change took place, he began a friendship with Giovanni Mardersteig of the Officina Bodoni at Verona which was to last until Mardersteig's death in 1977; he wrote and designed and published *Printing for Pleasure* in 1955 and *A Suite of Fleurons* in 1956, the year in which Francis Meynell and Desmond Flower drew him into the Double Crown Club.

The devoted production manager at The Bodley Head was the invaluable Len Lake, who had made his life with the firm since 1928, and who was by the time of Reinhardt's arrival looking after paper buying, printing, sending out of proofs, binding, stock-taking and acting as chief order clerk. By the mid 1960s, however, Ryder was splitting the production of adult and children's books with Iain Bain who went on to become manager of the publications department at The Tate Gallery, while Ryder became director of the design and production departments at The Bodley Head. As such he has put his stamp on the firm's publications. His principal insistence has been on legibility. This, combined with an instinctive eye for the printed page as the reader would hope to find it, did not make him a fashionable designer in the 1960s, when—and indeed since—legibility has played a low profile and fashions dragging back to the 1920s have become popular. Fashion, perhaps, is anathema to his ways of working and living.

He revived, together with Iain Bain, for as long as it was financially feasible, a dormant specialist publisher, Nattali & Maurice. This firm, established in 1825, was bought by G. P. Putnam in 1931. When it passed to The Bodley Head in 1962 Ryder prepared a number of new books, such as *Bewick to Dovaston, Letters, 1824–28*, Stanley Morison's *Letter Forms*, Giovanni Mardersteig's astonishingly complete account of the production of a medical book in 1447 at Padua. Ryder also discovered the plant of a famous and beautiful book, William Daniell's *A Voyage Round Great Britain*, in the shape of over 300 aquatint plates. After some experiments to reprint them successfully the plates were sold to The Tate Gallery as a national inheritance that had to have a proper home.

Ryder's combination of clarity, elegance and visually durable impact has given The Bodley Head books their unmistakable quality: exemplified especially in Graham Greene's new editions and collected works—not least the catalogue of *Victorian Detective Fiction* published in 1966—the new editions and collected works of William Trevor, the many volumes of Shaw's plays, letters and music criticism, two editions of James Joyce's *Ulysses*, each as far removed from the other in techniques of production as they possibly could be, and the one book of Maurice Sendak to be designed and made on this side of the Atlantic—drawings for Glyndebourne's version of *The Love for Three Oranges*.

These are the most obvious of Ryder's contributions to the spirit of The Bodley Head, on whose list he has also happily featured as an author, including the perennially popular *Printing for Pleasure*, in a version substantially rewritten.

In 1974 The Bodleian Library, Oxford, staged a major exhibition selected from all of Ryder's work, from the pre-war typewritten books, to current work at The Bodley Head and at The Stellar Press (of which he was then a director). Two years after the Oxford exhibition Ryder began a series of lectures which he later prepared for The Bodley Head to publish in 1979 as *The Case for Legibility*.

Of course no design director acts alone and Ryder would be the first to acknowledge invaluable help for many years from Judy Taylor. Iain Bain is to this day a valuable adviser, as are Christopher Bradshaw, John Dreyfus and Ron Costley. For most of this thirty-year period Michael Harvey, letter-designer of special distinction, has responded to countless projects and become a key figure in the design office much as Beardsley might have done had John Lane so wished it.

And design problems must be shared with printers so that experience of working together may benefit both printers and client. Ryder's closest relationships were formed with Bill Hummerstone (Stellar Press), Mark Clowes (William Clowes) and with Philip Evans (Tinlings).

Artists also play an important part in the planning of books with illustrations, decorations, lettering or devices. It is rare indeed for the book designer to have all these skills and talents. Ryder has worked with many artists and knows that the closer the association and understanding between artist and designer the more satisfactory will be the end result.

A less flamboyant but hardly less important figure in The Bodley Head had already joined Max Reinhardt by way of HFL Ltd in 1950, preferring this small and interesting firm to a larger one. John Hews, a young accountant, had served in the RAF during the war as a Beaufighter navigator. He has remained with the firm, or firms, and indeed with Max Reinhardt till now. From the office where, in Spicer & Pegler's building, the new-born HFL Ltd began its new life, Hews followed the flag to end up as Finance Director.

Apart from the day-to-day work of running HFL's commonplace financial affairs, Hews had soon had to grapple with Max's acquisition. The proposal for the acquisition of the firm had been complicated enough, and John Hews certainly proved a friend in need. The Bodley Head had been for sale at £72,000. This sum was to be paid by Ansbacher on loan. Max Reinhardt was to throw in MR Ltd which he guaranteed would produce £15,000, anything extra produced to go to him. The Bodley Head was to be owned half by Ansbacher, half by Reinhardt, thus starting his part-ownership of The Bodley Head with this sum, repayable with normal rates of interest. In the event, and with the co-operation of the Westminster Bank, he had soon been able to build a warehouse, improve the premises of The Stellar Press at Hatfield, and pay off Ansbacher's to gain control of eighty per cent of The Bodley Head.

Hardly had Reinhardt surveyed the unexciting premises and exciting prospects of The Bodley Head before he was offered, by a curious irony, the business of Werner Laurie: the very firm which, in the 1890s, had been The Bodley Head's principal rival as publishers of poetry, and the continued object of Richard Le Gallienne's scorn. Now, sixty years on, things had much changed, but it was with The Bodley Head that the crumbling firm found shelter. Its backlist was not without plums—chief among them, as it turned out, Winston Graham's Poldark novels. Graham was to become a great personal friend and transferred all those of his books originally published by Hodder to The Bodley Head.

The Bodley Head itself surged invisibly to the fore during the next few years. In 1962 another publishing house of unexceptionable respectability accepted The Bodley Head's umbrella. Hollis & Carter were generally known as a lay affiliate to the Roman Catholic publishing house of Burns & Oates. The Hollis of the firm was the writer and Conservative MP, Christopher Hollis. Along with biography, history and current affairs publications this firm had built up under the impulse of another Conservative MP and ex-naval officer, David James, an interesting list of books on sailing and navigation, which perhaps appealed to Max's intermittent enthusiasm for small boats.

In 1964, however, came what was initially a more difficult proposition. G. P. Putnam was a long-established American firm of considerable repute. Its London branch was allied but, by 1905, separate and controlled by the rigid figure of Constant Huntington, also an American, but more English than the English and (perhaps to outdo John Lane) also married to an American heiress.

Putnam's backlist in the early 1960s was not to be despised— though perhaps firmly pruned, especially of poets. Just as Hollis & Carter had a surprise list of navigational books, so Putnam had an even longer list of aeronautical books. These, extremely expensive to produce, relatively modest in price, were by no means money-spinners, but had a world reputation. The general list included Erich Maria Remarque's novel *All Quiet on the Western Front*, which has never been out of print since it was first published in 1929. The early works of L. P. Hartley, including the Eustace and Hilda trilogy, always received glowing reviews if seldom at that stage more than modest sales. Isak Dinesen, too (alias Karen Blixen), was in the right circles a name to conjure with, as was Bernard Berenson, the art-historical sage. Putnam's could also be proud of Dr Marie Stopes, pioneer of birth control, or at any rate of permitted, recognised birth control. Not least of the treasures accruing from the backlist was Ernest Newman, whose place in the galaxy of musical critics has never been challenged, and whose popular *Wagner Nights* was soon to be re-issued. Of transcending popularity remained that agreeable little hymn of praise to the American rural outside-privy builder, Charles Sale's *The Specialist* (1930), belatedly followed in 1982 by its sequel *The Master Builder*. On the list was also to be found Henry Williamson's classic for children, *Tarka the Otter*; when Sir Francis Meynell chose it for his Nonesuch Cygnets edition, some fifty years after its first publication, the author was still making corrections in proof.

By the 1960s, and Constant Huntington's death, the firm was owned by Roger Lubbock, nephew of Percy Lubbock, Italophile author of *The Craft of Fiction*. He himself was a product of Eton, the Navy, Cambridge and, modestly, journalism. He was, needless to say, a member of the Savile Club and a squash player. With him were Constant Huntington's nephew, John, formerly much put-upon by his unsympathetic uncle; James MacGibbon, who returned to Putnam's after working there in his youth—a most experienced publisher and sailor; and soon, brought in by Lubbock, John Pudney, the all-round man of letters.

In the Putnam basket were also to be found Bowes & Bowes the academic publishers from Cambridge, and Nattali & Maurice, already mentioned. One way and another, and despite its excellent backlist, Putnam's found itself awkwardly placed as a publisher and impossibly placed as a business proposition: so much so, in fact, that a prospective deal with Heinemann, who had already gathered

Secker & Warburg, Peter Davies and The World's Work under its wing, was firmly quashed.

So approaches were made to Max Reinhardt for an introduction to Ansbacher. Ansbacher said they would buy the firm if it were done through The Bodley Head. Employers and employees alike, they were a proud lot, and before very long all concerned got tired. The directors of Putnam's drifted off, not without acrimony at several levels. The rank-and-file, however, discovered that Reinhardt was an easy man to work for, and with, a paternal figure of unshakeable availability; they remained, to provide The Bodley Head with some sterling staff members, notably the plump, friendly and unerringly efficient orders clerk Rene Antink, who retired only in 1986, and the majestic late Fred Miller, of whom Max was heard to observe, during the first onset of computerisation, 'Fred is my computer.'

While all these acquisitions, and their personal problems, were going on, and under Reinhardt The Bodley Head was expanding and improving its personal skills, Max had encountered what perhaps seemed like a stroke of ill-fortune but was in fact a stroke of luck in more senses than one.

25

Graham Greene Joins the List

When Ansbacher's, in the person of L. A. Hart, put its proposal for taking over The Bodley Head to Max Reinhardt, it was only one of many financial institutions sniffing round independent publishing houses in search of either businesses under-exploited for lack of capital, or more simply as suitable channels for tax losses—and in some cases, for a chance to meet more interesting people than those normally encountered in the City.

This was certainly the case with Hart, a sharp but also a civilised businessman—and a more than competent painter. Initially this could not have been said of George Ansley of Ansbacher's, who could not understand why Hart was so keen to enter the publishing field: yet, to a man who eventually left a fortune of £30 million, and managed to avoid paying death duties, the money involved was barely worth bothering about. Hart and Reinhardt therefore devised a plan: to flatter Ansley by making him Chairman. The plan worked. Ansley became fascinated with books, or at any rate with the sort of people he now met through this to him otherwise trivial little business. Ansley lived in Paris and flew over to London for board meetings. It soon became clear to other Bodley Head directors that his presence ensured discussion, such as it was, of a purely financial nature, which most of them were ill-equipped to take part in, or even to understand.

One day Hart, still anxious to widen the spectrum, gave a luncheon party at Ansbacher's which included Graham Greene, always fascinated by and ready to exercise his novelist's curiosity about big business. By way of providing a more or less bookish link with Greene, Reinhardt was also invited. This proved a more significant

first meeting between these two men than perhaps Ansbacher, Reinhardt or Greene suspected. They got on well. Soon afterwards Hart
suggested to Reinhardt that Greene might become a director. He
was, in the late 1950s, not only a famous novelist but had already, so
to speak, qualified as a publisher, having been an editorial director of
Eyre & Spottiswoode. He could perfectly well, said Hart, go on
being published by Heinemann while he was a director of The Bodley Head; Greene thought so too, and everybody was happy—
except perhaps J. B. Priestley, another Heinemann author, who had,
at Max's suggestion, joined The Bodley Head's board in 1957. This
was the firm which in the 1920s had published all his early non-
fiction work, for whom he had long ago read manuscripts, and in
whose house magazine, *The Bodleian*, he had written so many early
blasts of commonsense, mostly at odds—as any commonsense views
so often are—with the received ideas of the time.

Neither Priestley nor Greene was particularly at home in this
literary frog-pond—nor were they naturally congenial to each other.
The parting of the ways was close at hand. It arose out of the publication of Vladimir Nabokov's *Lolita*. Published in Paris by the
notorious Maurice Girodias, this cunning evocation of sexuality and
the American way of life had been enthusiastically introduced to
Britain by Greene in a Sunday newspaper article; it was natural that
he should advance its claims for British publication by The Bodley
Head.

Alas, Priestley muttered round his pipe that he 'wasn't going to
remain a director of a firm which published muck like that . . . It'll
only encourage dirty old men.' In the event the book was published
by Weidenfeld & Nicolson, The Bodley Head having refused joint
publication, for reasons nothing to do with the disagreement between
Greene and Priestley.

At this time, too, another veteran Bodley Head author returned to
the fold. André Maurois was in any case an old acquaintance of
Reinhardt's. By way of cementing the reunion, he decided to give a
dinner party for Maurois and his wife. Happening to mention this
forthcoming event to George Ansley, he found the occasion taken

over by the financier. He would give the dinner party instead in Paris and in his own house, too: appropriately, as it turned out, for he lived in The Villa Saïd, formerly Anatole France's Paris house, in which Madame Maurois had grown up as a young member of France's unconventional household.

The occasion was a great success. Flushed with triumph, Ansley then proposed, and carried out, a singular plan: he organised a large Anglo-French literary lunch at the Plaza Athénée hotel, held with considerable pomp, attended and addressed by the British Ambassador, Sir Gladwyn Jebb. In the course of his speech Jebb mentioned (what was in most people's minds) that though this was an extremely agreeable occasion, its purpose was by no means clear.

Ansley, however, heartened by this further pseudo-literary success, was beginning to express opinions about books, or at any rate about the sort of books The Bodley Head was publishing. His principal concern was to avoid looking ridiculous in that self-regarding institution, the Paris Travellers Club. He became particularly anxious (not without reason) about another of Graham Greene's enthusiasms, *Candy*, a lively sexual frolic of the kind associated with the 1960s spirit. Though not noticeably anxious to expand his firm's interest in sexual frolics, Reinhardt's wish to lift the enabling shadow of Ansbacher's was reinforced, and was soon to be reinforced even further.

In that same Paris Travellers Club Ansley used to meet his fellow-tycoon Lionel Fraser. Fraser, as Chairman of Tilling, also controlled, or thought he did, the Heinemann Group, and lent a friendly ear to Ansley's suggestion of a merger between Heinemann and The Bodley Head.

Although it seems difficult to believe—so many were their big-selling names—Heinemann was in financial difficulties. Another plan, to sell it to the American publishers McGraw-Hill was also thwarted, not least by Heinemann staff, who were not consulted. Learning nothing from this experience, Fraser and Ansley went ahead with their idea of a merger with The Bodley Head; as the other firm involved was also British, perhaps there would be fewer objections to overcome, while the combined financial muscle of Ansbacher and Fraser—75 per cent to the Heinemann group, 25 per cent to the smaller Bodley Head—would surely make up a viable commercial prospect. Fraser became greatly enthusiastic. With Frere as chairman of Heinemann, Max would become Joint Managing-Director of the overall company, with Peter Ryder of Tillings. Graham Greene would be the publishers' literary adviser. Heinemann would have enough work to occupy its handsome printing works in the sylvan calm of Kingswood, in the Surrey uplands; it would no longer have to keep itself going by heavy overprinting of, for example, American family sagas, its charges for which did nothing to aid, and much to depress, the publishing house.

Reinhardt's obligations to Ansbacher's at this point left him no option but to agree. Besides, his new friend Graham Greene was all for it. In publishing terms the organisation would have been a very big one. There seemed no reason why the Bodley Head staff would suffer. All would be well. The principals—Fraser, Ryder, Reinhardt and Greene—met one Sunday night at Fraser's flat in Lowndes Square in an atmosphere of cordial optimism. Greene and the Reinhardts went off to dine with old friends, the actor Anthony Quayle (one of Max's original directors) and his wife at the nearby Brompton Grill. 'The deal is done,' said Graham Greene, over champagne.

But it was not. On the following day Fraser himself assembled Heinemann's staff to tell them the good news. As this was the first, rumours apart, that even the other directors had heard of it, perhaps it was not surprising that their reaction was hostile: so hostile that Fraser lost his nerve. He called on Graham Greene, and wrote to Reinhardt, Ansley and Hart backing out of the deal they had all supposed to be firm. The businessmen had failed to learn, in Wren Howard's words, that editors, like writers, 'were not to be bought and sold like cattle.' A shock for Reinhardt—but some would say a blessing in disguise. His commercial background, by family connection and education, enabled him to cope more successfully than most relatively small publishers with the complexities of trade; he would no doubt have continued to do so in the world of high finance, but he would have inevitably been transformed from a personal publisher into a mere businessman.

In the event Max's escape brought him not only back to the kind of publishing he liked, but an unexpected bonus. Graham Greene was outraged at Fraser's insensitivity and, much disliking the thought of being bought by 'a bus company'—a reference to Tilling's distant origins—he almost immediately transferred himself to The Bodley Head who published *In Search of a Character* in 1961. His friendship with Max was even more strongly bonded by this apparent reverse. And Frere, who survived the debacle only by being, as the saying goes, kicked upstairs, shortly left Heinemann; he did not join The Bodley Head, preferring the douceurs of the South of France; but he did bring to The Bodley Head's list a string of notable names—Eric Ambler, Georgette Heyer, George Millar (whose war-time story *Maquis* had launched at Heinemanns a successful string of adventurous travel books). Two Heinemann stalwarts refused to move: Richard Church, poet, essayist and highly successful autobiographer, and Priestley, who said 'They made me, I must stand by them now.'

No such problem, however, prevented another friend, Arthur Crook, lately of the *Times Literary Supplement*, from joining the firm as a consultant at about this time. He gave some sound literary advice and brought valuable authors to the firm, like M. R. D. Foot, whose book *MI 9* was a great seller, and Samuel Hynes, whose *The Auden Generation* had a splendid reception and who is now under contract for a further work, *The World After the War*.

Soon, Max Reinhardt found himself in a position to buy all Ansbacher's stock, from Ansley first and from Hart's descendants after his death.

26

Publishing for Children

'It was all fun,' said Max Reinhardt. 'Friends, meetings, ideas'—and, he might have added, families. Before taking over The Bodley Head, Max had decided to fly to New York (his life on this trip insured for a large sum by the ever-cautious Ansbacher) to propose to the elegant Joan MacDonald, an American and his present wife, who was then casting director in New York television. She has played a big supporting part in his publishing activities. A great capacity for pleasure illuminated Max's life and work, as it had John Lane's, but for Max, his wife and their two daughters came first. The family instinct, indeed, had been strong in him all his life, even though he moved away from the family business.

As his publishing interests took shape, it soon became clear that these too were to assume the outlines of a family, with Max as pater-familias. Many bright young men came under his influence before they moved on—John Goodwin, dapper in an open-necked shirt, who went on to be chief of public relations with the Royal Shakespeare Company; Colin Haycraft, before long running with exuberant eccentricity his own publishing house, Duckworth; Peter Green, scholar and biographer of Kenneth Grahame; Nigel Hollis, son of Christopher and, in due course, a director of Heinemann; Brian Glanville, novelist and sports writer and the ubiquitous, ever-friendly Laurence Cotterell, fertile in ideas.

Gradually, though, a group crystallised round the father figure. The young veteran Barney Blackley was of course already there, having been recruited by Greenwood in 1952, and was there to remain, like the young Iris Taylor, until now, congenially un-ambitious, though of course achieving one of those directorships which became the hallmark of The Bodley Head's increasing and famously long list of such inexpensive tributes. Barney Blackley always treasured two particular pieces of advice proffered to him by Stanley Unwin. 'Never', he said, 'remainder a book without careful thought.' As an instance of this, he realised 6d. a copy on a few hundred copies of Gray's *Elegy* otherwise valued scarcely above 1d. each, by seeking out the Vicar of Stoke Poges, site of the country churchyard celebrated in the poem, and doing a deal with him. (The Vicar realised one hundred per cent profit on resale.) The other piece of advice was, 'If you must meet an author, always wear your oldest suit.' Barney paid little attention to the last cunning injunction, whether or not he had to meet an author.

Soon Blackley was joined as an editor by Guido Waldman, son of Milton Waldman, whose association with The Bodley Head as reader and author dated back to the 1920s; an American—and also, perhaps it was only to be expected, a member of the Savile Club. His son still keeps a famously scrupulous eye upon the texts of slap-dash authors (including the author of this book).

Some three years later, in 1961, they were joined by the poet, translator and relaxed yet alert talent-spotter James Michie, who came from Heinemann as Chief Editor—a role which he relinquished, not without relief, when his talents were in danger of being swamped by the increasing mass of administrative detail in the rapidly-expanding firm, though he remained, and remains, as editor and literary midwife to some of the firm's most distinguished authors.

At Oxford he had read both classics and English. Fortune led him to Heinemann, where Frere's highly personal relationship with his authors appealed to him; so did his relaxed attitude towards Michie's agreeable notion of the freedoms within which he wished to work. Frere was asked by Michie, for example, for three months' leave of absence. He waited for Michie's hard-luck story: 'Well, I've never read *War and Peace*, and I should like to go to Greece and set about it.' Leave was granted. Later, when Heinemann was in financial difficulties, Michie also began to feel that Tilling's was not the sort of organisation to which he could easily give his loyalties. Then one evening Graham Greene, as a Bodley Head director, asked Michie to dinner, and suggested that he should think about seeing Max, which he did, and much liked him. In the course of the interview, by way of testing the water, Michie asked whether Max wished him to try to bring, for example, Anthony Powell or Olivia Manning with him. 'That's not the reason for the offer,' said Max. 'It's you, James, whose talents we're interested in.' So Michie came to The Bodley Head in its Earlham Street office. There he found an exceptionally agreeable atmosphere in older and younger colleagues alike, with Max a paternalistic figure, completely in charge. And when, says Michie, anyone had any personal problem, Max was 'a rock of support and practical help'.

The atmosphere of high-spirited optimism engendered by Max was enhanced by the vitality and charm contributed by Euan Cameron. This lively Scot (brought up in Argentina) first came briefly, under the aegis of Max's publicity consultant Laurence Cotterell, and left, to return in 1968 as Publicity Manager, and before long, Director. In the mid-1970s he began to combine his promotional work with that of editor, for which he acquired both the taste and aptitude, recruiting a number of young authors such as Allan Massie, Ronald Frame and David Wheldon, as well as spotting the potential in Tristan Jones. When ultimately, in 1986, the Bodley Head and Cape publicity departments were to merge, he was to take the opportunity to seek a full-time career as an editor.

One constituent of Reinhardt's group of young publishers meanwhile grew even more rapidly, and today represents more than half The Bodley Head's output and turnover: the Children's Book Department, whose range encompassed pre-schoolers and teenagers, with a list that has acquired a considerable standing among librarians and teachers.

In the haphazard days of the Nineties, the firm published Kenneth Grahame's *Dream Days* and *The Golden Age*, and also (taking them over from Routledge) the Toy Books of the artist Walter Crane, whose poetry John Lane included in *The Yellow Book*. In due course Allen Lane too published a scattering of children's books, including those popular but loss-making Walt Disney titles, and a number of volumes with lines enviably far apart, and margins too splendidly ample for today's economics, but with poorly printed colour.

One of Allen Lane's authors survives on The Bodley Head list. The sprightly near nonagenarian, Norman Hunter, was first discovered by Lane himself, or so he claimed, when listening to the BBC's Children's Hour. Some of his stories were read with suitable unction by a once notable raconteur, A. J. Alan. They had first appeared in the 1920s in a children's magazine called *The Merry-Go-Round*, published in Oxford. Lane thought they would make a book, and in 1933 appeared *The Incredible Adventures of Professor Branestawm*, illustrated by an old Bodley Head hand, W. Heath Robinson. This engaging debut of the mad professor and his zany, not to say surrealist, inventions, became with its successors an unquenchable source of delight for generations of young readers. So indeed was the author, for in a South London boyhood, and during a variegated time in journalism and advertising, he had become also a professional illusionist, who not only gave more than two hundred performances for that royal cenacle of illusionists, Maskelyne and Devant, but was still performing his conjuring tricks for Max Reinhardt's young daughters and their friends some twenty years ago. Both Hunter and Branestawm became a joint figurehead for the lighter (and far from unprofitable) side of The Bodley Head as well as making an early appearance in Puffin Story Books when Allen Lane demonstrated his continued interest in children's books by starting a paperback series in the dark war-time days of 1941.

But it was not until late in the day, after the Second World War, that Stanley Unwin, C. J. Greenwood, and the nebulous Yorkshireman, Martin Foster, began to realise the possibilities of children's books. Young Richard Hough also turned his attention to them and the openings for non-fiction with 'Men of the Modern Age', while his first wife Charlotte provided the illustrations for many of the children's novels. At the beginning of the Reinhardt years the first children's book editor was appointed: Barbara Ker Wilson was paid the then startling salary of £1,000 a year, and with John Ryder as head of design The Bodley Head moved smartly into the vanguard of a rapidly-changing and expanding world of children's books. Barbara Ker Wilson, having produced the first commercial catalogue of children's books, inaugurated many co-operative publishing ventures, and introduced the many volumes featuring that redoubtable pirate, Captain Pugwash, soon married and then went to work for William Collins. Judy Taylor, whom Richard Hough had brought into the firm on her return from her year in Canada, was still thought too young to take sole charge of what was clearly an important factor in the market. Antony Kamm came in for a while, but more importantly in 1959 so did Kathleen Lines. She never joined the staff of the firm, but seldom can the conveniently evasive title of consultant have been more accurately applied.

This immensely influential lady had come to Britain from Canada and the Toronto Public Library where she had trained as a children's Librarian under the redoubtable Lillian Smith. Once in England she had done work for the Oxford University Press: she had compiled *Four to Fourteen*, an annotated booklist of children's reading for the National Book League, which insisted—a novel notion then—on the same (or higher) literary standards for children's as for adult books. She had written about and reviewed children's books for *The Sunday Times* and was soon seen by Max Reinhardt as a potential ally in building the children's list.

It also became clear to him that in Judy Taylor—by now aged 27 —he had a notable publishing personality to hand. And with Kathleen Lines to consult, she became head of the children's book department. Very soon Miss Lines was playing Minerva to three graces, and a golden age of children's books set in.

Back in 1951 Jill Black, a young woman with a history degree from London and a certificate from the London College of Secretaries, went to work as a secretary (there were virtually no other jobs for women in publishing) with the highly respectable educational publishers, Edward Arnold. She was recommended to Reinhardt as a possible head of the children's department, but as she at that stage lacked the relevant experience, she was taken on as children's book editor, with the warm recommendation of such luminaries as Grace Hogarth and Kathleen Lines, who had preceded her at Abelard-Schumann, an American firm starting a small London office. When the position of deputy to Judy Taylor became vacant in 1959 she joined The Bodley Head with responsibility for books for older children, making in due course something of a speciality of commissioning the re-telling, by writers such as Rosemary Sutcliff, of myth and legend.

Then in 1961 came Margaret Clark. She could look back in exasperation at her own innocence as the ruthlessly exploited secretary to Allen Lane, but he had given her the chance to move into Penguin's editorial department where she had worked with Eleanor Graham on the Puffin list. Eventually steeling herself to make a move, she came to The Bodley Head for three months while Judy Taylor was visiting America for the firm and Jill Black, having married and started a family, wanted to work part-time. The three months in 1961 have extended themselves to the present.

And so that golden age took shape. Max was endlessly supportive of his children's editors, always ready to entertain their authors stylishly, always ready to reassure them, especially about money ('Don't worry about that, leave me to worry about that'). Kathleen Lines, known to them as K, was in her field no less so; she fostered the three of them, encouraged their good ideas, restrained their less promising ones, entertained them in her Sussex cottage, where many projects were cooked up over late-night drinks, and, above all, passed on to them her 'creed' that only the best books are good enough for children.

As for the market, it seemed that they could do no wrong. Suddenly money was available for libraries and schools. Suddenly a whole crop of immensely talented designers and illustrators flowered on every hand, their work instinct with stylish gaiety. Picture books like *The Happy Lion* and *Anatole* and Acorn Books encouraged the very young into reading at one end of the scale, and at the other, books were published for what the Children's Department called New Adults in the transitional stage. Gone, at any rate, was the manner of 'Great Men of the Counties': in the volume dealing with Kent, the life of Sir Philip Sidney had begun 'Every boy' (and, who knows, girls were included) 'loves his own County best and that is right. There are beauties and virtues in all.' The sentiment may just pass muster, the style will not.

Judy Taylor's unique talent in the creation of picture books brought to the firm artists of such standing as Mitsumasa Anno, Shirley Hughes, Pat Hutchins, Renate Meyer, Maureen Roffey and —most celebrated of all—Maurice Sendak. The publication of *Where the Wild Things Are* in 1967 was, perhaps, the most exciting event in the decade for the children's list, in more ways than one. In the first place, there was much discussion about whether it was right to publish this alarming work at all. True, all evidence from the United States, where it had been published in 1964, suggested that although adults were horrified by its savagery, children lapped it up. Not that this should have come as any surprise; fairy tales down the millennia have made it clear that children like nothing better than, like Dickens's Fat Boy in *The Pickwick Papers*, to give themselves the shivers. Even Judy Taylor's colleagues had misgivings, but of course she was right in recognising the book's qualities; right too in believing that it would merely 'stimulate them in their own wild rumpus.'

The other problem was that this large-format book, in a satisfactory production, with forty-eight pages printed in full colour, would have to be sold at too high a price. The only answer was to persuade publishers in other countries to collaborate by printing together as many editions as possible, changing only the black plate which embodied the translated texts. At the Bologna Children's Book Fair the previous year Margaret Clark was able to organise such an international co-edition, which was already becoming a staple of children's book publishing. The most favourable printing deal was obtained in Holland, and it was only unfortunate that currency exchange fluctuations prevented the firm making an adequate profit. This, however, was the beginning of an increasingly important source of revenue—the organisation of co-printing of picture books alongside the sale of translation rights in both picture books and children's novels.

The publication of Maurice Sendak's book in London on 10 April, 1967, brought the artist himself to Britain—a journey he had not undertaken lightly, since he loathed flying. After an appearance on a late-night television programme, he went the next day to Newcastle for another television appearance, in the course of which he began to feel acutely ill. A doctor summoned to the hotel where he and Judy were staying dismissed his symptoms as indigestion and it was only on Judy's insistence that he was taken to hospital where it was discovered he had had a heart attack. So the world's most famous children's book illustrator has good reason to remember that year and his first introduction to The Bodley Head.

Maybe less subject to the problems of costings were informational and general non-fiction books. School libraries created a vast market, which The Bodley Head was ready to fill with quality. Much of this, in the 1960s and 1970s, came under the wing of Jill Black, especially books for older children; there was often, as in Eric de Maré's history of *London's River*, or Christopher Headington's *The Orchestra and its Instruments*, little enough to mark children from adults. In 1972 Jill Black launched the Bodley Head Archaeologies, following up the interest aroused by the television programmes 'Animal, Vegetable and Mineral' and 'Chronicle'. Magnus Magnusson, later of 'Mastermind' fame, one of the moving spirits of 'Chronicle', was the general outside editor, and himself wrote the introductory book of the series, *Introducing Archaeology*.

Jill Black's principle was 'to get experts as authors, not children's book writers who regurgitated other people's writings', an example which has been increasingly followed by publishers during the last twenty years. Naturally enough this led her towards editing books increasingly for an adult readership. It was not long before Max appointed her editor of the authors closest to him, including Graham Greene. (It was also at this time that Stephen Watts, well-known journalist and Second World War correspondent, was brought in to edit a number of successful booklets on topical affairs in a series called Background Books. In addition, he produced an enchanting autobiographical book, *Moonlight on a Lake in Bond Street*. On the strength of that, he was commissioned by another friend of Max's, Charles Ritz, the owner of the Ritz Hotel in Paris, to write its history, which he did in his *New Yorker* style.)

In 1972 Max appointed Judy Taylor Deputy Managing Director, extending the range of her responsibilities beyond the children's department. She had become well known in the publishing world when elected to the Publishers' Association Council in 1972 (the first woman member of the Council) and had been awarded the MBE in 1971 in recognition of her services to publishing. Margaret Clark, who had been in charge of the list for older children, now took sole charge of the department. Many are the children's editors today who owe their professional formation to this charming and, when necessary, uncompromising personality.

In the late 1970s, after nearly thirty years with The Bodley Head, Judy Taylor reached a long-matured decision to leave the company, after marrying Richard Hough, and withdraw to lead a rural existence in Gloucestershire—a heavy loss to Max and to The Bodley Head. Judy only took the step, however, in the firm assurance that the Children's Book publishing programme remained in the surest hands to continue the work.

27

The Buoyant Sixties

Although the children's book department of The Bodley Head soon established its own place in the family, the rest of the firm still retained something of the old atmosphere which in the late 1940s brought Max Reinhardt, Ralph Richardson and Anthony Quayle together to found Max Reinhardt Ltd. Its board meetings were an assembly of like-minded people, and, led by Max himself, staved off the progress by which a publishing house becomes merely a useful adjunct to Big Business. Nevertheless, a business it was, and subject to the law of man-made nature that compels any organisation either to expand or contract.

Under Max, The Bodley Head took the road of expansion. The names joining the list at this time were a clear enough indication of direction. There were grand old names awaiting a new lease of life, as F. Scott Fitzgerald, reclaimed for a new generation by J. B. Priestley in the elegant set of volumes designed by Will Carter. (The publication of *The Bodley Head Scott Fitzgerald* was a tribute to J. B. Priestley's and Max's flair, for the books of this Jazz Age author could currently be picked up for a song from remainder dealers along the Charing Cross Road.) There was an author of rising reputation, J. P. Donleavy, who brought to the firm his novel *A Singular Man* (1964) and a volume of short stories *Meet My Maker the Mad Molecule* (1965). An unknown black teacher from British Guiana, E. R. Braithwaite, working in an East End school wrote a simple and moving account of his experiences, *To Sir, With Love*, now part of our cultural heritage. A man and his dog joined the list together in J. R. Ackerley's enduring novel, now considered a classic, *We Think the World of You* (1960); Joe Ackerley has already featured in this narrative back in the 1930s when, as editor of a collection of Escape stories, he had complaints to make on copy-editing (p. 252). The genial Alfred Hitchcock was also making a regular contribution in a great series of volumes of 'stories they would not let me do on television'.

The road to expansion was indicated, too, by the search for larger premises, which led to the move, in 1966, to 9 Bow Street, where the miniature empire could be housed under one roof, and even a good sample of stock could be accommodated to meet local trade needs. One of the first computers used in publishing was also installed.

Max achieved the singular feat of controlling commercial operations while remaining a personal friend of his authors. Many were the leading authors who regarded Max both as a good business manager and as a close personal friend. These included Graham Greene, even though he was no longer Max's fellow-director since he chose to move his residence to Antibes. The gap created in the board of The Bodley Head was handsomely filled in 1969 when the author's brother, Sir Hugh Greene, having stepped down as Director-General of the BBC, accepted to join the board as Chairman, in circumstances worth relating.

Even before Ansley had decided to sell his share in the business he had expressed a wish to retire from the board because of ill-health, which made his journeys to London more tiresome, and he suggested that Reinhardt should try and find a new chairman. At the same time Graham Greene thought it would be a good idea for Max to get in touch with his brother, who would have a story to tell, if only he could be persuaded to tell it. 'Why don't you give him a good lunch,' said Graham, 'and try and get him to write about his life, it is an interesting one.' The meeting was fortuitous for by the time they met it had just been announced that Hugh Greene was giving up the Director-Generalship soon. The proposition was put to him by Max, but he said he was still so immersed with the problems he had to solve before giving up the BBC that although he agreed to think about it he couldn't promise when. A halt had come to the conversation when suddenly Reinhardt had the idea of asking him if he would consider becoming Chairman of The Bodley Head when he left the BBC. His answer was typically clear: 'My dear Max, I would love it and I will accept immediately in case you should change your mind.'

And so it was that Hugh Greene joined The Bodley Head as Chairman in 1969, becoming Honorary President in 1981 and remaining as such until his death in 1987. In all these years he was certainly not a passive chairman. He was fond of reading and of collecting books and he had a particular passion for Victorian detective stories which he collected. He contributed a number of books to the Bodley Head list. After a short biographical book of essays as Director-General of the BBC there were four highly entertaining and profitable collections of detective stories called *The Rivals of Sherlock Holmes*, *More Rivals of Sherlock Holmes*, *The Crooked Counties* and *American Rivals of Sherlock Holmes*.

He also introduced to Reinhardt Jack Ashley who had worked for the BBC and then become an MP and who, through an unsuccessful operation, had become completely deaf. He was encouraged to write his autobiography which was highly successful and made Jack Ashley and his wife great personal friends. Jack Ashley soon became a great expert in the House of Commons on all sorts of disablements. There were also books from active or former BBC colleagues like the autobiography of Grace Wyndham Goldie and these were followed by Hugh's own biography to which he contributed very much himself. Hugh enjoyed his relationship with publishing and particularly the fact that The Bodley Head were publishing his brother with whom he had edited some books jointly. He remained a good friend until the end.

Alistair Cooke was another author who regarded Max as 'his publisher' in a very personal sense; his books, like his broadcasts, have never failed to attract attention—his *Above London*, an aerial meditation on the capital, in which the lucidity of his prose is supplemented with striking photographs by Robert Cameron, is a constant bestseller. Winston Graham, a close friend, gave strong backing with his Cornish books.

There was Georgette Heyer, too, who took her time in moving from Heinemann to The Bodley Head but when she did (through 'Frere's friend Max Reinhardt'), she soon wrote to her new publisher:

'Dear Mr Reinhardt: No, on second thoughts I'll alter that to dear Max, because now that we have entered into what I hope will prove an enduring association the sooner we abandon formality the better. I was always very formal with Ralph Hodder-Williams, and look what came of it! Well, probably you don't know, but we split brass rags.'

And of course Charles Chaplin, in whose memoirs the elements of publishing drama ripened into a lasting friendship with him and his wife Oona. Max first heard of the possibility of Chaplin's memoirs in 1957. He was not alone, this comparative newcomer to the big publishing scene, and actually getting a contract signed was by no means plain sailing. In fact, at one of those board meetings Dwye Evans—still there, though a director of Heinemann—announced firmly that Max wouldn't succeed—they were going to Heinemann. 'In that case,' said Graham Greene severely, 'you shouldn't be on this board.' And before long he wasn't. Laying out the very large sum needed to secure the world rights was a breathtaking step for this relatively small firm, and meant, win or lose, further dependence on Ansbacher's. In the event, of course, the success of the book made it all the easier to pay off the bankers.

Even when the deal was made, the business was by no means over. Chaplin was living in Switzerland, and for the next five years or so Max was required to visit the man upon whose memories so much depended. At first Chaplin distrusted the idea of a secretary-typist, and wanted Max himself to take down his recollections—an idea which, whatever depended upon it, had to be as swiftly and tactfully disposed of as possible. It was; but reassurance was frequently necessary, to say nothing of a string of technicalities over the agreement—at first a purely verbal one, which baffled Ansbacher's understandably. The reassurance was equally taxing.

(327)

Seven years and four sets of galley-proofs later the book was ready after innumerable anxieties and delights. Among the latter was the evening early in the relationship when Max, his wife and Graham Greene were invited to visit Chaplin for dinner. A most enjoyable evening followed; none of those present was by nature ascetic. Eventually the ladies went to bed. At 1 a.m. Chaplin proposed that he should read the early part of his book, that most memorably dealing with his early years. At 3 a.m. Greene and Reinhardt found themselves, as the latter put it, 'drunk and moved': clearly they would have been moved in any case, drunk or not.

Hardly less of a strain was Max's later dealing with the Russian Nobel Prizewinner and prophetic scourge of East and West alike, Alexander Solzhenitsyn. It was in fact James Michie who first brought news of this controversial figure's typescript of *Cancer Ward*, news gathered amid the beneficent clicking of a roulette wheel at which he and Alexander Dolberg were seeking distraction from the cares of the world. Between them they added substantially to the cares, as well as the high standing, of The Bodley Head. Having written to a Czech contact, asking him to do what he could for *Cancer Ward*, Solzhenitsyn then put it out that the book had been published without his permission (which led to an attack on The Bodley Head by that eager polemicist Paul Foot). Soon, however, Solzhenitsyn was being represented by an agreeable Swiss lawyer, Dr Heeb, the only Communist member of the Swiss Parliament. World rights in *Cancer Ward* were confirmed to The Bodley Head later. *August 1914* was bought from Dr Heeb, by a German firm. This firm approached not Collins but The Bodley Head, who had sold them *Cancer Ward* and who thus acquired not only *August 1914* but also *November 1916* with options for *March 1917*, to say nothing of a spate of plays, broadcasts and other salutary and well-deserved exhortations to the West—and a series of exigent requirements from this towering figure.

Once Solzhenitsyn had reached the West, Reinhardt thought it expedient to visit him. Accordingly, with the co-operation of Dr Heeb, he set off for Switzerland. The meeting was not wholly successful. Solzhenitsyn's appearance was itself intimidating. After the exchange of civilities, 'Now,' said Solzhenitsyn, 'I will ask you a few questions. Thirty, to be precise.' He did so. The first question lasted almost half an hour. Reinhardt felt constrained to suggest that he might answer that question first since by the time he had listened to all the questions it would be difficult to remember what the earlier ones had been about. Solzhenitsyn agreed. The answer to the first question, Max said, is: 'You are wrong in every case. Next question please.' After five hours of discussion a semi-friendly parting took place. Many years later, when Solzhenitsyn came to London to give a lecture at the Guildhall and the two met again at Claridges, he greeted Max most affectionately and has since remained with The Bodley Head.

28

---◆---

A Federation of Publishers

'The theatre of war was sometimes terrifying,' wrote John Ryder in
The Case for Legibility (1979), 'but the present terror of being overwhelmed by illiteracy and blinded by illegibility is just as real.' That
it should be thought necessary to make the case for legibility at all
was an indication of how strident British standards of presentation
had become in the late 1960s and 1970s, a stridency reflected in publishing by promotional techniques designed to ensure that books—
some books, at least—continued to be bought in ever-increasing
numbers, if not perhaps actually read. Given the battery of distract-
ing competition already directed at the printed word by television
and what became known somewhat earnestly as the leisure industry,
this kind of marketing was short-sighted.

The Bodley Head, already fighting a permanent campaign on
behalf of clear design, took the battle for literacy beyond the schools
to its source, the family at home: philosophically in Margaret Meek's
Learning to Read (1982), practically in Dorothy Butler's influential
Babies Need Books (1980) and its successor, *Five to Eight* (1986),
which sold the astonishing number of 15,000 copies in less than a
year, doubtless to many mothers themselves brought up as Bodley
Head babies, on the gospel according to Dr Spock. This is but one
example of the way in which a children's list may sometimes respond
fastest to the demands made by social and political change.

Survival, eventually in some confidence and strength, was
achieved through the last fifteen years of the firm's first century
despite problems of viability and effectiveness common to all publishing houses of this size, and against a volatile background of recession and boom that seemed to revolve like a thunderstorm that never

quite died out and returned each time with a strength more danger-
ous than before. It was achieved in two ways: by new structures
designed to protect the firm and allow it to grow, and by the con-
tinuity of the people who had worked for Max almost from the start
in 1957, giving the imprint the identity and definition it had.

The crisis faced by all publishers in 1986 was a global one which
had been foreseen for many years—a matter, among many things, of
a reduction in Britain's historic share of world markets, of piracy
abroad and unredeemable debts. The Bodley Head had by then
slimmed itself drastically and was optimistically prepared, in new
premises and under a new owner, to rise to the storm. The crisis
facing the firm in 1973, on the other hand, was almost in reverse:
markets were large, books in demand. What was missing was the
logistical means to get the books to the market. Sales were declining;
prices and overheads were going up. A strong backlist and the
margins to be made on reprinted titles were no longer sufficient to
keep an eclectic and literary list in the black through a season when
new books were not selling well.

Fortunately the problem was not Bodley Head's alone. Many
publishers at the time had to secure their financial base at some
sacrifice to their independence. The most promising and least pain-
ful form of rationalisation seemed to be to pool resources and to
share marketing, warehouse, distribution and accountancy services
with other publishers similarly placed. In August 1973 therefore
The Bodley Head entered into an agreement with Chatto & Windus
and Jonathan Cape, who had already signed one of their own. All
three houses (Chatto smaller than The Bodley Head, Cape larger)
shared similar philosophies of literature and publishing; each lacked
the clout to compete on their own with the mustering conglomerates.
Accordingly, a kind of conglomerate was established (later joined by
Virago) under the title of Chatto, Bodley Head and Jonathan Cape
Ltd, the shares held by the principal publishers. Max became
Joint-Chairman with Graham C. Greene, the novelist's nephew and
Managing Director of Cape, and with Ian Parsons of Chatto.

Joining forces with equals, after an uninterrupted history of absorbing smaller fry, could have been difficult for The Bodley Head, but if there were teething troubles in setting up the three companies' joint services, the exercise had already proved itself by 1980 when the Booksellers' Association voted all three Publishers of the Year, and repeated the honour the following year. Editorial independence was the cornerstone of the affiliation, to the point where they might even be competing for the same books. Design, production, publicity and subsidiary rights also remained separate, but the new holding company built a large warehouse at Grantham on the A1 to contain stock and all facilities for selling it to the trade.

John Hews and Iris Taylor found themselves placed overnight in charge of, respectively, financial management and authors' royalties for three middle-sized companies, having to familiarize themselves not only with a huge range of unfamiliar titles and authors but with a new generation of computers. John Hews and Judy Taylor joined Max as the Bodley Head members of the new Group Company board. As Managing Director of the Service Company, John Hews was largely responsible for setting up the Grantham warehouse and the expanded trade department and computer services. The dynamic Quentin Hockliffe, who four years previously had joined The Bodley Head from Paul Hamlyn as Sales Director, was placed in charge of the Group's export marketing, and at once began to ginger up overseas representatives in a series of visits they did not know whether to anticipate in joy or alarm.

Without the affiliation, senior editors say, The Bodley Head would never have survived the inflationary crisis of 1975/6, nor the temporary one that succeeded it on the change of Government in 1979. Fears that it might in the end compromise personal publishing have not, on the whole, been met.

The history of The Bodley Head between 1973 and 1987 was characterised by the consistency with which members of Max Reinhardt's original editorial team (or those arriving shortly after he did)—Barney Blackley, John Ryder, Margaret Clark, James Michie, Guido Waldman, Jill Black—were not only still working with him as the centenary approached, but, with the significant addition of David

Machin and Chris Holifield, were producing a list of books which consistently maintained the strength and individuality of the imprint in the eyes of the outside world.

Max continued to run his team as a benign enabler. His manner of handling authors had always been gentle persuasion combined with an assurance that made them feel welcome and able to get on with the book they wanted to write. Even more important, he left his editors alone to build up a creative working relationship with the writers committed to their care. Jill Black ('I don't much care for the market place. I put books together and edit them!') looks back on the early 1970s as 'the palmy days' of Max's regime, 'wonderfully heady, champagne years'. Among her particular specialities were popular archaeology and music; this enabled her to build up professional partnerships with Magnus Magnusson (*Introducing Archaeology*, 1972; *Vikings!*, 1980; and *Iceland Saga*, 1987), Christopher Headington (*The Bodley Head History of Western Music*, 1974 and *Opera: A History*, 1987), and Rupert Christiansen (*Prima Donna*, 1984 and *Romantic Affinities*, 1987).

Such editorial sympathy and skill was exercised when Georgette Heyer died in 1973. She left unfinished the first volume of a projected trilogy on John, Duke of Bedford, gifted but forgotten third son of Henry IV, a project she had been researching for years. *My Lord John* (1975) was assembled for publication by her widower and Jill Black. Perhaps a more lasting tribute to Heyer's influence and gifts was The Historical Novel Prize set up in her memory (1977) and administered by Jill with Diane Pearson of Corgi Books. Endowed by both publishers (one-third each), and the Heyer Estate (the novelist's son Sir Richard Rougier, one-sixth, Booker McConnell, one-sixth) the £2,000 prize has raised the respectability of a perpetually popular genre, and guarantees publication by both The Bodley Head and Corgi.

The prize was first awarded to Rhona Martin's Tudor novel *Gallows Wedding*. The most successful winners so far have been Valerie Fitzgerald's *Zemindar* (1981) and Susan Kay's *Legacy* (1986), much seen on holiday beaches and the London Tube.

Zemindar attracted an American advance of a quarter of a million dollars in 1982, one of the highest in the history of the firm. In its second year an author's courage and the judges' shrewdness were vindicated when the winner turned out to have been submitted pseudonymously by the veteran Norah Lofts who, once unmasked, permitted *Day of the Butterfly* to be published under her own name, and brought her next historical novel to the firm.

Each editor made a distinct mark on the list. James Michie's sensitive editing and personal concern ensured the consistent loyalty of William Trevor to The Bodley Head. Michie signed him up, unknown, in the 1960s (with *The Old Boys*) and nurtured him through a series of novels and short-story collections whose excellence came to be taken for granted by readers and reviewers and therefore, from time to time, rated below its worth. *The Children of Dynmouth*, however, won the Whitbread Award, 1976, and was filmed for television ten years later. Michie also acquired for the list Robert Pirsig's improbable, exotic and wildly successful *Zen and the Art of Motor Cycle Maintenance* (1974), the seminal voyage of self-discovery and 1970s romanticism which reconciled the two cultures of art and science in a manner unforeseen by Lord Snow. A mature friendship with Graham Greene and James Michie resulted in Muriel Spark joining The Bodley Head list in 1981 with her novel *Loitering with Intent*.

One of the splendours of English publishing at this time was *The Bodley Head Bernard Shaw*, edited by Dan Laurence: seven volumes of the collected plays and their prefaces, and three of his musical criticism; in addition a monumental edition of his *Collected Letters*, ultimately to make four volumes, was being issued. The house editor behind the masterly and meticulous editing of Professor Laurence was the unfathomably patient Barney Blackley, whose tolerance for large-scale projects was intermittently put to work on Lord Harewood's ever-augmented editions of Kobbé's *Complete Opera Book*, (at the latest count, 1,424 pages). Flexible as ever, Barney Blackley was also the one to persuade Max that the twenty-six dog-eared pages of typescript submitted via a theatre friend of

Max made a publishable proposition: duly embellished, the handsome little volume of *Old Wives' Lore for Gardeners* by the sisters Maureen and Bridget Boland sold 130,000 copies and still sells. The photographic albums, whether Sam Haskins's nudes, Bill Brandt's creative, impressionistic camera-work, or John d Green's egregious and lucrative *Birds of Britain*, also came under his careful editorship.

Guido Waldman describes himself as the firm's resident polyglot: books of Continental origins generally fetched up on his desk. Raymond Queneau (*Zazie*) and Primo Levi (the tremendous *If This is a Man* and *The Truce*) joined the list, as did a contemporary Russian master of comic irony, Alexander Zinoviev (*The Yawning Heights*). Guido's brief was wide: he might find himself discussing details of nineteenth-century religious history with Newman's biographer in the morning and, as nautical editor, the finer points of the Collision Regulations with The Royal Institute of Navigation in the afternoon.

If most authors came and stayed—the Nobel poet George Seferis, attracted by his friend and translator Rex Warner; Jerome Weidman; and Derek Traversi, mentor, with books such as *An Approach to Shakespeare*, to generations of English-literature students—Eric Ambler, Isabel Colegate and Paul Theroux each moved elsewhere after they had written some of their best work for The Bodley Head.

The fiction list indeed firmed up remarkably in the years 1973 to 1987, led by a marvellously productive Greene, Solzhenitsyn, Trevor, Spark, Zinoviev, the mystery writer Peter Dickinson (*The Last House-Party*, 1982) and young novelists like Allan Massie and Ronald Frame.

The long and glorious Indian summer of the novelist Graham Greene—flourished in a whole variety of forms, but above all in four remarkable novels, which came after *The Comedians* and *Travels with My Aunt* and take their place beyond any doubt in the canon: *The Honorary Consul* (1973), *The Human Factor* (1978), *Doctor Fischer of Geneva* (1980) and *Monsignor Quixote* (1982). They are distinguished by tenderness, anger, an Olympian comic sense, an

(335)

unsparing pursuit of the wicked and charity towards the meek. In 1985 came a short novel *The Tenth Man*, published jointly with Anthony Blond, who had called the author's attention to the fact that the manuscript had lain unfilmed, unread and undisturbed in the MGM archives ever since it was commissioned in 1944.

While Greene continued to write with apparently effortless crafts-manship and ease, Solzhenitsyn wrote and rewrote his massive sequence on the Russian Revolution and the Great War: the majestic *August 1914* was expanded, and retranslated (by H. R. Willetts who was at work on the entirely new volume, *November 1916*).

What remained unchanged through fifteen troubled and transi-tional years was the breadth and diversity of the general list: music, archaeology, printing, photography, history, biography, public affairs. Americana, for example, ranged from Henry Brandon's *The Retreat of American Power* (1973, nearly four hundred pages at the pre-inflationary price of £3.75) to Shirley MacLaine's memoir of show-biz and positive thinking, *You Can Get There from Here* (1975) and Donald Spoto's pioneering life of Tennessee Williams, the first to count, *The Kindness of Strangers* (1985). A further revised edition was on sale of *Venice for Pleasure*, J. G. Links's little, almost apolo-getic guidebook which has acquired an indispensable place in the luggage of any tourist bound for the lagoon-city. Another hardy perennial was the series of autobiographies by Helen Forrester, whose stark and vivid recollections of an impoverished wartime childhood in Liverpool caught the popular imagination and assured a continued success for *Twopence to Cross the Mersey* and its sequels. An unfailing producer of good narrative, too, was Tristan Jones, a one-eyed (and eventually one-legged) sailor who had, among other exploits, spent a year locked in the arctic icepack in the company only of a three-legged dog called Nelson. Tristan Jones brought The Bodley Head his first book, *The Incredible Voyage* (and many people did find it precisely that) and went on to produce a book a year ever after, each one stretching the imagination and building a devoted readership.

The same season—1986—which saw the corrected edition of

Joyce's *Ulysses* by Hans Walter Gabler, with Wolfhard Steppe and Claus Melchior (not to mention a miraculous computer at Tübingen), with more than five thousand changes from the imperfect version first published in 1936, also saw *The Army and the Curragh Incident, 1914*, part of a new military history series published for The Army Records Society.

The Bodley Head nose for the spirit of the times, which had first brought the house into being in 1887, had presented the poets and artists of *The Yellow Book* to the smart public of the 1890s, E. R. Braithwaite's *To Sir, with Love* to a Britain newly aware of its immigrant communities at the end of the 1950s, *Baby and Child Care* to the 1960s, unearthed a best-seller for the early 1970s in Alvin Toffler's millennarian harbinger of the stress caused by rapid technological change, *Future Shock* (1970). When the spirit of the times moved towards a nostalgia for lost craftsmanship and a perhaps less healthy interest in the revival of personal wealth and what new money could buy, great attention was given to John Martin Robinson's *The Latest Country Houses* (1984).

In this respect books like *Learning to Read* and *Five to Eight* were also responding sharply and directly to a public mood and need in the manner of John and Allen Lane. The Bodley Head children's list, indeed, has as often led as followed the spirit of the times, fighting the decline of formal teaching and the drastic reduction in public expenditure on books for schools by making their titles more attractive, producing them in Greek, Turkish, Gujerati, Urdu and other immigrant languages, widening the subject-matter of fiction to touch on wife-beating (Betsy Byars's *Cracker Jackson*, 1985) and survival after nuclear attack (Louise Lawrence's *Children of the Dust*, 1985). The author of *Baby and Child Care* finally met his nemesis, alas, from within the lists of The Bodley Head itself, in Aidan Chambers's *Breaktime* (1978) when an adolescent love scene was interspersed with what was actually going on in the boy's mind and what was supposed to be happening, clinically, according to Dr Spock.

If some taboos fell, hypersensitivity often increased, and America was, as ever, different. Americans deplore nudity, the British bad language. Margaret Clark took it all in her stride, believing that the innovations in the list were now done with more confidence and in a less earnest and patronising manner than was the case in the 1960s. The Bodley Head continues to publish the resonant Japanese conundrums of Mitsumasa Anno (*The Earth is a Sundial*, most austere of pop-up books, 1986), and books which present information in a light-hearted way using, for instance, cats as the different characters in a publishing house in Aliki's *How a Book is Made*, 1986, as well as extremely funny ones, as that about a pig who refuses to help set the table (*It's Your Turn, Roger!* by Susanna Gretz, 1985). This last was one of a growing number of books created by Rona Selby who had joined The Bodley Head in 1976.

Then there is Maurice Sendak, a jewel in the Bodley Head crown officially confined to the children's list until his brilliant stage work on Prokofiev's opera *The Love for Three Oranges* at Glyndebourne. These Tiepolo-inspired designs made up the first Sendak book ever to be originated outside the United States, and the artist was delighted with it. Sendak's books had, of course, been collected by grown-ups in Britain and America ever since *Where the Wild Things Are*. This turned out to be the first of a dream-trilogy with *In the Night Kitchen* (1971) and *Outside Over There* (1981). In the second book a small boy loses all his clothes (consternation in the States) whilst falling *upwards* through a shadowed city constructed entirely of drygoods and cooking utensils, to land in a cake being mixed by three sinister-smiling chefs in the shape of Oliver Hardy. Mickey escapes by kneading the dough in a fat little brown aeroplane, tumbles *down* into his clothes again and wakes up with a bump.

In *Outside Over There* Sendak drew on the intense stillness and compacted violence of German Romantic painters like Philipp-Otto Runge and Caspar-David Friedrich to cast a spellbinding pastel nightmare around the theft of a plump baby by two hooded shades and its rescue by sister Ida and her magic wonder horn. Father has gone to sea, and Mother cares for nothing but to wait in the trellised arbour for his safe return. It is a book into whose psychological and allegorical possibilities only the very brave would dare to tread.

As The Bodley Head approached its centenary year children's publishing was proving somewhat more resilient than the adult side. There were some seasons, indeed, when new general titles proved slow sellers, and the business only remained healthy through a children's list which frequently accounted for more than fifty per cent of the firm's turnover by this time. The Bodley Head team returned in April 1987 from 'the best Bologna we'd had for years', a large number of rights transactions put in hand. Notable was the success of two books produced by Rona Selby, now Senior Editor, who—from her own experience with two young children—saw a gap in the market for an updated book of nursery rhymes with colourful illustrations by a young artist Sarah Pooley (*A Day of Rhymes*, 1987) and a collection of stories for reading aloud, *Listen to This*, made by Laura Cecil and illustrated by Emma Chichester Clark. The first was sold instantly to Random House, the second to Greenwillow in New York. Both represented a change of direction in children's book publishing, away from books for the institutional market with its restricted budgets towards books for the increasing number of parents concerned for their children's literacy.

Subsidiary rights grew enormously in importance over every area of the business, becoming indeed a central factor in determining profit or loss on most books. Each new proposal had to be costed more carefully with this in mind. Book clubs became major purchasers of new books, but most important of all, the centre of gravity, particularly in fiction, shifted away from the standard hardcover novel familiar to John Lane to the cheap paperback that would follow it a year or so later—a consequence that had grown, of course, from the establishment of Penguin Books by Allen Lane.

Advances on novels with best-seller potential began to rise out of reach for all but the 'vertical' publishing firms, i.e. hardcover houses with a paperback imprint of their own. It was with this in mind that The Bodley Head and its two affiliates entered into a special relationship with Granada Publishing in 1975. CBC and Granada set up Triad, which had first call on all new books published by the group in hardcovers, always subject to the author's approval and sharing both profit and costs of the paperback. Authors were, however, free to honour existing loyalties; Greene, Trevor, Fitzgerald and *Ulysses* continued with Penguin. The scheme worked well enough, but the Group often found itself in competition with Granada for the acquisition of new books. In 1985 CBC entered into a similar arrangement with Pan.

The exact nature of the identity so effectively defended by The Bodley Head in the 1970s and 1980s varied somewhat from year to year; the firm was watchful of the dangers of living on past achievement. That it would not be primarily as a publisher of mainstream middlebrow fiction was suggested by the experience of Maureen Rissik, recruited as a lively expert in that field at Hodder & Stoughton to be Editorial Director for Adult Books at The Bodley Head in 1978. Max had decided that his firm should move into the more dynamic 'popular' section of the market.

Maureen Rissik—a woman of enormous charm with a wide circle of friends in publishing on both sides of the Atlantic—soon acquired a number of popular authors, frequently American, of whom the most notable was Thomas Harris: *Red Dragon* was an outstanding success in hardcover and paperback. But the recipe rarely worked so well, and when another experienced popular editor was brought in to bolster the list, Maureen left, to become a successful novelist in her own right: *Relative Strangers*, for rights in which large sums of money exchanged hands, was published in 1987. She was succeeded in 1985 by Chris Holifield, with the title of Adult Publishing Director, one of the brightest young women in British paperback publishing, who had already completed five years as Editorial Director of Sphere. But this is to jump ahead.

That the firm would one day have to survive without Max Reinhardt was evident. Judy Taylor's departure, described in Chapter 26, was very difficult for Max, who had come to regard her not only as the chief architect of his children's list, but also as his possible successor as head of the firm. Parting left them the best of friends, but Max was looking once more for an experienced executive to relieve the administrative strain and free him for the old pleasure of publishing authors he liked. The world had grown a little colder and a great deal tougher in the thirty years since Max bought John Lane's historic house. Although Max had relished the market place in the past, he did so less and less and it was no longer the same place. There was an intruder in the game.

The greater assertiveness of the literary agent—David Machin had been one himself—was a phenomenon which sprang from the movement for authors' rights, from abuses by unscrupulous publishers in the past, and from the market values that seized hold of British life after 1979 and made many hitherto innocent of the knowledge realise that it was possible to make a killing out of anything, even a *book*. The number of multiple submissions—the system long common in the United States whereby an agent sends copies of a new manuscript to as many publishers as possible, who then compete in an 'auction' for the book—rose so fast that the historic patterns of direct patronage between publishers and authors became harder and harder to find.

Some account of all this was taken by the appointment of David Machin in 1981, first as Joint Managing Director with Max, then as sole Managing Director of The Bodley Head, thus allowing Max himself to become Executive Chairman. Machin's background was invaluably diverse—in his own words, he had 'jumped back and forth across the barrier' several times. During a career which began in 1957, the year in which Max bought The Bodley Head, he had been an editor with Heinemann, an agent with A. P. Watt, Deputy Managing Director of Cape, and General Secretary at The Society of Authors. It was there that Max found him, and he was still only 47.

A wry, conciliatory, philosophical and much-amused man of many enthusiasms, he possessed both the breadth of vision and the ability to get on with all manner of people that would be essential in anyone taking on the workload and mantle of Max. Like Max, he enjoys the commissioning and editing of long-terms projects like Martin Duberman's biography of Paul Robeson and a volume by the wizard-archivist Kurt Gänzl which will do for the underdocumented area of musical theatre what Kobbé and Harewood did for opera.

Under his direction, both development and retrenchment took place. A hard look at profitability led to a pruning of the list where too much editorial and production time was spent to little purpose save, perhaps, that of prestige. The excellent but costly aeronautical list was sold off. Into The Bodley Head list came Peter Dickinson, Michael Davie's very successful account of *The Titanic* (1986) and distinguished public figures such as Lord Devlin, who gave a highly privileged account of the Bodkin Adams trial in *Easing the Passing* (1985). There was a flair, here, for the slightly sensational subject presented with scholarship and authority.

Chris Holifield complemented Machin's style and herself lost little time in giving the list a broader perspective after her arrival in 1985, enriching both the literary and commercial ends of the fiction (from Guy Vanderhaeghe to Peter Lovesey), recruiting a number of promising new young novelists and drawing on her own interest in a wide range of non-fiction in books on the secret world of intelligence (*Break In*), conservation (*State of the Ark* and *Beyond the Frozen Sea*) and business affairs (*Too Good to Be True*). She broadened the travel list and introduced a new kind of popular biography with such books as Jacqueline Weld's life of Peggy Guggenheim and Dora Bryan's autobiography. Above all, she assured the outside world that The Bodley Head was still in the business of publishing books of quality on almost any subject.

One distinguished author to join the Bodley Head list in 1985 was the famous actor-director, Sir Richard Attenborough, a friend of Max for over twenty years, as both are working together on the Council of the Royal Academy of Dramatic Art. His autobiographical books on the making of his recent films, *In Search of Gandhi*, *Chorus Line* and *Cry Freedom* confirmed the strong links with the world of the stage and screen that Max had forged—and incidentally achieved remarkable sales.

After almost twenty years in Bow Street, the convenience of the group was considered best served by The Bodley Head's moving into the Bedford Square offices vacated, in June 1985, by Jonathan Cape. In 1986 they moved again: from number 30 to number 32. The Bodley Head is back in Bloomsbury, in a handsome and imaginatively modernised town house on perhaps the most beautiful square in London, with a distant view of the pale green copper dome on the Reading Room of the British Museum, that great crucible of the making of books, a quarter of a mile away. From David Machin's office only the motorised traffic would in any way surprise the visiting shades of Mathews, Beardsley and Richard Le Gallienne.

For a business which began the first forty years of its life as an inspired, if bloodyminded autocracy, enjoyed thirty more (1957–1987) as an enlightened monarchy and which has throughout shown an historic sense of itself, the documentation of The Bodley Head has become sadly dispersed. The file copies have gone to Grantham; the documentary archive is at the University of Reading, the design archive at the Bodleian Library. John Lane's correspondence from c. 1881 to 1921, inherited by Allen on his uncle's death (Allen himself died in 1970) was sold by his Trustees at Sotheby's in 1985 for £170,000 and ended up in the Humanities Research Center in Texas. It included a great deal pertaining to *The Yellow Book*, no fewer than 1,367 letters from the unstoppable William Watson (how did he ever find time to write a poem?), 113 from Stephen Leacock, 74 from Laurence Housman and the one from Henry James pointing out that Lane was paying him roughly half what he was getting paid elsewhere. He was, as we have seen, lucky to get paid at all.

The second move in Bedford Square had not been foreseen. The financial stability of The Bodley Head had always depended on sufficient regular income from the sale of books and rights to meet overheads, with enough to spare for investing in the forward list. Like other manufacturing sectors, publishing suffered from the recession in the British economy during the 1980s, characterised by high unemployment and high interest rates. Income failed to meet costs; overdrafts of all the companies in the group soared. The reduction of overheads involved, among other things, staff redundancies, anathema in a company with an exceptional record of (reciprocated) loyalty between management and staff.

Production, design, publicity and rights departments were merged with those of Cape, leaving the autonomy of each confined to independent editorial departments each looking for books suitable to its own character and style. The heads of the merged departments were all directors of Jonathan Cape; their Bodley Head counterparts negotiated redundancy agreements and sought new work outside. A false impression was created that The Bodley Head had to some extent been absorbed by Jonathan Cape. But Cape made their new Bodley Head fellows welcome from the start and gave Bodley Head books and authors a priority, care and attention equal to their own. What was undoubtedly preserved, however, was the total independence of The Bodley Head's Adult and Children's editorial departments under Chris Holifield and Margaret Clark, which essentially continued to enshrine the vitality and traditions of the firm.

ENVOI

On 7 May 1987, the staff of The Bodley Head and its fellow companies in the group were summoned by the remaining group Chairman, Graham C. Greene (Max's resignation as Joint-Chairman having been announced), to be told that, with the exception of Virago (which was about to buy itself out), the group had just passed into American hands. The new proprietor was Random House. This publishing company, with its associates Alfred A. Knopf and Pantheon Books, was the closest to CBC in quality, tradition and style. After several unprofitable seasons, Chatto, Bodley Head and Cape all needed fresh capital to continue their recovery and build up new programmes, and the new owners were readily recognised as like-minded publishers who would value their British companies for what they had made of themselves and what they would continue to be.

*

AFTERWORD

J. W. Lambert died suddenly in August 1986 while working on this book. He had completed more than three-quarters of the manuscript, reaching 1957 in detail and 1973 in outline notes. Like all literary journalists, Jack had been trying to write what we wistfully think of as a 'real' book all his working life, but more immediate tasks had always intervened. It was for me therefore both a pleasure and an honour to edit and complete this history in order that it might appear during the centenary year of The Bodley Head.

Jack was my first editor in Fleet Street, where I worked as his deputy in the literary department of *The Sunday Times* between 1962 and 1967. No apprentice could have had a finer master: he was technically the best and personally the most exhilarating I have ever worked with, and taught me all I know about sense, cutting, musical rhythm and narrative shape. I have therefore cut and shaped the main body of the book according to what I hope are Lambertian principles (such was Jack's delight in the subject that the first seventy years of the firm alone had already reached the size of the planned, complete book); I have constructed a narrative, essentially his, from the sketches for 1957–73, and I have written the final chapter, with the invaluable help of Guido Waldman at The Bodley Head, myself.

Michael Ratcliffe

PUBLISHER'S NOTE

The author wishes to acknowledge the help of the following who made documents or their own recollections available to him: the present and former directors and employees of The Bodley Head, including Mr Reg Gowers, Mr Frank Harris, Mr and Mrs Richard Hough, Mr Michael Legat, Mr L. A. Lake, Mr Eric Norris, Mr Ronald Whiting, and Mr Edward Young; Mr M. P. Rhodes and the Trustees of the John Lane Archive and the Allen Lane Foundation; Dr J. A. Edwards and Mr Michael Bott, The University of Reading; Mr David Whitaker, *The Bookseller*; the National Book League; Mr William L. Joyce and Mr John Stinson, New York Public Library.

If Jack Lambert had survived to complete his book, he would have wanted to include a scrupulous list of all those who helped him in his research, or from whose books he has quoted passages. In the event, it has been possible to assemble what may be only an incomplete list; the Publishers ask the forbearance of those who could rightfully claim a note of acknowledgement but are not listed here—their help is much appreciated.

A note on the booklets

These twenty-four booklets were all printed at The Stellar Press, including illustrations and covers, under the direction and typographical skill of Bill Hummerstone. The texts were set in Ehrhardt metal types excepting No. 5 which appeared in Baskerville (169). A special paper was made for the press at Hollingworths' mill in Maidstone and became known as Stellar Laid. The chain lines and the laid lines were unusually close and a watermark (reproduced in No. 15) of the sun symbol and the letters SP was designed and wired to the dandy-roll. This distinctive paper was first used in No. 8 and thereafter in all issues except Nos. 12 and 14. After booklet No. 3 a standard format of 190 × 112 mm was established. No. 19 was produced in a variant size to accommodate Anno's drawings.

The booklets were issued to friends of the authors and the publisher.

APPENDIX

The Bodley Head booklets
1961-84

[1] *Concerning Ulysses and The Bodley Head*

Six auto-lithographs by Charles Mozley, printed in sepia (two with
a second printing in pale mauve), trimmed to bleed and tipped onto
jap vellum paper. Each drawing accompanied by a brief quotation
from James Joyce's *Ulysses*. Sewn into tinted paper covers with the
title in black. Edition: 165 copies, 1961. Private issue to celebrate the
twenty-fifth anniversary of first publication of *Ulysses* by The Bodley
Head.

[2] *The Sin of Father Amaro*

An extract from chapter xv of Eça de Queiroz's novel *O Crime do
Padre Amaro* in Max Reinhardt's English edition published in 1961
and illustrated with five pencil drawings by José de Almeida. Sewn
into paper covers printed in purple and black. Edition: 200 copies,
1962. Private issue to celebrate this first English translation.

[3] *The Revenge*

An autobiographical fragment by Graham Greene. The text,
amended slightly, became chapter 3, section 2, of *A Sort of Life*
published by The Bodley Head in 1971. Sewn into dark green paper
covers with the title and author printed in black from a drawing by
Michael Harvey. Edition: 300 copies, 1963.

[4] *The Jealous God*

An extract from Eric Ambler's *A Kind of Anger* published by The Bodley Head in 1964. Sewn into paper covers, title printed in a private typeface, Grot R, drawn by Michael Harvey. Edition: 200 copies, 1964.

[5] *A Balloon Incident from Frederica*

An incident from the novel *Frederica* by Georgette Heyer published by The Bodley Head in 1965. Sewn into dark green paper covers with a balloon drawing by Arthur Barbosa printed on the front cover, (Brick red overprinted 8 times from a litho plate). Edition: 200 copies 1965.

[6] *A Voyage Round Great Britain*

A note by Iain Bain on the production of William Daniell's *A Voyage Round Great Britain* (1814–25) together with an account of the original aquatint plates found, in 1966, in the printshop of Thomas Ross but belonging to Nattali & Maurice, and subsequently purchased by The Tate Gallery. Illustrated with details from seven of the pictures in monochrome, a folding plate in colour and a photograph of one of the copper plates. The illustrations also include a portrait of William Daniell and the endpapers show production details from the original ledgers now in Longman's archives. Edition 200 copies, 1966, plus 100 copies for sale.

[7] *Poems from William Blake's Songs of Innocence*

Seven poems by William Blake with drawings by Maurice Sendak printed in sanguine. Sewn into paper covers printed in black and dusty purple using one of the drawings enlarged and reversed left to right. Edition: 275 copies, 1967. This item was made to celebrate Maurice Sendak's recovery from a serious illness he suffered whilst in England. The drawings have not been reproduced elsewhere.

[8] *Thomas Bewick: from the letters of 1823–28*

Extracts of letters from *Bewick to Dovaston, Letters, 1824–28* published by Nattali & Maurice including a draft of a letter from Dovaston to Bewick (dated 13 November 1823) which is the only surviving Dovaston letter in this correspondence. This and other letters from Bewick and from his daughter, Jane, are published here for the first time. They were found in the Shropshire Record Office but the main collection of letters was sold to the British Museum in 1938. Edited by Iain Bain and John Ryder. Sewn in white paper covers printed in blue and black, Bewick's magpie on the front and a detail from a portrait of Bewick by James Ramsay on the back. (Seven engravings by Bewick are included in the text.) Edition: 200 copies, 1968. One hundred copies of this item were made available for sale.

[9] *Mr Visconti*

An extract from Graham Greene's novel *Travels with my Aunt* published by The Bodley Head in 1969 with a frontispiece by Edward Ardizzone, a pen-and-ink with wash drawing of lively sensitive wit. Sewn into yellow paper covers with the frontispiece printed in black. Edition: 300 copies, 1969.

[10] *The Bodley Head, 1887 to 1957*

A short account of the founding of The Bodley Head by John Lane and Elkin Mathews up to the time of Max Reinhardt's acquisition of the firm and its subsidiaries. Written by John Ryder and issued only in this private edition. The title-page includes a colour reproduction of the Nicholas Hilliard miniature of Thomas Bodley painted in 1598. Sewn into laminated white paper covers with the Hilliard miniature on the front. Edition: 500 copies, 1970.

[11] *Nonesuch Again*

Being most of chapter xx of Sir Francis Meynell's autobiography *My Lives* published by The Bodley Head in 1971. From 1935 to 1951 the Nonesuch Press was owned by George Macy: in 1986, on 5 November, Max Reinhardt bought the imprint and its copyrights from Dame Alix Meynell with intent to revive this famous enterprise. (Bennett Cerf of Random House, and George Macy of the Limited Editions Club, had been distributors of Nonesuch books in New York.) Sewn into green paper covers with an enlarged detail of one of Reynolds Stone's devices for Nonesuch printed in brown on front and back. Edition: 200 copies, 1971.

[12] *The Virtue of Disloyalty*

Graham Greene's acceptance address on being awarded the Shakespeare Prize at Hamburg in 1969, together with a prefatory note by the author. Sewn into white paper covers with a printed label on the front in green and black. Edition: 300 copies, 1972.

[13] *'Dreaming'*

A fragment from William Trevor's novel *Elizabeth Alone* published by The Bodley Head in 1973. Sewn into paper covers printed (4-colour offset) with a detail from David Hughes' jacket drawing for *Elizabeth Alone*. Edition: 225 copies, 1973.

[14] *The Land of Beulah*

An extract from *The Pilgrim's Progress* by John Bunyan with six pen-and-ink drawings by Edward Ardizzone and a note by the artist concerning his special interest in illustrating this text. Sewn into paper covers printed overall with a pen-and-wash drawing in black and grey-blue also by Ardizzone. Edition: 350 copies, 1974. The drawings have not been reproduced elsewhere.

[15] *John Ryder, designer and art director for The Bodley Head*

Written by Sonia Newby and Michael Turner for an Exhibition at The Bodleian Library, 1974–75, of the work of JR. Illustrated with archive material in black and several colours. The original cover for the booklet on sale at the exhibition featured a bookplate by Yvonne Skargon (black and two colours). A second cover was printed and wrapped over (detail from Loggan's seventeenth-century engraving of the library printed as a negative in blue-grey) in order to issue this as a Bodley Head booklet. Edition for this purpose: 225 copies, 1975. Privately issued (in this form) for friends of The Bodley Head.

[16] *Garden Lore*

Extracts from *Old Wives' Lore for Gardeners* by Maureen and Bridget Boland published by The Bodley Head in 1976. Illustrated with seven cuts from sixteenth-century herbals. Sewn into paper covers printed with a detail from the mountain ash (Mattioli, 1562). All cuts printed in dark green. Edition: 250 copies, 1976.

[17] *A Wedding Among the Owls*

An extract from Graham Greene's novel *The Human Factor* published by The Bodley Head in the following year, 1978. Sewn into grey Ingres paper covers printed with a typographical two-colour design using Bodoni braces. Edition: 250 copies, 1977.

[18] *Lovers of Their Time*

An extract from William Trevor's story of that title published by The Bodley Head in 1978. Sewn into buff paper covers and printed in sepia with a wash drawing of a Victorian bathtub in the Great Western Hotel, Paddington, by David Hughes—the title and author handwritten round the edge of the bath in black. Edition: 225 copies, 1978.

[19] *Anno/1979*

In 1978 The Bodley Head asked Mitsumasa Anno if he would contribute to this established series of booklets. Thinking that he might produce a drawing which could be folded into the standard format (*approx* 1 : 1·618 proportion) and issued perhaps with a title-page and editorial note, The Bodley Head was surprised and delighted when he sent a complete and original miniature picture book. The story is without words and printed in pale sepia and black. The format had to be adjusted by only a few millimetres to accommodate the two-page drawings. Sewn into paper (orange Ingres) covers with drawings printed in black. Edition: 280 copies, 1979.

[20] *Christmas in Vermont*

An extract from Alistair Cooke's *The Americans* published by The Bodley Head in 1979. Sewn into white paper covers with title printed in two shades of brown. Edition: 225 copies, 1980.

[21] *Bernard Shaw and Max Beerbohm at Covent Garden*

An article by Bernard Shaw (1889) on the opera season at Covent Garden and an essay by Max Beerbohm (1899) on a visit to Covent Garden as a social event. These two pieces were chosen to celebrate publication by The Bodley Head of *Shaw's Music* edited by Dan H. Laurence, 1981. Sewn into paper covers with a cartoon of Shaw and William Archer by Max Beerbohm on the front cover printed in blue and grey on light grey paper. Edition: 225 copies, 1981.

[22] *. . . one November day in 1980 the other Graham Greene burst through his shadow . . .*

Some answers by Graham Greene to questions put to him by Marie-Françoise Allain taken from *The Other Man: Conversations with Graham Greene*, translated by Guido Waldman and published by The Bodley Head in the following year, 1983. Sewn into slate grey covers with the long title printed at the tail of the front cover. Edition: 225 copies, 1982. On the title-pages of this and the 1981 booklet is a light sketch of Thomas Bodley by David Gentleman. The drawing also appeared in the Bodleian booklet (15), 1975.

[23] *From Edward Ardizzone's Indian Diary*

Extracts, mostly relating to Ardizzone's commission from Unesco to teach printing by silk screen, taken from *Edward Ardizzone's Indian Diary, 1952–53* published by The Bodley Head in the following year, 1984. There are nine drawings printed in red-brown in the text and three drawings on the covers, all by Ardizzone. Only five of these twelve drawings appear in the published version. Sewn into card covers printed in black and red. Edition: 225 copies, 1983. Issued to celebrate the artist's happy involvement, until his death in 1979, with his editor, Judy Taylor, at The Bodley Head.

[24] *The State of the Language*

A speech by Alistair Cooke (San Fransisco, 1979) from his collection entitled *The Patient Has the Floor*, published by The Bodley Head in the following year, 1985. Sewn into white paper covers with the title and author printed in brown and an engraved image of Thomas Bodley by David Gentleman printed in light ochre. Edition: 250 copies, 1984. *The State of the Language* was the last issue in this series up to the present time, 1987.

INDEX

Frere, A. S., 292, 293, 313ff., 316, 327

Gale, Norman, 38, 66, 90
Galen Place office, 263
Gallatin, A. E., 177
Gänzl, Kurt, 341
Garnett, David, 150
Garnett, Richard, 64, 90, 128
Gibson, Charles Dana, 178, 233
Gibson, W. W., 91
Gill, Eric, 239
Glanville, Brian, 315
Goldie, Grace Wyndham, 326
Gollancz, Victor, 232
Goodwin, John, 315
Gosse, Edmund, 59, 62, 64, 90, 140
Gould, Gerald, 234
Graham, Eleanor, 320
Graham, R. B. Cunninghame, 117
Graham, Stephen, 182
Graham, Winston, 307, 326
Grahame, Kenneth, 10, 43, 66, 68, 87ff., 90, 119, 123, 146, 165, 282, 317
Granada Publishers, 339ff.
Gray, John, 71ff.
Green, John d, 335
Green, Peter, 315
Greene, G. A., 38
Greene, Graham, 211, 230, 305, 310ff., 317, 322, 325, 327ff., 334ff., 340
Greene, Graham C., 331, 345
Greene, Sir Hugh, 325ff.
Greenwood, C. J., 272ff., 299, 315, 318
Gretz, Susanna, 338
Griffith, Hubert, 238
Grigson, Geoffrey, 234, 245
Groves, Ernest & Gladys, 234

Haldane, Lord, 182
Hallam, Henry, 39

Hamilton, Hamish, 267, 284
Hamsun, Knut, 99
Hanley, James, 243, 273, 274
Hardy, Thomas, 156
Harewood, Lord, 334, 342
Harland, Henry, 61ff., 80, 107, 123ff., 142
Harmsworth, Cecil, 181, 216
Harris, Frank, 61
Harris, Thomas, 340
Harrison, G. B., 210
Hart, L. A., 297ff., 310ff.
Hartland (Devon), 6, 9, 218
Hartley, L. P., 308
Harvey, Michael, 305
Haskins, Sam, 335
Hassall, Joan, 296
Haycraft, Colin, 315
Hazell, Raymond, 205
Headington, Christopher, 322, 333
Hearne, H. P., 175
Hedin, Sven, 190
Heinemann, William, 104, 119
Heinemann, Messrs, 85, 149, 152, 212, 250, 292ff., 308, 311ff., 315ff., 327, 341
Henley, of *National Observer*, 48, 56, 64, 85, 87
Herbert, Agnes, 181
Heseltine, Philip, *see* Warlock, Peter
Hewlett, Maurice, 118
Hews, John, 294, 306ff., 332
Heyer, Georgette, 314, 327, 333
HFL Ltd, 292ff., 300, 306
Hichens, Robert, 87
Hill, Vernon, 178
Hine, Muriel, 151ff., 162, 216, 235, 256
Hitchcock, Alfred, 325
Hobbes, John Oliver, 64
Hockliffe, Quentin, 332
Hodder & Stoughton, 213
Hodgkin, Mr, 13ff.